“‘My Life In You’ *by Jesus Christ*”

Volume I

...by the obedience of one
shall many be made righteous...

penned by Judith

" 'My Life In You' by Jesus Christ"

Appreciation to.....
My loving husband, Roy.
The Lord's choice for me and my best friend.
Second only to the Lord in my heart.
Thanks for all your support!

ISBN: 978-0-9849873-9-9

Cover by Judith L. Young
Scriptures KJV
Publisher/Distributor: Ministry Services, LLC, email: hsfkm@live.com,
www.hsfkm.info, www.kingdomministry.info

If you would like to include this book in your library, email or mail your request to Ministry Services, LLC.

" 'My Life In You' by Jesus Christ"

SPECIAL NOTE....

"...as I walked to the car just in awe of the working of the Lord, HE spoke these words in me "My Life In You by Jesus Christ".... I was seeing the life of Jesus Christ manifested in my own life and it humbled my soul and I was rejoicing in His Presence...."

My Father was writing His Perfect Book within me... The Book of Life Jesus Christ was and is being made known to us... not in the letter but by His Spirit.... His Blessings and Benefits words alone cannot express. It must be experienced by an encounter of the Father and Son revealing Himself to you. John 14:20-23. What an experience...to have your name written in the Book of Life and His name written in you.

So as you read this book I pray the Holy Spirit will give you an experience by an encounter of the Word of God which was manifested in the flesh and we now know in His Holy Spirit.

Join the Lord and me, and share this book...His message of His Victory and Good News of His Son for the salvation, peace, joy and much more abundant life for all.

Receive the Lord's blessing as He illuminates and blesses you in His Presence.

Abide in the Lord and let His Word abide in you.
Trust Him. His Love will not fail.

Take Your Next Step in God's Plan and Victory.
Expect Your Miracle!

His Love for You,

Judith

Furtherance of the Gospel...

The message of Jesus Christ is always free. Therefore you have received this book and/or media publication at no charge. A free copy can always be asked for by sending your request to the email or address below.

According to the Lord's will and guidance, Ministry Services, LLC aka Holy Spirit Family & Kingdom Ministries will continue to publish, preach, teach, minister, and administer the Good News of Jesus Christ and His Kingdom in His Power and Love to all that will receive Him.

If the Lord has put on your heart to support this ministry, then you may send that gift of support to

Ministry Services, LLC
Holy Spirit Family & Kingdom Ministries
PO Box 8222
Virginia Beach, VA 23450

Your Gift of Support has been and will always be appreciated.

Meeting information can be found at
www.hsfkm.info
www.kingdomministry.info
Email: hsfkm@live.com

Thank You.

INTRODUCTION

"'My Life In You' by Jesus Christ" is a composite of revelations (revealings) of Jesus Christ by the Holy Spirit. As the Lord had instructed me years ago that He wanted me to write as He gave it, and it was a couple of years later that more instructions came that lead me to the production of this book.

This is the first volume of a series which will declare Jesus Christ. I don't know what the next volume will say or what it will look like, but I do know that it will be lead of the Lord and it will be a revealing of Him to you. Expect your Miracle!

It is His life, and our lives are to be swallowed up in His. He is having this book written to reveal Himself to those that will receive Him, His Kingdom, and Righteousness for their Salvation and New Life in Him.

If you desire this book, then it is because the Lord is drawing you unto Him for a deeper understanding of who He is and of His Kingdom, and your place in Him.

So take your time, and allow the Lord to bring you into a deeper and more awesome experience and awareness of His Presence in You, and you in Him.

Christ Jesus In You... Your Hope of Glory!

CONTENT by REVELATIONS

** End Time Messages*

" 'My Life In You' by Jesus Christ"

REVELATION 1
Word of Faith Speak

Romans 10:9-10-11 (8-12)

But what saith it? The word is nigh thee, even in thy mouth, and in thy heart: that is, the word of faith, which we preach;

v9 That if thou shalt confess with thy mouth the Lord Jesus, and shalt believe in thine heart that God hath raised him from the dead thou shalt be saved.
(Saved: Healed, Delievered, Protected)

v10 For with the heart man believeth unto righteousness; and with the mouth confession is made unto salvation.

v11 For the scripture saith, Whosoever believeth on him shall not be ashamed.

v12 For there is no difference between the Jew and the Greek: for the same Lord over all is rich unto all that call upon him.

Our Father loves EVERYBODY and will prosper them in His Righteousness if they will call upon Him. The Riches of His Glory within the Soul!! Nothing better than that.

Soooo simple has the Lord made it for us to have blessings from Him! Yet that simpleness was provided through the birthing and suffering and death and resurrection of His Son, Yeshua – Jesus Christ.... all honor to the Father and Son. What team work! They are One.

Now the Lord in us- who have received the Spirit of the Son, sealed by that Holy Spirit - so that He can renew our minds and resurrect us from our grave of the dead soul that sinned, and be washed and cleansed and set in the place in Him, which is prepared for us through and by that working which Romans 10:8-12 speaks of. The New Man, the Quickening Spirit, the Lord from Heaven, the Resurrection, and the living Soul: The Lamb of God within... having taken over another soul.... redeemed by the Master's plan.! WE ARE ONE. (I hear a song...!)

Oh, Father.... continue the birthing and deliverance of every soul, bringing all into the blood redemption of your Son. ! .

A New Life... the Sure thing... An Eternal Life we live Today. What Joy, What Peace, My heart sings of Gratitude!!!

Amen.
RPJ

(Write your notes here)

" 'My Life In You' by Jesus Christ"

REVELATION 2
His Testimony Unveiled

Romans 10:9
v 9 That if thou shalt confess with thy mouth the Lord Jesus, and shalt believe in thine heart **that God hath raised him from the dead**, thou shalt be saved.

So, what does "that" mean to you? How does "that" affect you?

So what are you believing in your heart? Is it only words by memory, or has there been a "revealing" of His Presence (The Saviour) in your heart.... a revelation, a manifestation (John 14:20-23) of Jesus Christ, His true presence and coming, and appearing within you... that THAT affects you so dramatically that a change has taken place in your spirit and soul, and you feel a liberty and cleanness within.... and nothing can tell you it is a mistake or make-believe or a lie, because Your Reality has been changed!!! Oh Hallelujah!!! A New Life has begun in Christ Jesus, and HE is causing you to continue your journey of being born again and is placing you in that place in Him that has been prepared for you.

So.... is this what is causing you to confess and believe THAT GOD HAS RAISED HIM?

Can you hold it back? DECLARE the Saviour.... Let us Hear You!!! Speak and don't hold back of the transformation that HE has begun in you.... Enter into His Rest and your Liberty. You are His testimony unveiled!

Amen.
RPJ

REVELATION 3
Receiving His Inheritance 

Ephesians 1:17-23
v 17 That the God of our Lord Jesus Christ, the Father of glory, may give unto you the spirit of wisdom and revelation in the knowledge of him:
v 18 The eyes of your understanding being enlightened; that ye may know what is the hope of his calling, **and what the riches of the glory of his inheritance in the saints**,
v 19 And what is the exceeding greatness of his power to us-ward who believe, according to the working of his mighty power,
v 20 Which he wrought in Christ, when he raised him from the dead, and set him at his own right hand in the heavenly places,
v 21 Far above all principality, and power, and might, and dominion, and every name that is named, not only in this world, but also in that which is to come:
v 22 and hath put all things under his fee, and gave him to be the head over all things to the church.
v 23 Which is his body, the fullness of him that filleth all in all.

.... **and what the riches of the glory of his inheritance in the saints**

...in you is **God's Inheritance** which is His Testimony, His Word, Jesus Christ – **Eternal LIFE in You**

God is Receiving HIS INHERITANCE ! Christ in you, God's riches made manifest to the world.

Christ Has Apprehended Your Soul
and as the Chaff (Carnal Nature) is falling away
and the Glorious Presence of the Son Revealed...
...In That Happening – You are Being Born Again – You are being Changed, Transformed and In That Happening – God is Receiving

You into Himself setting you in that place He has prepared (John 14:1-4)

Once Set – You, the Son, and the Father now are One
Now Your Heaven and Earth are brought together in Christ, in You too!!! All of your spirit, soul and body are being swallowed up of Christ, so that it is His Life, God's Inheritance revealed to the world... even through you.

So, As He is, You now are also, in this world,
yet it is no longer you, but God !!!!!!
Oh Hallelujah!
(1 Corinthians 15:24-28 done.... Ephesians 1:22-23 confirmed) Today is your day... Faith Step or Jump!)

Amen.
RPJ

REVELATION 4
Lord, You are the Focus of my Eye 

Psalm 40:6-11 *8
Matthew 6:24-34 *32-33
Psalm 42:11

Psalm 40:8 "**I delight to do they will, O my God**: yea, they law is within my heart."

Matthew 6:32-33 **"...for your heavenly Father knoweth that ye have need of all these things."**
"But seek ye first the kingdom of God, and his righteousness; and all these things shall be added unto you."

Psalm 42:11 "Why art thou cast down, O my soul? and why are thou disquieted within me? **hope thou in God: for I shall yet praise him**, who is the health of my countenance, and my God."

The Lord is Your Riches, Your Source, Your Provision
* Focus on the Lord – Not the Need at hand
* Seek the Lord's Direction concerning the Need
* Be Consumed by God – Not the Need
*Have Faith in God – He said He knows already what you Need
*Be Obedient to His Word – Matthew 6:24-34 *33 "But seek ye first the kingdom of God, and his righteousness; and all these things shall be added unto you." Believe Him.
* TRUST HIM to FULFIL HIS WORD for YOU

He is Your SOURCE – Your PROVIDER – Your RICHES & WEALTH – Your HEALTH... not money.

Analyze Yourself, and See if you Need to Re-Position Your Focus – Goal – Desires ... why are you doing it?
And Look Unto the Lord, Your Father – and not unto money. Make Him Your Purpose for all.

" 'My Life In You' by Jesus Christ"

Let the Lord your Father be your souls delight.... and trust Him to bring the job, the funds, the people, the peace, the health, the joy, the wealth, ... He already OWNS it all! He is ABLE to provide, so keep your attention on Him, and bring all your concerns to Him.... and let out your Praises and Thank You's with a song in your heart .... for HE IS the DELIGHT OF YOUR HEART.
Matthew 6:24 No man can serve two masters: for either he will hate the one, and love the other: or else he will hold to the one, and despise the other. Ye can not serve God and mammon.

Re-Position yourself so your FOCUS and ATTENTION is doing His Delight and you will see a change in your condition. It may not come in the way you think it will, but it will come as He wants it to be... Can you accept that?

Amen.
RPJ

REVELATION 5
Holy Spirit Tell us more... for without you we could do nothing

Acts 17:28	1Corinthians 4:20	Luke 16:16
Colossians 1:17	Romans 14:17	John 3:3-5
Hebrews 1:3	Luke 17:20-21	John 1:12
Hebrews 9:8	Matthew 23:13	Luke 18:27
Ephesians 1:13-14		

Acts 17:28 For in him we live, and move, and have our being; as certain also of your own poets have said, For we are also his offspring.

Colossians 1:17 And he is before all things, and by him all things consist.

Hebrews 1:3 Who being the brightness of his glory, and the express image of his person, and upholding all things by the word of his power, when he had by himself purged our sins, sat down on the right hand of the Majesty on high;

As an example of Him, the Breath within us powers us to live...
Yet, so...The Breath of Him IS Power in us To Breathe and Live by. (His breath in you is more than just man's breath... hear what He is saying: Key!)

He is Power... He Is *The Key to the Kingdom*. *****
1 Corinthians 4:20 For the kingdom of God is not in word, but in power.

In His Word IS Power. He Speaks and it so. He Willed it, He breathed it ... purposed it forth.
Romans 14:17 For the kingdom of God is not meat and drink; but **righteousness, and peace, and joy in the Holy Ghost.**

... Now IN YOU! if so, the Holy Spirit is in you... then the Kingdom of God is come in you, and that means Jesus Christ is come in you too (because they are one: He's in the kingdom, right? right. - now His Kingdom that is Righteousness, Peace and Joy in the Holy Spirit is abiding in you).

Luke 17:20-21 (Jesus said).... The kingdom of God cometh not with observation: Neither shall they say, Lo here! or, lo there! for, behold, the <u>kingdom of God is within you</u>.

He said it, Do you believe it, do you accept it?

But Now.... We are to enter into His Kingdom that is in us, in Him. How is this possible.... ??? (Luke 18:27 ... with God all things are possible.)
You received that Holy Ghost/Spirit when you heard that word of truth, believed, and received the Son of God (Ephesians 1:13-14).... He Sealed you, and inhabited you, now renovating you, in and by that Holy Spirit .... Transforming and Renewing of the mind... birthing you. (John 1:12 power to become sons)

ONLY by that Holy Spirit (the completeness of Father & Son), the fullness of Him, within us, can we Enter into the
understanding and experience of this Kingdom and Holy Presence (Luke 16:16; John 3:3-5). Our Ability and Strength and Comfort.
He is the KEY to the Kingdom (Hebrews 9:8). Think about it. Every way you look at it, it stills comes back to this one truth: Without Him you can do nothing.

Amen.
RPJ

REVELATION 6
Speak Your Word, Father....

Luke 4:4
Matthew 8:8 (7-8)
Matthew 13:18-23 *22-23

It is therein, His Will Expressed, His Word Manifested, is our Wealth and Riches to get your situation resolved.

It is not money that you need, it is God's Word sent forth into your situation that will resolve it. (period)

Call upon Money – seeking it here and seeking it there – in hopes that it will be the answer to your problems....
OR
Call upon and seek after GOD - for His Word into your situation will bring what you need to resolve your pain.

Decide today who you will serve.

Luke 4:4 And Jesus answered him, saying, It is written, That man shall not live by bread alone, but by every word of God.

Matthew 8:8 (7-8) ...but speak the word only, and my servant shall be healed.

It is Not about the Word of the Carnal Mind, desiring to control and manipulate, declare itself as God.

But it is about The Word of God, breathed into your situation, where even the rich man's knees will have to bend and bow in reverence to the Almighty as Lord.

For God with one breath can dissolve all your material gains, and then where will your feet stand, rich man? where is your feet oh poor man that continues to seek material gain rather than the Will of God in your life. Don't let poverty consume you. People that are poor are sometimes more guilty of seeking material gain, than the rich.

Where is your heart today?

Our Father desires to supply you with what you need... and want.... but make sure your heart is abiding in His Love and Will for your moment.

Don't let the cares of this life, choke out the Word of God....

Matthew 13:18-23 *22-23 He also that received seed among the thorns is he that heareth the word; and <u>the care of this world, and the deceitfulness of riches, choke the word</u>, and he becometh unfruitful.
v 23 But he that received seed into the good ground is he that heareth the word, and understandeth it; which also beareth fruit, and bringeth forth, some an hundredfold, some sixty, some thirty.

Seek His face and Hear His Word for your situation, then hold fast in obedience to it, and Walk.

He will give you your instructions....

Amen.
RPJ

REVELATION 7
HIS GREATER GLORY in You ... Revealed

Romans 8:18-19
Eccl 3:10
Galatians 4:19
Romans 5:3-5
Hebrews 5:14

Romans 8:18 For I reckon that the sufferings of this present time are not worthy to be compared with the glory which shall be revealed in us

Ecclesiastes 3:10 I have seen <u>the travail</u>, which God hath given to the sons of men to be <u>exercised in it</u>.

Galatians 4:19 My little children, of whom I travail in birth again until Christ be formed in you.

Romans 5:3-5 And not only so, but we glory in tribulations also: knowing that tribulation worketh patience;

....patience, experience; .....

....experience, hope;....

....hope maketh not ashamed.... because the love of God is filled your heart (paraphrased).....

Hebrews 5-14 But strong meat belongeth to them that are of full age, even those who by reason of use have their senses exercised to discern both good and evil.

*** "Despise Not the current Tribulation because It Is Working His Greater Glory In You." Hallelujah!

Romans 8:18-19
v 18 For I reckon that the sufferings of this present time are not worthy to be compared with the glory which shall be ***revealed in us.***
v 19 For the earnest expectation of the creature waiteth for the ***manifestation of the sons of God****.*

Amen.
RPJ

REVELATION 8
CHARITY is a 5-letter Word = FRUIT 

Galatians 5: All (*22-25)
1 Corinthians 13:2-8

Galatians 5:1 Stand fast therefore in the liberty wherewith Christ hath made us free, and be not entangled again with the yoke of bondage.

FREE from What?
Free from Rome, or Government? – No
Free from Law of Sin & Death (current Religious Order)? – Yes
Free from Sin – Yes
Free from Missing the Mark of Righteousness, so as not to obtain the prize of Eternal Life, which is The Son of God: His Identity and Inheritance of God the Father – Yes!

Don't fall back under the power (working) of the Flesh... to try and deliver yourself or another from their Flesh.

The ones of old couldn't do it then by the flesh, and neither can it be done today, in that way.

Only by the Spirit of the Son can you or another be "liberated" from your/their flesh...

Only by the Spirit of the Son abiding in you can you be able to abide in Him...

Only because of the Spirit of the Son in us, Do we HIT the MARK of RIGHTEOUSNESS – Forever Done: Sustained in Him..., by Him..., and for Him. Now We also are declared His Righteousness, all because HE – THE RIGHTEOUS ONE, That SEED, abides in us. !!!!! What LIBERTY! amen.

So much could be said on this, so feel free to shout and say more!!!!!! Declare God's Righteousness and Liberate all Souls! Amen.

Now, that we Abide in That Spirit, we WALK .... Producing ...

Producing according to the Holy Spirit that is in us, and according to who We have submitted to: Which is That Holy Spirit of God, the Spirit of the Son, Jesus Christ....

Now HIS FRUIT will be manifested through us, for all to taste of.

Galatians 5:22-25 v22 But the fruit of the Spirit is love, joy, peace, longsuffering, gentleness, goodness, faith, meekness, temperance: against such there is no law....
v25 If we live in the Spirit, let us also walk in the Spirit. (Produce!)

1 Corinthians 13:2-8 ... and have not charity, I am nothing. And though I bestow all my goods to feed the poor, ...

Note here that Charity isn't about giving to the poor... it is clear that Charity is a condition of the heart projected in ALL our giving and/or activities. God likes a cheerful giver??? Is our heart murmuring in our daily walk in the Lord? Are we picking up our daily cross and enduring with Charity each step we take???

v 4-8 Charity suffereth long, and is kind; charity envieth not; charity vaunteth not itself, is not puffed up, Doth not behave itself unseemly, seeketh not her own, is not easily provoked, thinketh no evil; Rejoiceth not in iniquity, but rejoiceth in the truth; Beareth all things, believeth all things, hopeth all things, endureth all things. Charity never faileth:....
You know this.... God is just reminding us and encouraging us to continue in Charity and Love towards each other: within the body

and without...., and allow Him to refine those areas in us, so He may increase within us and through us to others.

Not according to our actions are we saved or born again... in Him only is this established and completed. But being born again, continue this journey, we walk in Charity and Love toward all, as His Presence consumes us and there is no more "I" but Christ, the visible image of the invisible God appearing through us to this world.

Amen.
RPJ

REVELATION 9
Jesus said... "Till I come"

John 21:15-23 (*22)
Matthew 10:19-23
Matthew 23:36; 24:34
Mark 13:30-32
Mark 8:38 – 9:1
Hebrews 10:9-10
Ephesians 2:7
Revelation 1:7

John 21:22 Jesus saith unto him, If I will that he tarry til I come, what is that to thee? follow me.

This was spoken by Jesus after the resurrection.
Jesus was talking of Himself coming back.

Now look at Matthew 10:19-23... Jesus is talking to the disciples instructing and warning them of events to happen soon during their generation.

Matthew 10:19-23
v 23 But when they persecute you in this city, flee ye into another: for verily I say unto you, *Ye shall not have gone over the cities of Israel, till the Son of man be come*.
Meaning: The Son of man will come, before His disciples would have time to go over the cities of Israel.

Oh Hallelujah!! Praise the Lord!! For His Word is Truth! He is Truth!

Now look at Matthew 23:36, Matthew 24:34, Mark 13:30-32, Mark 8:38 – Mark 9:1
Matt 23:36 Verily I say unto you, All these things shall come upon this generation.

Matt 24:34 Verily I say unto you, This generation shall not pass, till all these things be fulfilled.
Mark 13:30 Verily I say unto you, that this generation shall not pass, till all these things be done.

So His Coming in Judgment and Tribulation was to happen to that generation. Now look at this next scripture... It will show you even more that He was talking of "that" generation:

Mark 8:38 – 9:1 Whosoever therefore shall be ashamed of me and of my words in this adulterous and sinful generation; of him also shall the Son of man be ashamed, when he cometh in the glory of his Father with the holy angels. (9:1) An HE said unto them, Verily I

say unto you That there be some of them that stand here, which shall not taste of death, till they have seen the kingdom of God come with power.

First note that he spoke of them as that "adulterous and sinful generation."

Next, note that Jesus says here that the Son of man will come in the glory of his Father with the holy angels. In Other scriptures, Jesus speaks of coming in great power and glory, judging that generation.

But note also here that Jesus tells them that some of them standing there will not die UNTIL THEY SEE the KINGDOM OF GOD COME with power. !!! "THEN" was it to happen... not in our future... but in their present. Wow!

Jesus clearly is telling them of the judgment of that generation which was the conclusion of that order of the Law of sin and death; and it was the bringing in of the **New Order of the Blood**

of Jesus Christ: Grace and Life through the Righteousness of Jesus Christ...

Judgment was about to come to that Generation to fulfil that old order which was about to melt away. And The New Heaven and Earth – God's Glorious Kingdom was then about to be Eternally Established in Heaven and Earth. !!! ... by His Own Doing, the sealing – the consecration by the Blood Covenant of His Own Son... Eternally Forever Finished. Completed. Done.

Jesus Christ Came – to Complete the order and covenant that was active during that generation of time. He consummated it and finalized all judgment upon that generation. Then to establish the 2nd Order: the New Priesthood, King, Government ... as it says in many scriptures ... here is one of them:

Hebrews 10:9-10 Then said he, Lo, I come to do thy will, O God. He taketh away the first, that he may establish the second. By the which will we are sanctified through the offering of the body of Jesus Christ once for all. (Oh, Holy Ground! Praise the Lord!)

NOW – We are – Ephesians 2:7 we are in and among those – that are in "ages to come" that this scripture speaks of :

Ephesians 2:7 That in the **ages to come** he might show the exceeding riches of his grace in his kindness toward us through Christ Jesus.

"In the ages to come" is speaking of US! "he might show" is speaking of what he will show to the future generations/ages which is US ! And WHAT he will show is the "exceeding riches of his grace in his kindness toward us through Christ Jesus" !!!!!
Oh Hallelujah! For Wisdom, Understanding, and Knowledge by the Holy Spirit of the Father and Son!!! He is our Souls Delight and Liberty!

So be free of present and future tribulation worries, for that great tribulation and coming of the Lord Jesus Christ happened just as Jesus had said. And today we can ENTER INTO HIS
KINGDOM which is Righteousness, Peace, and Joy in the HOLY GHOST (the Spirit of the Father & Son) IN US who have received Him.

In Matthew 24:21 Jesus explains about that great tribulation that was about to come on that generation: "For then shall be great tribulation, such as was not since the beginning of this world to this time, no nor ever shall be." Jesus said it, that settles it, I accept His Truth in His understanding.

It's so wonderful to be free! Thank You Lord!

Amen.
RPJ

" 'My Life In You' by Jesus Christ"

REVELATION 10
Is this Your Administration from the Lord?

1 Chronicles 29: all (*9)
2 Corinthians 9: all (*7)

Look at the old testament on this and then the new.... and in this you will see that even though there has been a changing of the "Law of God" concerning His relationship with us, and it is so much easier for us to fellowship with Him, all by and in thanksgiving of the Blood Covenant of His Son, Jesus Christ ....!!! .... Yet, when it comes to giving for the support of the Lord's Ministries, our Father STILL DESIRES WE GIVE WITH A WILLING AND CHEERFUL HEART - OBEDIENCE. (period)

Soooo, We all have that administration of GIVING in obedience to our Father in all things. Yet some are given the administration of providing for the saints so that they can be about the working of the Lord rather than about making money or getting food and clothing or whatever necessities are needed for the working of His ministries, i.e. building, furniture, advertising, working vehicle, gas, and the list goes on......

No One Person should have to provide for any ministry. Some don't want to give because they have a HARD HEART. If that is you, then it is time to turn to the Lord in forgiveness and His love, and let Him soften and HEAL that hard heart up.

This Giving Administration can be shown in many ways. So whatever the Lord has caused You to be full of..... give CHEERFULLY, and WILLINGLY out of an OBEDIENT heart when HE SHOWS YOU that HE DESIRES to bless that certain person or ministry/minister.

Don't give because someone says you have to. Don't give because a minister makes you feel guilty or threatened..... There should be a heart within you that is having a love relationship with our Father and is seeking Him in every area of your life, for Him to flow through. You are His expression through His Son, to this World.....

Get your own heart soft towards the Lord our Father, and allow Him to guide you. Giving to someone when the Father says to, even if you know that person will wrongly use it, is better than not being obedient to the Father when He tells you to give, even if it doesn't make sense to you.... that person then will be dealt with by our Father in correcting their behavior, or maybe there's more to the story than you are able to see. Then God's Grace begins working in that person, through your obedience, and the limits are off to the thanksgivings unto the Lord that could come of this. !!!

Soooo, Read these scriptures above and ALLOW the Lord to talk with you.... let your Heart be right, open, willingly to do expediently as He reveals and puts within you His Desire.
The Lord is our Shepherd, we shall not want..... Trust Him and walk in His Faith. Give Him First – the Honor and Respect Due.... all the other necessities will be provided for.

HE Loves Us.

Amen.
RPJ

REVELATION 11
Your Covering

Isaiah 30:1 *... and that cover with a covering, but not of my spirit...

1 John 3:27 ... but as that same anointing teacheth you of all things, and is truth, and is no lie, and even as it hath taught you, ye shall abide in him.

John 14:20 At that day ye shall know that **I am in my Father, and ye in me, and I in you**.

Now THAT's The COVERING!

There are many scriptures in the Old Testament that speak of animal skins used as coverings. So by all understanding, we have Jesus Christ as our Covering... the Eternal Sacrifice, Lamb of God that has taken away, and is continuously washing and cleansing us until all our sin and sinful nature is no more. What a process it is, to be born again of His Nature, His Spirit.

Jesus Christ was the first fruit, the first to be birthed forth of the Spirit: all man in that sinful nature, yet without sin; All God in that glorious nature, and all victorious in accomplishing the redemptive actions for the rest of us...
as our Eternal Covering: the Eternal Sacrifice & Blood which speaks and declares Righteousness.

HE is the ONLY COVERING we need or should ever take upon ourselves.... The Only Name to walk by.... The Only Spirit to have leading our lives. So as the Lord sets and places each of us in position within HIS BODY, let us be faithful to follow the leading of the Spirit of the Lord only, in all our affairs. Yielding to Him only. If another tells you thus saith the Lord, but there is no witness in you to that.... you are not required to follow.

If you are not able to hear the voice of the Lord yet, or are still learning..... ask the Lord to give you HIS Shepherd/Pastor to help you.

Then when that one (or more) comes in to your life, He/She will be lead of the Lord's Spirit in causing you to grow up into Christ, and will know when to let you go or rather back off to let you learn.

Not an easy task for any of God's true Shepherds or Pastors, or any of the 5-fold hand ministry spoken of in Ephesians 4:11-13, and 1 Corinthians 12, but it is a necessity in the Body of Christ.

And YOU will have the assurance & peace of the Lord in your heart when that Shepherd/Hand Ministry Gift(s) is sent to help you in instructing and teaching you of the Lord, yet it will be by that SAME ANOINTING – SAME SPIRIT OF THE LORD that will be teaching, governing, instructing, guiding, and/or protecting you. Now if you are one of the rebellious ones... then, well, that is another working.

Pressing in to the Lord can be unsettling at times, as the Truth is revealed, which is so different from the traditions of religion.

The Lord is Patient and Kind. But His Fire does a perfect work. And sometimes what looks like Hell, is actually your hell
being shaken to release you into the finer things of the Kingdom of Heaven that is in the Holy Spirit.!

So submit to the Lord, that same Spirit. Know that HE, the Lord Jesus Christ, the Spirit of the Father is the only covering you need.

Then wherever you go, no matter what church gathering place you go to, no matter what name they associate themselves with, You Are Covered - In and By the Spirit of the Lord, the Lamb of

God, and the Blood that speaks better things than that of Abel. (Hebrews 12:22-29)

Can't get any better than this!

Amen.
RPJ

(Write your notes here)

REVELATION 12
The Travail of His Soul

Ephesians 3:19 (14-21)	John 15:4-5	1 Cor 15:44-47
2 Corinthians 5:1-5	Acts 13:23	2 Cor 4:14
Isaiah 53:11	2 Peter 1:4	John 1:12
Genesis 1:28	John 16:21	Galatians 4:19
Eph 1:22-23		

Jesus Christ offered the ultimate Travailing of the Soul. None can top what He did.

So why would our Father desire for us that are called by His Name and have become His Habitation to have to travail also in our souls?

First, being birthed as a member of His Son, and walking in the identity and co-heirs of His Son, and being filled with God's Holy Presence/Spirit – being filled with all the fullness of Him (Ephesians 3:19, John 1:12).... we have a responsibility to be Obedient to our Father's Desires... And PRODUCE after His Kind. (Genesis 1:28, 1 Cor 15)

So when the Father wants to "birth" His Son, an idea, His will, and/or purpose in and through us FOR THE PROFIT OF HIS BODY AND PEOPLE, then we should do as Jesus also did....

Travail in our minds, our Souls, Spirit for the manifestation of God's Will (not the carnal minds will or desires of the flesh).

Travail: (in my dictionary) means to labor, to toil, to suffer the pangs of childbirth.

From the biblical definition it is also referred to as "going through the birthing process" but as the parent mother, not as the child experience. Jesus talks of travail as the "seed" being planted and producing out of the earth.... (John 16:21). Then in Galatians 4:19 Paul says "My little children, of whom I travail in birth again, until Christ be formed in you." Again in the sense of the experience the mother parent must go through within themselves to bring forth the produce of the seed that is planted in them.

Now, take this to the next level! .... YOUR Soul is that Mother, that God has planted THE SEED (HIS WORD) to germinate within Your Soul and PRODUCE after That SEED WHICH IS CHRIST JESUS.

Jesus said in John 15:4-5 "Abide in me, and I in you.....I am the vine, ye are the branches; He that abideth in me, and I in him, the same bringeth forth much fruit: for without me ye can do nothing." So here He speaks as the One IN your Soul as The Spirit that is all Righteousness and Holiness, to impregnate your Soul with His SEED, Word, Spirit... to produce His presence IN you and then Through you to this world. ! . (So many scriptures to confirm this working)

Breaking forth through you is THE SON OF GOD swallowing up your nature body, yet it is The Holy Spirit: the Father & Son having produced themselves to, in and through you, having now SWALLOWED UP YOUR MORTAL BODIES having RENEWED and TRANSFORMED your MIND (the falling away of the chaff – that carnal mind). (2 Cor 5:5 1-5)

Oh how exciting is this birth, Oh how painful it can be most of the time! Don't give up now, it is too late to turn back now.... take a deep breath and push!!!! Joy comes in the morning!
So, Travail is a meditation on the Word that God has Planted in your Soul and Mind. Think on it. Meditate on it. SEEK the Lord In It Always!!!! Until His Nature is Revealed... Until His Will is Manifested in this world. (2 Peter 1:4; Gal 4:19)

Acts 13:23 states "Of this man's seed hath God according to his promise raised unto Israel a Saviour, Jesus:" 'this man's seed' is

Abraham's seed that God used to bring forth the Promised Saviour for Israel and us all.

But listen to what the Lord is saying here ----- That is and has been accomplished through Jesus Christ, yet NOW we are become that BODY of the Lord... not only in and by and as the Spirit of the Lord (1 Cor 15:44-47), but are The Church, HIS BODY, the fullness of Him that filleth all in all (Eph 1:22-23). God in the flesh, returned to the earth, the visible image of the invisible God, Heaven and Earth brought together in one, That

Lord and Saviour, The Son of God..... which HE has Caused Us to BECOME (birthed) in this world manifested through the natural man, that has now been and is still being, swallowed up of His Spirit and Kingdom. (2 Corinthians 5:1-5; 2 Cor 4:14).

Oh Hallelujah !!!!!

So allow the Travailing to continue in the Lord until the Lord's Desire is fulfilled through you.!.

Amen.
RPJ

REVELATION 13
"ESTABLISHED"

2 Chronicles 20:20 (perfect vision); v 17
Ephesians 6:10-18
Romans 1:16-17
Psalm 24:1-2
Proverbs 3:19-20
Matthew 13:18-23
Ephesians 1:17-18
2 Peter 1:1-12

2 Chronicles 20:20 And they rose early in the morning, and went forth into the wilderness of Tekoa: and as they went forth, Jehoshaphat stood and said, Hear me, O Judah, and ye inhabitants of Jerusalem; **Believe in the Lord** your God, so shall ye be **established**; believe his prophets, so shall ye prosper.

If you read the rest of the chapter you'll find that they were going through a tough time... a battle. But in verse 17 the word of the Lord to them was to stand fast and believe in the Lord. Here's what v 17 states:

v17 Ye shall not need to fight in this battle: set yourselves, stand ye still, and see the salvation of the Lord with you, O Judah and Jerusalem: fear not, nor be dismayed; tomorrow go out against them: for the Lord will be with you.

Today we are in Grace; the Battle is over and won; so HEAR what the Lord's instructions for you are today, and WALK in that FAITH of HIS Word for You.... THEN you will SEE the VICTORY of the Lord come forth to your Favor. BUT HEAR HIS INSTRUCTIONS.... SEEK HIM on that .... THEN GO ...
BELIEVE in the Lord your God ... So shall you be ESTABLISHED. SET in Place..... Unmovable.

Ephesians 6:10-18 instructs of standing fast in the armor of God which is the wisdom, understanding, and knowledge of Jesus

Christ! This IS the LORD'S PRESENCE IN US – His Power in this World. (Romans 1:16-17)

So, When the Lord ESTABLISHES you In Truth, You Can Not Be Moved.... or depending on the circumstances, you can say... Once the Blessings of the Lord are ESTABLISHED in Your Heart, AND YOU IN THE BLESSINGS, then your outcome in every situation will be BLESSINGS! FAVOR! VICTORY every time!

So how to be Established? First the LORD MUST REVEAL HIS WORD TO YOU... Then there must be the Lord's Understanding Revealed in Your Mind/Soul of His Word and Will for your situation, which may come right away, or may require that you spend time asking the Lord questions and LISTENING to HIS VOICE in revealing the MEANING of His Word.... wait until that Experience/Revealing is given to you. Then BELIEVE and WALK in That Understanding of His Word concerning your situation. Read 2 Chronicles 20:20 again.

Now read Psalm 24:1-2.....
Psalm 24:1-2 The earth is the Lord's, and the fullness thereof; the world, and they that dwell therein.

v2 For he hath founded it upon the seas, and <u>established</u> it upon the floods. <u>Once the Lord ESTABLISHES the Victory for you, it is done...</u> secured.... unmovable.
YET Now He wants YOU to be ESTABLISHED in the VICTORY.... HOW? Read this......

Proverbs 3:19-20... The Lord by wisdom hath founded the earth; <u>**by understanding**</u> hath he <u>**established**</u> the heavens. By his knowledge the depths are broken up, and the clouds drop down the dew.

UNDERSTANDING will ESTABLISH YOU <u>IN</u> the LORD'S BLESSING. Read Matthew 13:18-23 below...

Matthew 13:18-23
v 19 When any one **hear**eth the word of the kingdom, and **understandeth** it **not**, then cometh the wicked one, and catcheth away that which was sown in his heart. This is he which received seed by the way side......
v 20 But he that received the seed into stony places, the same is he that **hear**eth the word, and anon **with joy receive**th it; v21 **Yet** hath he **not root** in himself, but dureth for a while: for when tribulation or persecution ariseth because of the word, by and by he is offended.
v 23 But he that received seed into the good ground is he that **hear**eth the word, and **understandeth** it; which also beareth fruit, and bringeth forth, some an hundredfold, some sixty, some thirty.

When you don't understand what the Word of the Lord means, that revelation/revealing/manifestation/appearing of Jesus Christ within your soul/mind, IF it is not understood, it falls to the ground, the way side, profiting you nothing (not being mixed with Faith). It is as if you hear and receive the word with joy, but because there is no root (understanding of it) to secure you, then the trials and cares of the world choke out the benefits of the blessing.

But when you Hear it AND Understand what the Lord is saying, you then have "conceived" God's word that is Spirit and Life and it is bringing forth your soul out of death and into life... and your body reaps of this too. It is revealing HIS Son to and in you, and then as you have received Him, you are entering in to Him and His Life.... (Eph 5:26-27) Reconciled, Redeemed. You are being born again by His living word that is Jesus Christ. God is writing His Blood Covenant in your heart and putting in your mind the new law (Heb 8:10). When you behold Him in His Glory (victory) you will be changed into the same image... yet by the Holy Spirit doing the work (2 Cor 3:16-18).

So ASK for HIS UNDERSTANDING and WISDOM along with His KNOWLEDGE. (Ephesians 1:17-23 *17-19)

Solution: You will Need to Hear, Receive & Understand = a Revelation (revealing) of Jesus Christ Manifest** in your Soul = This only comes by the Holy Spirit Teaching*** those that are willing to be taught.....

*** an **encounter**; no longer a word from the doctrines/traditions of man trying to be God; but instead the **experience(encounter)** within your soul of the manifestation of the Power of God which Is Jesus Christ – God's Salvation that was manifested in the Flesh, in the form of the sinful man, yet was and is the Lamb of God, the Eternal Sacrifice that takes and took away our sin, decay and death, so that we may LIVE in HIM who is the LORD, the Quickening Spirit, that is LIFE ETERNAL today. That by HIS WILL we are ONE with the ETERNAL GOD ALMIGHTY, yet as a child and student still being taught and learning continuously of His and Our Kingdom, We abide in HIM who governs all things,
and we walk humbly in reverence of our Father and God of All.... and you & I could go on, and on, and on to Declare such Righteousness abounding!!!)*

**** A Teacher can never force themselves on a student – in order for the student to prosper in the teaching, the student has to be willing to be taught, AND Ready to make the time for the Teacher to teach.*

Again... To the STUDENT: ASK of the Lord to give you: Wisdom, Understanding, and Knowledge of Jesus Christ.

Ephesians 1:17-18 says the perfect prayer to **ask of the Father**:
v 17 That the God of our Lord Jesus Christ, the Father of glory, **may give unto you** the **spirit of wisdom** and **revelation** in the **knowledge** of him:

v 18 **The eyes of your understanding** being **enlightened**; that ye may know what is the hope of his calling, and what the riches of the glory of his inheritance in the saints,....

Understanding is PERFECT VISION... Perception... Comprehension, which comes only by that Holy Spirit which is the Lord.

Receive His Word Today, and UNDERSTAND (see clearly what he is saying and means), and BE ESTABLISHED IN THE PRESENT TRUTH. (2 Peter 1:1-12)

Amen.
RPJ

REVELATION 14
Innovation: The Lord's Will Be Done

Corporate mentality has been destroyed... and is being removed from the True Church." What does this mean? To Incorporate or Corporate means to bringing together of many as one body, and as one mind ..... so this mentality should STAY and INCREASE By & In The Government of the Lord. But what about those that have an issue with incorporating in the state, or with the laws of the land? Some say yes, some say no don't do it. Does that mean we cannot use the benefits of the state and federal government of the land, to benefit the Body of Christ? If the earth is the Lord's, then isn't He the one that is in charge of the governments of the land.... Didn't God put us in this earth to declare His Righteousness and His Government in this land. Yes. So don't give away that authority the Lord gave us. Instead, Get Up and Stand in Your Place that the Lord has put you in, and Do the Work, ministering the Gifts He has given you. Even in the days of Jesus, didn't he permit taxes to be paid, to go along with their rules, and keep the peace..., as long as they never interfered with the Order and Government of His Father. So if paying taxes was okay, then not paying them (thru the benefit of the government by being a 501c3 status) is also okay today... does anyone really care about getting a tax deduction? Oh, you do care!

Then be sure our giving is to the Lord and out of obedience, first and for most.

Getting a tax deduction is not wrong or against God, but it is 'the motive' or reason for the giving that needs to be looked at. Maybe there are those that are so wealthy that they could use a tax deduction and want to give to help the Lord's Ministry, too. Then let them give with a cheerful heart, as the Lord puts on their heart to give. And if another that is wealthy wants to give only because of a tax deduction, then let the Lord be praised by the Body of Christ in that giving, for the scriptures reveal that the wealth of the sinner is stored up for the just.... But it is a choice to make, yet only after seeking diligently the direction the Lord, as He directs YOU to do.

Money shouldn’t determine what you do. Being Free from paying taxes shouldn’t be the reason to create a local assembling place for the Body of Christ. But yielding to the Lord’s decision on how to create that gathering... and if He wants to pay taxes, so be it. ... if He wants it to be 501c3, so be it.

The Word of God in our situation is sufficient to bring us what is needed.

It was the Religious System that gave Him the most problems. Put the Lord first in our lives. Acknowledge Him in all our ways. Let HIM be the reason for all we do.

So ask the Father how He wants YOU to work the ministry He has put in your hands.

If the Lord tells you to make it as a corporation, or a sole proprietor, or go and minister in your daily lives with no company of the land at all, or just have meetings in your home (we have that privilege in the USA to ‘freely assemble.’) ... whether able to give tax deductible receipts or receive only “gifts non taxable” or even pay taxes on the support you get...
the decision comes down to what and how our Father wants us to do His Will.

Don’t allow Money to determine our motions!
Let the Word of God be established in every move.

So go and do as He instructs. Whether a corporation set up as a local assembling, or free church set up or whatever... just do it because He our Father says to.

And Ask the Lord how He wants you to give your gifts of support to His Ministries…. then just do it. Teamwork. No one is better than another in the Body of Christ.

We Need Each Other!

Just go and do what He tells you to and be settled in that, and let love flow.

If any grumble or complain, let them take it up with our Father, who has made Jesus Christ, that eternal Sacrifice and Soul of God, our true HEAD and Authority in all places that He takes us.

Time to Be about our Father's Business and Go to Work…. So let the Father's Government Reign in our Souls first, and then it will flow in this land that we live in…

And we will see the change for the better in this land.
Trust God. Have Faith In God. He Deserves all Honor, Glory, and Thanksgiving from All.

Amen.
RPJ

REVELATION 15
BRANDED By the Lord

Ezekiel 9:2-4
Exodus 12:3-17
Revelation 21:11
1 Corinthians 5:7
Hebrews 8:10
Ephesians 1:22-23
Ephesians 5:23
John 1:12

Oh what a Saviour we have, Oh what a Lamb to partake of, who has marked us with His Blood, Branded Us with His Name, Oh what a Saviour to Proclaim!

Have you been branded by the Lord? Allow Him to Brand you with HIS NAME, and Mark and wash you with HIS BLOOD.... No Harm is allowed to touch this Place. Let the EVIDENCE (FAITH) cause you to stand and walk upon this Truth.

Ezekiel 9:2-4 tells us of the 'man' with the inkhorn that went about the city to "mark" each of those men that sigh and that cry because of all the abominations that were done there... they lived there but did not participate in it. So the Lord had them 'marked' on the forehead to protect them from the wrath to come. It's interesting to see that there was one man among the six that was clothed in linen, which was the one with the writer's inkhorn by his side. Read this passage and hear the many revealings of the Lord here. But to stay focused on the topic of today, let's look at verse 4:

v 4 And the Lord said unto him, Go through the midst of the city, through the midst of Jerusalem, and <u>set a mark upon the foreheads</u> of the men that sigh and that cry for all the abominations that be done in the midst thereof.

Then look at Exodus 12:3-17 verse 7, 11-13 reveals:
v 7 And they shall take of the blood, and strike it on the two side posts and on the upper door post of the houses, wherein they shall eat it.

v 11-13 And thus shall ye eat it; with your loins girded, your shoes on your feet, and your staff in your hand; and ye shall eat it in haste: it is the LORD's Passover. For I will pass through the land of EGYPT this night, and will smite all the firstborn in the land of Egypt, both man and beast; and against all the gods of Egypt I will execute judgment: I am the LORD. And the blood shall be to you for a token upon the houses where ye are: and when I see the blood, I will pass over, and the plague shall not be upon you to destroy you, when I smite the land of Egypt.

Note, the 'marking' of the blood on each two side posts and the upper door post (three areas) of the entry of that family or household. The EVIDENCE of the Lord's lamb sacrifice for the safety of that household. That BLOOD that speaks better things than that of Abel or any animal sacrifice, is noted on our forehead: body, soul, & spirit (three areas) to declare us Private Property of the Lord – No Trespassing allowed.

So upon your forehead the brand or mark of the Lord rests on us that have received the Lamb of God, to declare us as His Property, to COVER us from all harm, disease, wrath of God and judgment. All harm, death, decay, disease, AND JUDGEMENT is to PASSOVER us. THIS IS our BLESSING and INHERITED RIGHT through That Blood of Jesus Christ, the FATHER's Eternal Sacrifice that **Consecrates** us forever in His Glory, Grace, SAFETY, and PEACE…. THAT LOVE & LIBERTY. We, by HIS WILL, are CO-Heirs of all His Kingdom and Rights as Priest and King over all other kingdoms and domains and names….. Wow! Yet always knowing HE IS HEAD FOREVER of us. What an excitement within on this!!

Also, Note that JUDGEMENT is now PASSED OVER…. GRACE ABOUNDS in His Mercy towards us, sufficient for us to continue our "being born again" journey (out of Egypt into the promised land: Eternal Life which is Jesus Christ). Continue to allow Him to wash us, teach us, train us, mature us, renew us, transform us…. until He sees only that 'clear as crystal' Glory of Himself which is spoken of in Revelation 21:11: Having the glory of God: and her light was like unto a stone most precious, even like a jasper stone, clear as crystal......

So some of you may say "I'm born again" when I accept Jesus Christ as my Saviour. ?? Actually, that is only the Beginning of your journey of Being Born Again. Yet, you are secured in Christ Jesus at that moment, that if you were to pass on (die) today, you would enter in to heaven.... he anchored you and became the way for you to enter in. BUT there is more to it than this.... MUCH More that is pretty heavy to look into, but if you desire, the Lord may show you, if you ask and are willing to allow Him to prepare you to receive it.

God is Awesome, yes? Yes!!! We couldn't and wouldn't be able to receive such awesomeness all at once. Yet He Desires to reveal all of Himself to us, yet there is a processing of our soul to allow us to be able to receive Him without being 'overcome' of Him. I thank the Lord for the BLOOD of Jesus Christ BY WHICH WAY WE CAN COME BOLDLY INTO THIS THRONE OF GRACE, AND BEHOLD HIM... and be CHANGED, TRANSFORMED into HIS SAME IMAGE – HIS SON, JESUS CHRIST. We are His Body, He is our Head. (Ephesians 1:22-23; Ephesians 5:23; John 1:12)

So, don't be passive at the first step into God's Presence and Kingdom, But Continue on Into His Presence TODAY! Don't wait, because Today is Our Day of Salvation..... ENTER into His Glory Today and EAT From His Table.... Learn and be Taught of our Saviour Jesus Christ the Eternal Lamb of God that was dead, but now lives forever.... creating OUR WAY to have true FELLOWSHIP and COMMUNION with our LORD and FATHER.

1 Corinthians 5:7 Purge out therefore the old leaven, that ye may be a new lump, as ye are unleavened. For even Christ our Passover is sacrificed for us: Therefore let us keep the feast, not with old leaven, neither with the leaven of malice and

wickedness; but with the unleavened bread of **sincerity** and **truth**.

Remember, a LIE of doctrine... is Not Truth. So continue the journey and PRESS INTO HIS KINGDOM by the BLOOD OF THE LAMB and allow Him to Reveal TRUTH.

Lay down all you think you know of Jesus Christ, and let Him WRITE UPON YOUR FOREHEAD THE LORD JESUS CHRIST – GOD'S ENGRAVEN PROMISE AND WILL OF ETERNAL LIFE .... upon and in your Mind & Heart. (Hebrews 8:10) Allow Him to Brand you with HIS NAME, and Mark and wash you with HIS BLOOD.... No Harm is allowed to touch this Place. Let the EVIDENCE (FAITH) cause you to stand and walk upon this Truth.

Amen.
RPJ

REVELATION 16
Peace of God is Jesus Christ: The Lord's Valentine to Us

Luke 2:14 (10-15); Ephesians 2:14
Luke 2:14 Glory to God in the highest, <u>and on earth peace</u>, good will toward men.

Ephesians 2:14 For <u>he is our peace</u>, who hath made both one, and hath broken down the middle wall of partition between us,... Although this passage we all have read plenty of times, yet when the Lord speaks concerning it, then it becomes engraved within our souls, and is alive within.... God's testimony, breath, Spirit working within us .....

So it is with these two scriptures and the Lord's message today of "on earth peace." In Luke the passage from verse 10 -15 speaks of the moment the angels appeared to the shepherds in the fields to tell them of the birth of the Son of God.

The world looks for peace. Every Soul longs for peace. Seriously, all souls long for peace, no matter what religion or belief they say they are of. Yet, that answer to their longing has arrived!

That peace is Jesus Christ to all men!.! You know that, I know that.... but many just know Him as a religion that isn't a real person, presence. They just haven't EXPERIENCED or ENCOUNTERED Him yet. Then they too will be changed, and abide in true PEACE.

Our Peace was ordained of God, and made manifest in the earth. Now, forever set is OUR PEACE. Ephesians 2:14 tells us he is our peace.

So as the song goes, "what the world needs now is love" can be changed or rather added to it "peace;" cause truly the world needs to EXPERIENCE God's Peace – Jesus Christ.

If all the World and people in the world could be awakened to this truth, and ENCOUNTER the Love of God through Jesus Christ, then His Peace would keep them.

And how can the world ENCOUNTER and EXPERIENCE the true presence of Peace? By that Holy Spirit appearing through His many membered body and revealing that "good news" that is their peace, and joy in this earth. Ephesians 1:22-23 tells us that we are the fullness of him that filleth all in all. We are the walking, visible body of God's Son in this earth, not by our choice, but by God's choice that we are.... So, grow up into the Head which is Jesus Christ, the Son, the firstfruit of the Spirit. Now let the Head, be birthed through you: His mind and character ... Co-Heirs of His Kingdom... as His woman, help mate, body to work through in this earth.

As Luke 2:10 states "And the angel said unto them, Fear not: for, behold, I bring you good tidings of great joy, which shall be to all people."

Give the best love gift of all – Jesus Christ revealed by the Holy Spirit through us.

What the world needs now is Peace.... and He is Come.
Let His Light Shine through You Oh Body of Christ!

Amen
RPJ

REVELATION 17
Raised Us Up Together

Ephesians 2:5-7	Romans 8:10-11	John 6:63
Romans 8:1-4	Ephesians 5:26-27	John 15:3
2 Corinthians 3:17	1 Peter 1:22-23	Hebrews 7:12
Ephesians 1:17-18	2 Corinthians 3:18	1 John 5:20
John 3:3-5	Matthew 7:21-23	Ephesians 3:9
John 1:12-14	John 14:3	John 15:4-5

Ephesians 2:5-8 Even when we were dead in sins, hath quickened us together with Christ, (by grace ye are saved;) And hath raised us up together, and made us sit together in heavenly places in Christ Jesus: That in the ages to come he might show the exceeding riches of his grace in his kindness toward us through Christ Jesus. For by grace are ye saved through faith; and that not of yourselves: it is the gift of God: Not of works, lest any man should boast.

"...raised us up together, and made us sit together in heavenly places... In Christ Jesus... " Is This True? Yes! Today it is so.

It sounds like that false doctrine called rapture, but this verse above is truth and is no lie. Rapture theology is a lie, a false doctrine that has stumped many that have not studied it out for themselves. So if this statement bothers you, then, Study it out.

We ARE raised up together in Christ Jesus.... Hallelujah! And there is soooo much to see and experience in this new life out of our Grave..... yes Grave. We all were dead because of sin.
But there is a new Spirit within us, now that we have received Jesus Christ (Romans 8:1-4). And this Spirit is the Holy Spirit which is the Lord which is Jesus Christ which is God (read 2 Corinthians 3:17; 1 John 5:20). Now there is a new law and order WORKING WITHIN us to Wash us and Cleanse us as Ephesians 5:26-27 talks of. (Hebrews 7:12)

Ephesians 5:26-27 That he (Christ) might sanctify and cleanse it (his bride/church) with the washing of water by the word,

WASHING OF WATER....BY HIS....THE WORD that is Spirit and Life. John 6:63; John 15:3, 1 Peter 1:23.

So allow the Lord to Wash you and Cleanse you by His Word being spoken to you through Him, in those ministers he sends your way.

You cannot be cleansed by or in a lie. Only the Truth can wash and cleanse and set you free.
Come on up higher. Ask and allow the Lord to Raise You Up ... So that where He is You are too...A Place that has no lies. Today is your Day of Salvation. Today your Sins have ended, and God's Clean up begins to Release You from your grave clothes, and reveal to you The Heavenly Realm of His Kingdom.

Ask for Wisdom, but with Wisdom, Get Understanding. Ephesians 1:17-18. He hasn't called you just to show off in the gifts... He wants Fruit of the Spirit Produced. He said he never
knew them – meaning those that just show off in the gifts, but are not reproducing after His own Seed through an Intimacy with HIM: Understanding that to "know one" is as Adam "knew" Eve and conceived... Intimacy that resulted in Producing after Him the Son. Jesus Christ is the Head which comes first in the birthing. God held this mystery in secret Eph 3:9 for a long time, until it was "time" to be revealed.... NOW the BODY COMES FORTH.

Yes, His church then came forth, but every age after are those that are also called and elected to this very election of Grace and Sonship which is to be and needs to be Revealed to this Age/World. .... You are Engrafted/Birthed in to the determined place of His Body John 14:3... and oh, there is so much more to reveal... continue your journey... PRESS .... John 3:3-5 be born again. Matthew 7:21-23; 2 Corinthians 3:18; John 1:12-14; Romans 8:10-11....

Galatians 2:20 I am crucified with Christ: nevertheless I live; yet not I, but Christ liveth in me and the life which I now live in the flesh I live by the faith of the Son of God, who loved me and gave himself for me.

Romans 8:10-11 And if Christ be in you, the body is dead because of sin; but the Spirit is life because of righteousness. But if the Spirit of him that raised up Jesus from the dead dwell in you, he that raised up Christ from the dead shall also quicken your mortal bodies by his Spirit that dwelleth in you.

We are His Body, now joined to Him the Head, to bring PEACE & Love to this age/world. RISE UP oh BODY. But You Must Be Joined/Submitted to the Head.... For without Him, you can do nothing John 15:4-5.

Maybe take time and think, meditate on all this with the Lord.

ENJOY!

Amen.
RPJ

REVELATION 18
The Great Assembling 

Daniel 6:22	Ephesians 5:26-27	2 Cor 1:9-10
Hebrews 2:8-9	Matthew 11:27	Heb 2:9
Rev 19:7-8	2 Timothy 1:10	1 Cor 15:24

In the midst of our dilemma, innocence was found and safety was demanded.

In your blood, or pollution, God has seen you and has sent help & rescue is on the way. For some, the Deliverer has arrived and the land is quiet. But for those that don't yet see everything put under your feet, just hold on to His Assurance for INNOCENCE is found within you and He will deliver you. (Hebrews 2:8-9)

Hebrews 2:8-9 Thou hast put all things in subjection under his feet. For in that he put all in subjection under him, he left nothing that is not put under him. But now we see not yet all things put under him. **But we see Jesus**, who was made a little lower than the angels for the suffering of death, crowned with glory and honour; that he by the grace of God should taste death for every man.

In Daniel 6:22 the word Innocency is 2136 kakuw meaning purity. If you study further a few more connecting words with this you'll find that it means: transparent, to be translucent, to be innocent, to be transparent, or clean (physical or moral).

That Innocence is Jesus Christ the Lamb of God: that Blood/Spirit/Righteousness of the Lamb, declaring in you your Liberty. His Power is that Living Word working God's Will in you... (!!!)

In Revelation it tells us that the Lamb’s wife hath made herself ready, and she was **clean** and white, arrayed in fine linen (righteousness).

Revelation 19:7-8
7 Let us be glad and rejoice, and give honour to him: for the marriage of the Lamb is come, and his wife **hath made herself ready**.
8 And to her was granted that she should be arrayed in fine linen, **clean** and white: for the fine linen is the righteousness of saints.

So what is the Lord telling us today….

God’s word is the cleansing agent for us spiritually, and physically. When He, the Spirit (Holy) speaks, within your own soul or through another to your soul, it has the same affect…. It quickens, makes alive, cleanses, washes, purifies, sanctifies, sets apart/consecrates, justifies……..heals, delivers, makes free.

HE makes You Ready (able) to be received by the Father.

Also, the Father is that Spirit doing the work in you, and through you, just as He did in Jesus. By whom also was the same Spirit that was in Jesus that raised him from the grave, which is what the Father is also doing in you… for this cause He is come in you. (!!!)

Yet by the Lamb, we go thru that VEIL, which is his Flesh….. then once all of our self is subdued to the Son, then cometh the end and we too, with all before us, go on to the Father…. (!!!) What a Working!

Heaven & Earth brought together…

Ephesians 5:26-27 25 Husbands, love your wives, even as Christ also loved the church, and gave himself for it;

26 That he (Jesus) might sanctify and cleanse it with the washing of water by the word,
27 That he might present it (wife) to himself a glorious church, not having spot, or wrinkle, or any such thing; but that it should be holy and without blemish.

Jesus Christ is that Prophet, the spirit of Elijah working IN YOU to PREPARE you to be received and joined to the Father. That Holy Spirit that speaks and reveals Jesus Christ to you, washing you, preparing you, and the whole time this is happening, you are being received unto the Father, himself.

Matthew 11:27
27 All things are delivered unto me of my Father: and no man knoweth the Son , but the Father; neither knoweth any man the Father, save the Son , and he to whomsoever the Son will reveal him.

1 Corinthians 15:24 (secrets are within this passage... do not pass it by quickly)
22 For as in Adam all die, even so in Christ shall all be made alive.
23 But every man in his own order: Christ the firstfruits; afterward they that are Christ's at his coming.
24 Then cometh the end , when he shall have delivered up the kingdom to God, even the Father; when he shall have put down all rule and all authority and power.
25 For he must reign, till he hath put all enemies under his feet.
26 The last enemy that shall be destroyed is death.
27 For he hath put all things under his feet. But when he saith, all things are put under him, it is manifest that he is excepted, which did put all things under him.
28 And when all things shall be subdued unto him, then shall the Son also himself be subject unto him that put all things under him, that God may be all in all.

The Great Assembling is happening, and will continue throughout all ages. Reconciliation of all things, from age to age. All things of your life: Spirit, Soul, Mind, And Body... all being transformed by That Living Word: from which all things are created and are established.

But while the "process" is going on, and you find yourself in a dilemma, remember... Innocence is found within the soul, where the Lamb of God sits to make whole. In Hope, we may be found to have apprehended Him who has apprehended us, for this very cause....

...that we may continue the journey, going forward, that we may come to the place where all is now put under our feet, and all is subdued unto the Son, whom now reveals and delivers us to the Father, that HE may be manifest in the earth.... thru us.

Oh, by the way, **that last enemy has been defeated already**.... He took care of that for us too... "tasted death for all."

2 Corinthians 1:9-10 But we had the sentence of death in ourselves, that we should not trust in ourselves, but in God which raiseth the dead: **Who delivered us from so great a death , and doth deliver: in whom we trust that he will yet deliver us;...**

Heb 2:9 But we see Jesus, who was made a little lower than the angels for the suffering of death , crowned with glory and honour; that **he by the grace of God should taste death for every man.**

2 Timothy 1:10 But is now made manifest by the appearing of our Saviour Jesus Christ, **who hath abolished death**, and hath brought life and immortality to light through the gospel:..

For the death of the testator lives in us! and because He Lives, and Lives In Us, we now can Live that new life of the Divine

Nature (no sin or death) here in this earth. Now heaven and earth is brought together... The Great Assembling!

Amen
RPJ

(Write your notes here)

REVELATION 19
How to Walk in the New Law

Psalm 103:10-12	Heb 7:15-17 *17	Heb 12:All *10-11
Hebrews 8:10-13	Romans 8:2	
Hebrews 7:12	Romans 5:20-21	

Psalm 103:10-12 He hath not dealt with us after our sins; nor rewarded us according to our iniquities. For as the heaven is high above the earth, so great is his mercy toward them that fear him. As far as the east is from the west, so far hath he removed our transgressions from us.

Hebrews 8:10-13 *12-13 For I will be merciful to their unrighteousness, and their sins and their iniquities will I remember no more. In that he saith, A new covenant, he hath made the first old. Now that which decayeth and waxeth old is ready to vanish away.

"I will be **merciful to their unrighteousness**, and their sins and their iniquities will I remember no more"

There is a new law and new priesthood, right? Right. But what are the rules and what are the guidelines. ??

Here is the short version, but to study this will do wonders within our souls....

The commandment is to love one another. As Christ gave his life for us, we should lay down our lives for each other, if it is necessary. Wow. That's a heavy statement. There are lots of scriptures to give us guidelines to how Jesus Christ has instructed us to live. The gospels are full of them, and so is the rest of the new testament.

Then there is the priesthood that is now after the order of Melchisedec rather than Levitical priesthood. Hebrews 7:15-17 *17 For he testifieth, Thou art a priest for ever after the order of Melchisedec.

Then there is the change of the law. Romans 8:2 For the law of the Spirit of life in Christ Jesus hath made me free from the law of sin and death. The law of the Spirit of life in Christ Jesus now works within us declaring His Righteousness for our liberty. Read Romans 8 and be blessed in the Lord. There are other places it reveals of the changing of the law... Let's look at a couple more in Hebrews.

Hebrews 7:12 For the priesthood being changed, there is made of necessity a change also of the law.
Hebrews 8:10-13 which tells us of the New Covenant too. And this is where we can see that the Lord wants to put His Laws into our minds and write upon our hearts...... THIS is part of
that "process" of being born again.... A New Law is put in you, and WRITTEN by His Own Hand/Spirit in you. Engraved. Engrafted.

AND in the New Covenant He tells us that our sins and iniquities will no longer be remembered! He doesn't see SIN in this new law for those that have this new covenant. It isn't part of the equation, if you have now received and allowed Jesus Christ to be your Saviour. He removed it out of the way. ! . Instead GRACE is seen! And in this GRACE there is now His Righteousness Standing Fast to declare US Righteous so that we may abide in Eternal Life.... now.

Romans 5:20-21 Moreover the law entered, that the offence might abound. But *where sin abounded*, <u>grace did much more abound</u>: **That as sin hath reigned unto death, even so might grace reign through righteousness unto eternal life by Jesus Christ our Lord.**

Hallelujah! A New Law within us now, so that we Walk by the New Law in the Spirit of Life by faith, not the old law that revealed sin and produced death through the works of the flesh man.

Now As We Walk by faith into this Grace in which we stand, and as we are pressing in to His Kingdom from faith to faith and glory to glory..... say... we... stumble and fall by that unregenerate carnal mind that you might not have been fully freed from yet.... What Happens?

In This NEW LAW.... GRACE Abounds where sin once was, and Eternal Life where death once was. MERCY is speaking on your behalf... because you have invited and received and allowed the Lamb of God to set up house within your soul. That Blood of Jesus Christ is speaking in you, and upholding you in every situation and step of your walk. In your Soul and Conscience, where the covenant is, it is revealed to you that you've done something out of character... or out of the Spirit of Christ, and you feel remorse. This MERCY is providing you the Path to correct that issue or problem or concern without FEAR of being separated from our Father and Kingdom.

"...merciful to their unrighteousness..." but does Mercy mean no correction? NO NO NO.... trust me on this.... Our FATHER does Give Correction especially in this New Law. But His correction is not to destroy. It is to bring forth More Righteousness... less of the carnal mind and more of Christ's Mind taking over... being subdued unto Him! Hallelujah!. Look at Hebrews 12:All. Here are verses 10-11

Hebrews 12:10-11 For they verily for a few days chastened us after their own pleasure; but he for our profit, that we might be partakers of his holiness. Now no chastening for the present seemeth to be joyous, but grievous: nevertheless afterward **it**

yieldeth the peaceable fruit of righteousness unto them which are exercised thereby.

Oh Praise you Father! For such Love and Assurance! We love you!

So, we can come boldly to the throne of Grace and receive Mercy to fix the issue. It is now about a RELATIONSHIP, and COMMUNICATION with THE FATHER, out of a Just & Humble Heart. BELIEVING what He Tells Us. Just TALK and COMMUNE with the FATHER, and LEARN of HIM his Ways. Be Obedient.

Listen, Learn, and REST in the Son/Father. Let obedience and a willing heart come forth in all Wisdom, Knowledge, & Understanding of His Will for you. ENJOY your NEW Life IN the Kingdom of the Lord. LEARN of Him and find Rest for your souls. Matthew 11:27-30

Amen.
RPJ

REVELATION 20
Being Born Again – God's Way to Him 

Titus 3:5-6
Not by works of righteousness which we have done, but according to his mercy he saved us, by the washing of regeneration(rebirth), and renewing of the Holy Ghost
v 6 Which he shed on us abundantly through Jesus Christ our Saviour;

Being Born of God is God's way to Him (entering His Kingdom)
Mediate with the Lord on these scriptures....

John 3:3-5
1 Peter 1:22-23
James 1:18
Romans 1:16-17
John 1:11-14 *12
Ephesians 1:19-20
Ephesians 3:20
Ephesians 5:26-27
Romans 8:9-11
1 Corinthians 15:19-28 *22-23

Luke 16:16 pressing into the kingdom

Hebrews 10:19-22 ...by the <u>blood of Jesus</u>, By a <u>new and living way</u>, which <u>he</u> hath <u>consecrated for us</u>, **through the veil, that is to say, his flesh**;... Let *us draw near* with a true heart in full assurance of faith, **having our hearts sprinkled from an evil conscience, and our bodies washed with pure water**.... hold fast the profession of our faith without wavering;....
pure water... this is the water that is the word of God: that is spirit and life (John6:63)

He BECAME us........

He BECAME us as the old priesthood, that we may BECOME the new priesthood.

HE was BORN into our World, so that We Can Be Born into His World.

If he hadn’t taken on the natural man and overcame it for us, then we would not be able to be Born Again ... Enter into His World. But He penetrated the Veil between the two Worlds so making the Two One World. (Oh Hallelujah!)
Continue to ENTER…. and BEHOLD HIS GLORY!

Amen.
RPJ

REVELATION 21
He Became Us

Romans 7:4-6
Wherefore, my brethren, ye also are *become dead to the law by the body of Christ*; that ye should be *married to another, even to him who is raised from the dead*, that we should bring forth fruit unto God, ...
...For when we were in the flesh, the motions of sins, which were by the law, did work in our members to bring forth fruit unto death. .....

The Law of Sin & Death required the flesh man's ability to do God's will: a working of the flesh. Jesus Christ became US, the natural man, in all aspects of our fallen nature; to accomplish God's will under that first Law.

We, the fallen, sinful, nature just could not do it. But that too was God's plan ... it had been hidden in His heart/mind for a long time to reconcile us back to Him: The Mystery. Now God's Mystery has been revealed, it has come and appeared in the earth: Jesus Christ, His Son.

He accomplished all God's plan to fulfill and bring in God's new order of Grace, Mercy, & Faith that we may walk and live in Righteousness and Eternal Life, now by His Spirit In Us working, rather than man's own ability of flesh.

So.... He BECAME us........He BECAME us as the old priesthood, that we may BECOME the new priesthood.

HE was BORN into our World, so that We Can Be Born into His World.

If he hadn't taken on the natural man and overcame it for us, then we would not be able to be Born Again ... Enter into His

World. <u>But He penetrated the Veil between the two Worlds so making the Two One World.</u> (Oh Hallelujah!)

He accomplished the working of the flesh (man's ability) to fulfill all Righteousness and Judgment contained in the old laws ordinances. Yet being all God, He became Man, that lower kingdom's ruler – Man.... known as the SECOND Man, to take the controls into His own hands and cause all things to be put in its proper order. <u>He was all earthly man, yet all God's presence combined into One</u>.

The Second Man IS the LORD from Heaven, and He is the LAST ADAM. The last Adam was made the QUICKENING SPIRIT, where as the first Adam was made a living soul, but died due to the act of disobedience. (1 Corinthians 15, Romans 5)

So if Jesus was a quickening spirit, did He not have a Soul? Yes He did. And that Soul was made ALIVE by that Quickening Spirit in Jesus!.... Oh Hear what the Lord is saying and showing us!

Hebrews 9:14 says...
How much more shall the blood of Christ, who <u>through the eternal Spirit offered himself without spot to God</u>, purge your conscience from dead works to serve the living God?

That Soul – the Lamb of God – was made Righteous BECAUSE OF THE <u>SPIRIT OF LIFE THAT WAS IN HIM</u> FROM THE VERY BEGINNING OF HIS BIRTH.... THAT KINGDOM WAS COME IN HIM.... THAT GRACE ABOUNDED... BUT THERE WAS ANOTHER LAW IN HIS MEMBER and more than that, which had to be overcome.

He was In Charge. And had to put down all rule and authority of that fallen Man's Soul. And when that was done, the whole creation was affected.... oh I see and hear the breathing of the Lord!!

So Jesus Christ the Lamb of God went through EVERY Ordeal that the Soul of Man went through... and Jesus Christ put every Ordeal in to its proper Order. By the obedience of one... God was and is that SPIRIT of LIFE that was in Jesus to assure that HE Would Not Fail.

Now, That is WHO is IN US to be our ASSURANCE to complete HIS WILL in us. God's Operation. Do not despair, for that very same SPIRIT of LIFE is in you and RAISING You out of the Grave and Death by His Word working in you... unlocking every lock and sealing His Will upon your forehead, and presenting you to Himself Glorious... seated in Heavenly places even in the earth. He has prepared this place for you, He has ordained this working for you, and purposed you to come forth for this hour.

Romans 5:19 (15-21) and 1 Corinthians 15:21-21 reveals to us that by the disobedience of one man all were made sinners, and by the obedience of one shall many be made righteous.

Jesus Christ was obedient in every ordinance and statute of His Father's first law, so to complete it. Then to bring in and establish the Second law, that was upon better promises, and the new order of the law and priesthood, and King-ship. He Established His Kingdom IN THE EARTH, within Himself first, now to be done within each and every one of us... as He puts down all rule and authority within your own Soul.... subduing everything of your heaven and earth into HIM. His Kingdom Is Come and HE IS RULING AND REIGNING IN THE EARTH AND HEAVEN. !!! Oh Rejoice all the land, Rejoice!

RECONCILIATION is what HE calls it.... Heaven and Earth brought together in One, Lord and Christ. Then ALL of yourself is submitted and joined to the Father........ all in all.

God appeared for our salvation as Jesus Christ... to redeem all creation. Jesus Christ became us as the natural man.... now He apprehends us that we may realize and grasp ahold of why He is in us, ... so that we may be In Him... and then He and us become one vessel/body/church In this world... yet it Is Him as us. (heavy but true Hallelujah!)

The New Man – Second Man – Quickening Spirit – Lord from Heaven. New Heaven and New Earth where God dwells.

Praise the Lord! and Thank YOU!

Amen.
RPJ

REVELATION 22
God Will Provide

God will provide..... so SEEK HIM for the INSTRUCTIONS AND UNDERSTANDING. God will provide for your situations, and necessities. You can be SURE in this. It is a SURE THING that He will provide. Now that "that" is said enough... TRUST God.

Matthew 6:33
But seek ye first the kingdom of God, and his righteousness; and all these things shall be added unto you.

Here are some thoughts to ponder...
Nourish the relationship you have with our Father. Communication is an important part of any relationship. Don't just talk, but talk with Hearing and Understanding what the other is saying.

In this case, what our Father is saying and meaning. Don't rush. Take time to daily hear and understand His instructions and heart for that day. And when He does give you instructions to do something, do not assume anything, but daily make sure you are not going beyond or behind HIS PLAN. He will and does tell you if there is more to it, or if you've got it right, or even to just do what you want to do...

If you are having trouble hearing and understanding, then ask your GIFT of GOD to help you... Apostle, Prophet, Evangelist, Pastor and Teacher. That is what they are for. They are Not to be wallowing in the problem with you, what good does that do either of you.

Rather, they are to help mature you so you can hear for yourself, and/or to give you God's (hand) solution to get out of the problem or issue at hand. Communication... True Relationship... True Fellowship....

True Family... Always desiring for each other's good and well being. Always desiring for each other's best.... according to the Father's Will. He is our Standard to Measure by. Being perfect as our Father is perfect. Matthew 5:48.

We've heard of those times that someone hears God's revelation or instructions, without the UNDERSTANDING of what HE is SAYING, then they go about to do it their way without waiting for God's understanding in each step, then they step out and end up going beyond or behind on exactly what His Plan is. Or greed gets in and makes it stink. Or pride gets in and it's hard to receive. Or your own carnal opinion of what they are doing gets in your way of receiving God through them. Oh, Thank God for Grace abounds always with Mercy towards us all... Thank you Lord!

Let Every One have a Humble Heart, because All we have and are, is from the Lord.

REFRESH your communication skills with Him... NOURISH the fellowship with Him... Make SWEET the walk with Him and ENJOY your life with Him. Allow the Lord to HEAL you in those areas that are in need. DRAW CLOSER.... and let the Lord SWALLOW YOU UP in HIS LOVE. *All You Are and All You Have Is the Lord's... don't hold back. Then the Fullness of Him can flow*
through you to others. Increase. (Isn't that what you were asking for?)

OUR FATHER WILL PROVIDE. Our Father LOVES us and is PERFECT in EVERYWAY.

So allow Him to WORK A PERFECT HEART IN YOU.
Now, let PATIENCE have her perfect work in you.

HIS BLESSING and PROVISION is a SURE THING. But if it's not coming in, then perhaps there is a "hindrance:" within you, or outside yourself.... so SEEK GOD for INSTRUCTIONS & UNDERSTANDING, then obey. God Will Provide.

Amen.
RPJ

REVELATION 23
The Bread of Life

How does God eliminate disease, sickness, false doctrines, traditions of man, and other various hindrances to the people of God that is keeping back the wealth of God's kingdom from them?

By the Weed Zapper? No, not really. Not by some method or gimmick, but by His Word.
John 6: ALL (*56-58) Meditate on whole chapter and Receive the Lord's Blessing

What you really need is the Bread of Life, God's Heavenly Bread that cures all things. It is the ultimate Nourisher and Healer for the Body, Soul, and Spirit Man. No Gimmick, Just your ears to Hear God's Word, so Faith is produced and Receives God's Liberating Grace.

Faith Comes by hearing, and hearing by the word of God. Romans 10:17
Faith IS GOD... have you ever thought about that. He Created It. It's the <u>character</u> of God <u>produced in us</u>. One of the Evidences of the Divine Nature Birthed in Us. !!!

That Divine Nature IS our Inheritance.
My Inheritance is not something that can be bought or sold.... I LIVE by and off of It Daily. There is no monetary value that can be placed on my Inheritance, yet My Inheritance provides my daily monetary needs and necessities. Read John 6... truly You Will Receive His Blessing.... and if you don't ... Read it again and Meditate with the Lord... Listen and Receive.

My Inheritance is God. He is my dwelling place, and Source for daily living. Yours too.

I bet you can say the same thing of yourself. But if you can't yet, then read John 6 and let the Holy Spirit penetrate your soul with Eternal Life.

In John 6 there is a feast of heavenly manna to enjoy and be enriched by. Take a look at verses 56-58, to start with:
John 6:56-58
He that eateth my flesh, and drinketh my blood, dwelleth in me, and I in him. As the living Father hath sent me, and I live by the Father: so he that eateth me, even he shall live by me. This is that bread which came down from heaven; not as your fathers did eat manna, and are dead: he that eateth of this bread shall live for ever.

For Heaven and Earth is brought together by One and In One, for they are One. For we/I dwell In Him, and He in us/me.... So HE HAS SAID, and MADE IT SO.

Let the Word of God work in you .... Destroying every false doctrine and traditions of man that hinder you from entering the kingdom of God, and reaping the harvest of Jesus Christ.

Amen.
RPJ

REVELATION 24
Spirit of the Father

Matthew 10:19-20
John 14:20-24 (*24)
John 14:10
2 Corinthians 3:16-18 (*17)

Matthew 10:19-20 But when they deliver you up, take no thought how or what ye shall speak: for it shall be given you in that same hour what ye shall speak. For *it is not ye that speak* but the Spirit of your Father which speaketh in you.

John 14:10 Believest thou not that I am in the Father, and the Father in me? the words that I speak unto you I speak not of myself: but the Father that dwelleth in me, he doeth the works.

John 14:20-24 At that day ye shall know that I am in my Father, and ye in me, and I in you. ..... and I will love him, and will manifest myself to him.... and we will come unto him, and make our abode with him. He that loveth me not keepeth not my sayings: and the word which ye hear is not mine, but the Father's which sent me.

2 Corinthians 3:16-18 v 17 Now the Lord is that Spirit: and where the Spirit of the Lord is, there is liberty.
Ephesians 4:4-6 There is one body, and one Spirit , even as ye are called in one hope of your calling; One Lord, one faith, one baptism, One God and Father of all, who is above all, and through all, and in you all.

For *it is not ye that speak* but the Spirit of your Father which speaketh in you....
and make our abode with him....

The Father and Son are not in the sky way up high, but has become The Spirit that is holy and righteous and is eternal life IN YOUR SOUL. It's a heavy thing to comprehend, but then that is why He desires to make himself 'manifest' to you as it says in John 14:20-24. To reveal himself to you and make himself known to you.... it is a love story. And He wants to write it in your Soul and Mind.

In this testimony being written within your soul, there will be an awakening or rather a quickening... a coming alive of yourself out of your death and grave, and into the living presence of That One – Jesus Christ that is being revealed within. It is called a marriage. A Birthing (2 Cor 3:18). And there are many other scriptures and terms to explain and express the working of the Holy Spirit in us all.

The Reconciliation of all things... Have your heart's delight and way, my sweet Father!

Amen.
RPJ

REVELATION 25
Mercy and Faith are walking hand in hand…. Grace abounds.

Psalm 103:8-12, 17, 19
James 2:12-26
Psalm 103:8 The Lord is merciful and gracious, slow to anger, and plenteous in mercy….

v 10-11 He hath not dealt with us after our sins nor rewarded us according to our iniquities. For as the heaven is high above the earth, so great is his mercy toward them that fear him.

v 12 As far as the east is from the west, so far hath he removed our transgressions from us.

v 17 But the mercy of the Lord is from everlasting to everlasting upon them that fear him, and his righteousness unto children’s children.

v 19 The Lord hath prepared his throne in the heavens; and his kingdom ruleth over all.

Even before Jesus Christ completed the work of Grace into the world for all mankind, Grace was still there, but yet, we could not get to it or it to us. It was only through the “veil of flesh” that God had set up and placed in His order of things, could we as man, even attempt to reach God. And even then, it had to be through God’s then divine order of the working of the flesh through the Priest.

Now, God’s order and laws of old have been fulfilled, and removed out of the way, as He has established a better Covenant of Blood for us to stand in and move by. Although there Is still a Priest-hood, and King-ship, and Kingdom of God put in place of divine order; yet, we find that God our Father has made a better 'way' for us all to be able to reach Him and have fellowship with Him.

Grace is Abounding……. and Mercy & Faith are working as we enter in to this Fellowship and Life that is our Lord, Saviour, and Father.

Come boldly to the throne of Grace…… Enter in through the Veil, that is to say His Flesh….. Have Communion and Fellowship with God, whom is our Father & Best of all Friends.

So EAT UP of Jesus Christ, and become One with the Son… Learn of Him in all facets of who He is and why…… And Enter into the Presence of our Father and ENJOY His Eternal Life In You…. now You In Eternal Life.

This is our new Life… WE ARE THE NEW MAN WALKING…. The Last Adam, Second Man, Quickening Spirit, & Lord from Heaven….. God's firstfruits of His Spirit that was harvested when this new order was established.

Is it your time/turn…. 1 Corinthians 15:22-23

So, Walk in FAITH and let MERCY prevail in all situations, for GRACE has taken care of the Sting, and removed death out of the way. Enter in to the Promised Land.

Amen.
RPJ

REVELATION 26
Faith Comes By Hearing

Romans 10:17 (13-18)	John 14:2-3	Ephesians 2:4-7
Matthew 12:13-23	Titus 3:4-6	Romans 12:2
Ephesians 5:26-27	John 3:3-5	1 Peter 1:22-23
2 Corinthians 3:16-18	Phil 3:21	

Romans 10:17
... so then faith cometh by hearing, and hearing by the word of God.

But how can they call upon the Lord, if they have not heard and understood the Good News of Jesus Christ? So a CERTAIN ONE is sent and SPEAKS and they hear, receive, and understand, then WALK by the belief of God’s word... Now THAT is FAITH. When you Call upon the Lord, FAITH is working. Because if you had not heard of His Goodness, then you wouldn’t Call upon Him, because you would not know that He is Your Help in all situations.

So, here the Lord reveals that HE NEEDS HIS PREACHERS to SPEAK forth to the world that Gospel of Jesus Christ or rather the Good News of Jesus Christ and of His Kingdom.

This is the Lord causing FAITH to fill the world by the word of God being spoken and received.... the planting of Faith for another harvest.

HIS PREACHERS are those that His (Holy) SPIRIT abides in, and are planters of His Good News... The SEED of GOD.... Jesus Christ... being Planted in the MIND and SOUL of individuals.... God’s Field.

Not all will receive or hear or understand... as explained in Matthew 12:13-23. Please read this when you get a chance (too long to put in this message). But those that do hear and receive with understanding will be healed and many more blessings will flow freely in their land (soul, mind, body, family...etc.)

FAITH comes by hearing, and HEARING by the WORD OF GOD. Lies preached, theologies preached, false doctrines and traditions preached, mind over matter beliefs preached will Not produce this FAITH and Liberty. Only the preaching by the Lord's Spirit through His Elect Ones will Produce God's beloved Fruit and Nourishment of Love with Peace.

We walk by FAITH, and from Faith to Faith, and Glory to Glory. Our Growing up into Jesus Christ our Head is a Step by Step Process. A continual WASHING and CLEANSING and RENEWING of the Mind as it is spoken of in many places in the scriptures. Here's a few to study: John 3:3-5, Ephesians 5:26-27, 1 Peter 1:22-23, Titus 3:5-6, Romans 12:2, Phil 3:21, 2 Corinthians 3:16-18,...)

Think about it... What would have happened if the Jews, upon being freed from Egypt, just stood still, having been freed, and rejoiced, but figured "alright now! we are free at last, let's party, and give thanks to God here, He'll protect us here!" yet they never came out of Egypt, nor UNDERSTOOD that they needed to continue the WALK in to a Better Place that was (is) to be there INHERITANCE and DWELLING Place that Jesus Christ has prepared for YOU. They would have been disobedient to God, because He wanted them to continue into the promised land. ....

Can You Hear This? If so, God is CALLING YOU to WALK in FAITH in to a PLACE He has prepared for you with IN HIMSELF. BEING BORN AGAIN: WASHED, CLEANSED, REGENERATED, RENEWED and RECEIVED UNTO HIMSELF -ESTABLISHED in Better Dwellings. (Read Ephesians 5:26-27)

Titus 3:4-6 But after that the kindness and love of God our Saviour toward man appeared, Not by works of righteousness which we have done, but according to his mercy he saved us, **by the washing of regeneration, and renewing of the Holy Ghost**; Which he shed on us abundantly through Jesus Christ our Saviour;

John 14:2-3 In my Father's house are many mansions (dwelling places): if it were not so, I would have told you, I go to prepare a place for you. And if I go and prepare a place for you, I will come again, and receive you unto myself: that where I am, there ye may be also.

There it is.. The Place.. and Where that Place is... Read Ephesians 5:26-27 That he might sanctify and cleanse it with the washing of water by the word, That he might present it to himself a glorious church, not having spot, or wrinkle, or any such thing; but that it should be holy and without blemish.

Ephesians 2:4-7 v5-6 Even when we were dead in sins, hath quickened us together with Christ, (by grace ye are saved;) And hath raised us up together, and made us sit together in heavenly places in Christ Jesus;...

To those that have ears to hear and receive from the Lord, THEN you can abide within that Truth and Revelation (revealing of Jesus Christ).

Jesus Christ, the Spirit of the Son, the Father, God has entered Your Heart to Redeem You Unto Himself By His Word, Jesus Christ.

Then What?... Then you that are One with the Lord, come and go as the Spirit moves you to Set Others Free. Read Joshua 1:14-15
Joshua 1:14-15 ... but ye shall pass before your brethren armed, all the mighty men of valour, and help them; Until the Lord have given your brethren rest, as he hath given you, and they also have possessed the land which the Lord your God giveth them: then ye shall return unto the land of your possession, and enjoy it, which

Moses the Lord's servant gave you on this side Jordan toward the sunrising.

Oh Hallelujah ! all you Priest and Kings in the Lord! Go Go Go.....!.

That is what this whole thing is about.... He has FINISHED the Work of Salvation, so that you may come freely and without hindrance into this New Life that is Eternal THROUGH THE VEIL, the WAY, THAT IS TO SAY THE FLESH OF JESUS CHRIST – THE LAMB OF GOD. No more a Wall of Separation between Earth and Heaven... at least not in Christ Jesus. EAT AND DRINK of the LIVING SACRIFICE. Eating of the sacrifice of the old testament days was said to make you One with the Sacrifice. That is why it wasn't good to eat of idol sacrifices. But eating of the Lamb of God, you become One with the Son. So eat His Word – His Body and Drink of His Spirit – His Blood.

Yet, are you standing in the same place of your mind that you were in when He freed you, or are you still dealing with some of those areas in your mind that keep wanting to put you back in prison of lack....???
Go forward! Start, or rather Continue to Walk in His FAITH,... it is DONE and SETTLED for YOU to have the VICTORY in every situation that HE HAS PUT YOU IN. Let Him WASH YOU, CLEANSE, FREE YOUR MIND from that adamic carnal nature and mindset. Freeing you from that mind and nature that will only try to cheat you out of your God-given blessing and inheritance.

ASK God to speak to you His ANOINTED Word that will SET YOU FREE into your God-given Inheritance. Don't follow God's ministers in the natural things, but you will know them by their Fruit; Just RECEIVE God's SPOKEN WORD of Jesus Christ and Be Free. We are here for each other.... a many membered body of Jesus Christ in this world. ... still growing up... mercy, grace & love abounds.

Now, if you have gone off course, then just apologize and ask the Father to “fix” your situation and put you back on the right track... then hang on to His Love, as He delivers you out of harm’s way and sets you in Peace.... GRACE is Working.

All that are in Christ Jesus can REAP of the Harvest of HIS Faith, and enjoy the Victory.

Continue Your Walk in His Faith, and ENJOY your Life IN His. Let the Kingdom Increase.

Amen.
RPJ

REVELATION 27
Youth Renewed

Psalm 103:5
Isaiah 40:31

What you eat has an effect on your natural body, right? Yes. So it is with what you eat spiritually will affect your spirit man.... AND your natural body.

If a person will eat of the Lord daily, his countenance will be renewed like the eagle's. If he/she eats of bitterness and/or unforgiveness, etc. his/her countenance will show this too.

Psalm 103:5 Who satisfieth thy mouth with good things; so that thy youth is renewed like the eagles.

God's people that are dedicated daily to eat of Him and be refreshed in Him, have a "glow" about them. There is an inner youth look. We have some older friends in the ministry that are in their 80's and the Lord's blessings are in their countenance. An Inner Glow... a reflection of God's working. Sure, there are wrinkle's, age spots, gray hairs, etc... but LIFE is pulsating in them and God's strength is revealed.

God's people that eat of bitterness, defensiveness, contentions, fights, etc... are stressed out and "look" stressed out.

They are EATING of the wrong kind of spiritual nutrition. So, EAT OF THE LORD's BREAD Daily.

Have FELLOWSHIP and COMMUNION with Him in the Anointing DAILY.... ALLOW HIM to flow through you to others and within yourselves.

ABIDE IN HIS LOVE, and TRUST HIM to PROVIDE for You. Seek His Righteousness and Kingdom, Ask of Him concerning Himself.... ENJOY your Walk with Him. Matter of fact... do just that. Take time out of your day to just let Him Talk to you..... That's what a Relationship is all about. Not just texting, but encountering each other face to face and communing.

Don't you think so?

Isaiah 40:31
But they that wait upon the Lord shall renew their strength; they shall mount up with wings as eagles; they shall run, and not be weary; and they shall walk, and not faint.

Strength, Peace, Shield, Help, Deliver from harm......

Psalm 28:7-9
The Lord is my strength and my shield; my heart trusted in him, and I am helped: therefore my heart greatly rejoiceth; and with my song will I praise him. The Lord is their strength, and he is the saving strength of his anointed. Save thy people, and bless thine inheritance: feed them also, and lift them up for ever.

Psalm 29:11
The lord will give strength unto his people; the Lord will bless his people with peace.

Psalm 37:39-40 and Psalm 68:34-35 (and many more scriptures of God's strength, & provision)

Psalm 68:34-35
v35 O God, thou art terrible out of thy holy places: the God of Israel is he that giveth strength and power unto his people. Blessed be God.

" 'My Life In You' by Jesus Christ"

Commune, Fellowship, Eat of the Lord and Your Countenance will change with Life. Don't let bitterness and unforgiveness cheat you out of life.

Amen.
RPJ

REVELATION 28
From Captivity Captive to Sonship

So we go from mindset of a prisoner of the Lord, to a servant, until He has reformed us into the image of His Son.... Renewed in the Mind of Christ Jesus, the Obedient Son Revealed... Born of God.

There are those that are still in the mindset of the servant. Then those that consider themselves a Friend of God. God is using them and they enjoy being around the one with the blessings and the one that has the riches, but they are not hearing that calling yet to press toward the mark of the high calling of God in Christ Jesus... to be a Son with The Son.

The Son of God is Jesus Christ. He is the head of the many member body of Christ... which we by the grace of God can now receive and become. We are Co-Heirs of Eternal Life.... His Life. An awesome Inheritance! Hallelujah!

Philippians 3:12-15
Not as though I had already attained, either were already perfect: but I follow after, if that I may apprehend that for which also I am apprehended of Christ Jesus. Brethren, I count not myself to have apprehended: but this one thing I do, forgetting those things which are behind, and reaching forth unto those things which are before, I press toward the mark for the prize of the high calling of God in Christ Jesus.

Romans 8:17-18
And if children, then heirs; heirs of God, and joint-heirs with Christ; if so be that we suffer with him, that we may be also glorified together. For I reckon that the sufferings of this present time are not worthy to be compared with the glory which shall be revealed in us.

Ephesians 4: ALL
Paul begins telling us that he is the 'prisoner' of the Lord in verse one and then encourages the Ephesus church to continue to walk worthy of the calling (vocation).

In verse 7 he says every one of us are given grace according to the measure of the gift of Christ. And then makes that statement...

v8 Wherefore he saith, When he ascended up on high, he led captivity captive, and gave gifts unto men.

Why from captivity to captivity? Why wasn't it expressed as "he led the captivity free" instead back in to "captivity"?

Romans 6:18 'Being then made free from sin, ye became the servants of righteousness.' So, we were prisoners of the dark side (sin & death), but now, having been apprehended by Jesus Christ, we have become prisoners, servants, or we can say that we are HIS PURCHASED POSSESSIONS, and now HE is – has - will clean us up in spirit, soul, and body so that all that we are, are transformed, changed, metaphorised (or whatever word you want to use) into the image of God's Son, Jesus Christ. One Body. One Spirit. One Mind. Oh Hallelujah!! Harmony at last!!!!!

So God gives to us all, and gave us grace according to the measure of the gift of Jesus Christ (Ephesians 4:7).

Each member has a part and place in God's Operation.

Christ Jesus was God's Firstfruit of the Spirit, then each of us to come forth, in God's appointed divine order to be birthed by the Spirit of the Son (1 Corinthians 15:20-23).

Jesus Christ the head, then each of us joined to Him as He apprehends and delivers us from the grave and captivity. Then, after He has washed and cleansed us from the effects of sin &

removes all smell and garments of death, He sets us in His Body, the church, which already exists (Hebrews 12:1, 22-29; Ephesians 3:21).

Jesus Christ went into the lower depths of the earth to release those that were a prisoner of sin and death and the grave, and to take a hold of them (apprehend), and raise them up with Him into His heavenly places of liberty; but at first, we seem to be His prisoners or rather SERVANTS unto Him for HIS PURPOSE.... BOUGHT out of slavery of sin, to BE HIS SERVANTS OF RIGHTEOUSNESS. (Romans 6:13-14, 18)

But then, we find that it isn't to be a prisoner or servant at all, but that He wants to Keep Us Protected from more Harm. We will see destruction no more.... He wants to protect us, and clean us up, and produce His Son IN and THROUGH us, being One with Him. John 1:12-14 ... gives us power to become sons of God.

So being made captive is not a captivity of harm, but the very opposite... a captive of LOVE.... He captures our Heart by Love.

Sounds like Marriage – the Lamb's marriage to His Wife! We are made to be His, exchanged (sold out) by the price of a woman (30 pieces of Silver, price of the field), but purchased by the Price of the Lamb (male, the man, 50 number for Jubilee)... He is our Saviour! Our Hero!

Now to declare & establish our Liberty, our JUBILEE and new beginning of LIFE for all SOULS.

The old man – the law of sin & death that God's elect were married to have died, now they and we Gentiles are free to marry the Second Man, the Lord from Heaven, and take on His Name and benefits!!

Even more... we BECOME His Flesh & Bone and Spirit & Soul as it is spoken in Ephesians 5:29-30. Heaven & Earth brought together in One. What a revelation of Jesus Christ & the church! Thank you Father. (Ephesians 1:10, Colossians 1:20)
Ephesians 1:10-11
That in the dispensation of the fullness of times he might gather together in one all things in Christ, both which are in heaven, and which are on earth ; even in him: In whom also we have obtained an inheritance, being predestinated according to the purpose of him who worketh all things after the counsel of his own will:...

Colossians 1:20
And, having made peace through the blood of his cross, by him to reconcile all things unto himself; by him, I say, whether they be things in earth, or things in heaven.

Even though the dispensation of the fullness of times came, and His Kingdom is established, yet from age to age since then, the Good News of Jesus Christ & His Kingdom is still preached, and still each soul, in God's appointed time, are being awakened unto His Righteousness and are being changed and reconciled unto the Father through the Son Jesus Christ... still by that Word of God preached by His Holy Spirit.

Philippians 3:18 Who shall change our vile body, that it may be fashioned like unto his glorious body, according to the working whereby he is able even to subdue all things unto himself.

2 Corinthians 3:18 But we all, with open face beholding as in a glass the glory of the Lord, are changed into the same image from glory to glory, even as by the Spirit of the Lord.

As our healing and deliverance from the affects of sin and death are accomplished, each person is set in their appointed place that the Lord Jesus Christ has prepared for them.

They are given His Garments of Royalty and Priesthood, and allowed to walk in the new life of the Son, in this world and heaven with Him, as Him...His help mate... His Body... His expression of Glory revealed.

Amen.
RPJ

(Write your notes here)

REVELATION 29
FIRE: Hell or Purification

FIRE.... Hell or Purification...

Even though there are many scriptures to reveal God's FIRE to you, I'm only picking a few to preserve space. But study this out and you will find many more scriptures to show you this truth, as you are lead of the Holy Spirit in your studies.

Matthew 3:10-12 And now also the axe is laid unto the root of the trees: therefore every tree which bringeth not forth good fruit is hewn down, and **cast into the fire**. I indeed baptize you with water unto repentance: but he that cometh after me is mightier than I, whose shoes I am not worthy to bear: he shall **baptize you with the Holy Ghost, <u>and</u> with fire**: (My note here: did not say OR, but AND)

Whose fan is in his hand, and <u>he will throughly purge his floor</u>, and <u>gather</u> his wheat into the garner; but he will **<u>burn up the chaff</u> with unquenchable <u>fire</u>**. Yes, He was talking of that generation back then, for they were about to go through the great tribulation and judgment of God that had been prophesied.

Jesus tells us in Mark 9:45, how the fire is used, and <u>the SALT</u> spoken of here **IS FIRE**:

Mark 9:45 And if thy foot offend thee, cut it off: it is better for thee to enter halt into life, than having two feet to be <u>cast into hell</u>, *into the fire that never shall be quenched*: Where their worm dieth not, and the fire is not quenched. And if thine eye offend thee, pluck it out: it is better for thee to enter into the kingdom of God with one eye, than having two eyes to be <u>cast into hell fire</u>: Where their worm dieth not, and the fire is not quenched. <u>For every one shall be **salted with fire**</u>, and <u>every sacrifice shall be salted with salt</u>. Salt is good: but if the salt have lost his saltness, wherewith will ye season it? Have salt in yourselves, and have peace one with another.

FIRE is a Hell for some AND a Purifying Presence for others: A means to remove all unrighteousness.
FIRE is the TRIAL you go through ... rather, that GOD puts you through to WORK YOUR FAITH. God's operation.

But for those that have not the righteousness of the Lord, they are consumed in it. It will burn up anything that is not of God's Righteousness. One scripture says that all souls belong to God; then says that the soul that sinneth dies (Ezekiel 18:4). Then another place it tells us not to be concerned what man can do to us, but rather give reverence and submit to the one that can destroy your soul in hell fire.
Matthew 10:28 And fear not them which kill the body, but are not able to kill the soul : but rather fear him which is able to destroy both soul and body in hell.

Ezekiel 18:4 Behold, all souls are mine; as the soul of the father, so also the soul of the son is mine: the soul that sinneth, it shall die.

Even though this is said under the old testament, the Lord shows us that still under Grace, those that receive the Son which is God's Salvation to ALL the World, will receive Life and Grace abounds; but those that do not receive Him, but Rejects the Word of God (breath of life***) stay dead. They are condemned already because they have not received His Breath of Life, Jesus Christ who IS Eternal Life. They have rejected Him.... the Word of God.

2 Corinthians 13:5 tells us Examine yourselves, **whether ye be in the faith**; prove your own selves. Know ye not your own selves, how that **Jesus Christ is in you, except ye be reprobates**? Reprobates means Reject of God.

God is not able to breathe life into them, because they don't want Him. .... There is so much we could talk on here!!!! But let's go back to the FIRE.

Hebrews 12:22-29 **God is the consuming fire** that will remove from God's people, ALL things that are not of His Kingdom; and cause them to RECEIVE His Kingdom.... But ONLY those that go thru the Water and Spirit can ENTER GOD's KINGDOM..... Being Born Again by His Water and Spirit.... (John 3:3-5) Yet **God the Spirit IS FIRE**, too.

Ministers are flames of fire. Hebrews 1:7 And of the angels he saith, Who maketh his angels spirits, and his **ministers a flame of fire** .
The Lord brought Abraham out of the land called Ur.... Ur comes from the word that means: 'flame; hence (in the plural) the East (as being the region of light).' FIRE/LIGHT.... makes sense.

Now, look at Isaiah 33:10-24. Please read for full understanding. Here I will quote a couple of verses:
Isaiah 33:14-15 The sinners in Zion are afraid; fearfulness hath surprised the hypocrites. Who among us shall dwell with the devouring fire? who among us shall dwell with everlasting burnings?

God is asking this. WHO shall dwell with the devouring fire and everlasting burnings? Then verse 15 He reveals who can dwell in the Fire:
v 15 He that walketh righteously, and speaketh uprightly; he that despiseth the gain of oppressions, that shaketh his hands from holding of bribes, that stoppeth his ears from hearing of blood, and shutteth his eyes from seeing evil;...

And we know that no man is truly able to be Righteous in God's eyes perfectly, but only the Son, Jesus Christ.... and ALL THOSE THAT RECEIVE HIM, have HIS RIGHTEOUSNESS to stand in the presence of the Father, holy and unblameable and perfect. What a GIFT! So WE CAN ENTER the Kingdom and Go thru the FIRE and not be burned, for the Perfect One is with us to SUSTAIN US. That's Grace through Faith working.

BUT HERE IS WHERE WE SEE GOD'S LOVE TO US AGAIN! He Has Given of Himself in the Righteousness of His Son Jesus Christ, the Lamb of God, to Abide in that special place within our Souls, so that HE may CAUSE US to go forward IN HIS RIGHTEOUSNESS and go through the FIRE/Purification of GOD...Without getting destroyed, but WITH HAVING ALL THE CARNAL NATURE AND MIND TO BE REMOVED (chaff, stubble, wood, hay, false doctrines, hatred, bitterness, jealousies, envy, strife, covetousness, greed, etc....), leaving ONLY HIS DIVINE NATURE THAT IS OF HIS SPIRIT and KINGDOM REMAINING... AND YOUR SOUL, YOU, IN HIM BEING 'SET' IN THE PLACE HE HAS PREPARED FOR YOU.... IN HIM.

His Spirit In You... is the nuclei ... to plant His Word - Seed, DNA, the Anchor of your Soul, to assure you to come forth as Gold (His Divine Nature) tried by the Fire (Himself).

In a forest fire, this is where the seeds fall to the ground and open up to germinate and reproduce. I'm sure you can think of other ways in the natural that fire is good. There's an Operation of God working In You.

Let the Holy Spirit take you through the Fire. His Presence is that consuming fire. As the Son within you Preserves you till the day (moment) that all that you are is subdued to the Father, in God's Kingdom. What a Processing!

YOU ARE ASCENDING, being SUBMITTED TO THE FATHER, IN THE SECURITY OF THE LAMB,.....

LOOK INTO THE MIRROR (by the Mind of the Spirit)... WHO DO YOU SEE... BE CHANGED/TRANSFORMED in the twinkling of that Moment (revelation/revealing) of SEEing Him. ENTER IN. So much more could be said, but for now.....

Amen and Amen, Father.
RPJ

(Write your notes here)

REVELATION 30
Provoking Unto Love

To provoke unto love... Hebrews 10:24-31
And let us consider one another to provoke unto love and to good works:

Speaking the truth in love.... Ephesians 4:15-16
But speaking the truth in love, may grow up into him in all things, which is the head, even Christ:... From whom the whole body fitly joined together and compacted by that which every joint supplieth, according to the effectual working in the measure of every part, maketh increase of the body unto the edifying of itself in love.

Faith that worketh by love... Galatians 5:6
For in Jesus Christ neither circumcision availeth anything, nor uncircumcision; but faith which worketh by love.

Vengeance belongs to the Lord... Heb 10:30-31
For we know him that hath said, Vengeance belongeth unto me, I will recompense, saith the Lord. And again, The Lord shall judge his people. It is a fearful thing to fall into the hands of the living God.

Bless and Pray.... the Lord Will bring forth His Righteousness in the situations that cause you trouble.

Don't Take on Bitterness and/or Unforgiveness, but pray for those that cause you trouble. Pray for God's Truth and Righteousness to be revealed in their situation(s) and mind. Pray for healing for all involved. Pray for God's perfect plan and will to be done.

Now **Rejoice** and **be thankful** to the Lord, and let your own mind **be healed** .....

Abide in God's Love…. John 15:9-12
As the Father hath loved me, so have I loved you: **continue ye in my love**.
If ye keep my commandments, **ye shall abide in my love**; even as I have kept my Father's commandments, and abide in his love.
These things have I spoken unto you, that **my joy** might **remain in you**, and that **your joy** might **be full**.

This is my commandment, That ye love one another, as I have loved you.

Amen.
RPJ

" 'My Life In You' by Jesus Christ"

REVELATION 31
LOCKED SEALED READY

All that the Lord draws to the Son, Must receive that Word that is Spirit and is Life, and Be SEALED…. LOCKED by the Lord for His Working in you to begin… Redemption…

The Lord PAID FULL PRICE FOR YOU – HIS PURCHASED POSSESSION. So GIVE HIM YOUR ALL – FULL ACCESS TO EVERY AREA OF YOUR BEING AND LIFE.

Ephesians 1:13-14 In whom ye also *trusted*, after that ye *heard* the word of truth, the gospel of your salvation: in whom also after that ye *believed*, ye were **sealed with that holy Spirit** of promise, Which is the earnest of our inheritance *until the redemption* of the purchased possession, unto the praise of his glory.

We Trusted, Heard, Believed, and Sealed by the Holy Spirit of promise…. promise that we will enter in to the promised land, our inheritance, Eternal Life… which is Jesus Christ, the true God (1 John 5:20).

Then it says 'until the redemption…' This word redemption means the "full, complete" redemption; so until God fully redeems, or can say, "brings every bit of our person: mind, spirit, soul, AND body in to His Presence… transformed in the likeness of His Son, and one with Him and the Son." What a processing!

We are Sealed by the Holy Spirit of promise, then the working begins – a process to release us from that carnal mind, by the Revealing of Christ Jesus in each mind and soul. He establishes us in Himself by the process of Him (Holy Spirit) RENEWING and REGENERATING and RENOVATING our minds IN/BY His Word, which is to secure us, and guarantee our success to enter His Kingdom. This is that process of being born again of His Spirit and

Water. We also find that God is a consuming fire, so we also are 'salted with fire' during this process.

Some will bring forth 10% of His character, some will produce 30%, 60%, 80% or the full 100%. Much depends on what YOU will ALLOW HIM to do/work in you. Sometimes it is not 'comfortable' as the carnal mind is being cut away (falling away), but the after affects are PEACE as HIS Character (Presence) of RIGHTEOUNESS shines forth and is our new divine born again nature. !...... oh Hallelujah!! What a WAY to be CHANGED.

And That Character is actually HIS PRESENCE APPEARING in You, and you realize that you and Him have truly become One. At this moment, HE has SWALLOWED UP Your Mortality, and ETERNAL LIFE is Revealed!! Oh Hallelujah! Thank you Father. Amen.!

Your Mind becomes God's Garden to Birth His Divine Nature in, and cause you to become a son of God.... Yet wisdom tells us, that there is ONE SON, yet many members of that One
Son. so each member can grow into the Head.... meaning can grow to manifest 100% of the character of Jesus Christ, IF they will continue in His Faith and allow the Lord to work that redemptive process of being born again, in their mind.

Look at Deuteronomy 30:11-14 and Romans 10:4-10.
The Lord reveals in Deuteronomy that the Commandment of Him in that day to that generation was near them.... 'Commandment which I command thee is very nigh thee.... in thy mouth... and in thy heart... to do it.'
In Romans it is revealed that the 'Righteousness which is of faith is nigh thee... in thy mouth ... and in thy heart... the word of faith which we preach.'

** Now, look closely to this.... Verses 6-7 of Romans as it shows us that you don't have to ascend to heaven to get CHRIST, nor descend to the deep to bring CHRIST up, BUT that CHRIST (the word) IS IN THY HEART, AND IN THY MOUTH. ! . THAT WORD .... IS.... JESUS CHRIST ... REVEALED ... MANIFESTED IN YOU.

The Word that is Spirit and Life which the Lord, that Holy Spirit, has SPOKEN... rather REVEALED IN YOU AND YOU TRUSTED HIM, HEARD HIM, RECEIVED HIM, AND SEALED OF HIM.... again. Why again? Because you go from faith to faith, glory to glory, victory to victory.... from one experience of redemption to the next... UNTIL the FULL, COMPLETE Redemption of your whole being is seated in the Father. What a Working of the Father through His Son.... His Word. ! .

Amen.
RPJ

REVELATION 32
Forgiveness Is Eternal

Even God has had to deal with a disobedient, and or a quarrelsome family. Read the old testament and you'll see all He had to put up with, AND how He dealt with disobedience then. Thank you Father for Grace now.

Grace doesn't give us permission to be disobedient; instead, Grace just makes it easier for us to walk in the 'way' that God wants us to.

Forgiveness Is Eternal. God has Eternally Forgiven us of sin: missing the mark of righteousness by our own ability in the flesh. He has provided the Eternal ... On-going Sacrifice... His Lamb – Jesus Christ – that was alive, died, was revived, and lives forever more.... He is Our Righteousness to stand by, and our Eternal Forgiveness. Amen.

Forgiveness Is Eternal.

God has already Forgiven You... done deal.

Just stop doing those things that are wrong... or not of His nature/character....

God has already Forgiven You Eternally... Done ..... sooo...

Just Start doing what He tells you to do....

Just Start walking by the Spirit of Love and produce HIS Fruit.
If you find yourself having to say "Lord, I'm sorry, please forgive me" over and over... Then it is time for you to realize that He Has Already Forgiven You Forever....... So you don't have to plead for forgiveness, just acknowledge to Him the wrong, and desire to change.... RECEIVE His Forgiveness and TURN - CHANGE Your

Mind. Don't forget to Thank Him and Praise Him for the forgiveness.... it's just the polite thing to do.... He's your Father, so reverencing Him is proper. Sure, there are various ways to communicate to Him on this, but the Truth of the matter stays the same.

Ask Him HOW to behave in those situations you keep getting in. Obviously, if you keep behaving inappropriately, then you need to LEARN OF HIM the proper way to behave.

So, Ask Him How. Then wait for the answer. He will show you HIS WAY, then say Yes Lord I will, Please Help me to do Your Will. Now, of course, you can talk to the Father any way you want to.... this is only an example. But the Father WILL show you the proper mind to walk by.

Be FREE from that carnal mind set. LET – ALLOW the Lord to RENEW your mind in His Spirit. The Change comes by His Spirit in the EXPERIENCES of your walk that cause you to seek the Lord and desire to be Obedient to His Will and Word in everyday situations. This will cause you to SUBMIT to the Lord, which means you are resisting the devil (the one that kills, steals, and destroys) and giving GOD PLACE in your situation.

Submitting to God means you BELIEVE in HIS WORD and Walk by that Word. Jesus Christ was manifested to destroy the devil and the works of the devil. Do you believe this? So, since Jesus Christ I your Head and Authority, then the devil is destroyed. Now, walk in Faith of the Son... Praise Him, Thank Him and know that victory is won.

Even in Revelation 20:10 it tells us that God has thrown the devil, aka Satan and the false prophet into the lake of fire and brimstone, and that this is where they will be for ever and ever. Another DONE Deal. DO YOU BELIEVE GOD'S WORD? It Is Done.

It is your own and others carnal minds that have not been fully REGENERATED (BORN AGAIN) that is producing behaviors that 'kill (verbally and/or physically), steal, and destroy'.

BE FREE from the ruling force of the carnal mind of first adam, and RECEIVE the Mind & SPIRIT of the LORD and Your Liberty. Declare with your mouth and believe in your heart that Jesus Christ is Lord of your Life.... that is giving Him Place as the Ruler and One who Reigns in your life. (2 Corinthians 3:16-18; Hebrews 9:14-15; Romans 12:1-2; Titus 3:4-7; Hebrews 2:14; 1 John 3:8-9; and many more...).

Amen.
RPJ

REVELATION 33
Through Jesus Christ 

There's only one WAY, one Door, one Avenue, one "method" or "means" .... to do Anything.
Jesus Christ is the Way, the Truth, and the Life, right? Right.

There's only one Way to the Father and that is THROUGH the SON. And you can't come to the Son, unless the Father Wills for you to.

So, what about Healing? How does Healing Come? In a short response to this, Healing comes by the Father, through the SON, Jesus Christ.... by that same Spirit working THROUGH Faith in You to another.

By Faith in God's Word, which is Jesus Christ, His Son, we can lay hands or pray for the sick and they will recover. Or we can pray for the Lord's guidance in the situation, to receive wisdom for them so they that are sick may be free, or, or, or .... there are lots of situations to see how Jesus Christ went throughout the land healing and setting people free. But there is ONE set Truth in every situation.... it was the Father in the Son that allowed the work to be done. Yet the Father gave the Son His Honor and Authority, but the SON acknowledges that the Father is Greater than He. Oh What a Relationship Here!!!

The point here is.... The Father is the source of Life and has given all to the Son to work, but the Son can do nothing without the Father or without the Father's permission. Likewise we can of ourselves do NOTHING.

NOTHING, NOTHING, NOTHING... Unless the Father THROUGH the SON will do it through us. Submit to the Head from which all blessings flow... Humble and Yield yourself to Him and HIS WILL for the given situation... If Jesus Christ is not in you, If the Father is not in you, If the Holy Spirit is not in you.... you can do nothing.

They are One – that Holy Spirit is the Lord, and there is only One Lord (2 Cor 3:17). They, the Father and Son come and make their abode IN YOU (John 14:20-24). Many verses in the gospels read that Jesus tells us that it is the Father that doeth the work, and speaks through the Son to that generation. Although He knows His place and authority, He always knows and gives acknowledgement and REVERANCE to the Father, and the Father acknowledges and Honors the Son. What a Team!

So must we do. KNOW that it is the LORD IN US that does the Healing, Miracles, Blessings of all kinds, etc.... Give the Lord HONOR, and REVERANCE in all His workings through us. Humble Mind, Meek and lowly in heart... just like the Son to the Father.

Without Him we can do Nothing.... John 15:4-5 Abide in me, and I in you. As the branch cannot bear fruit of itself, except it abide in the vine; no more can ye except ye abide in me. I am the vine, ye are the branches: He that abideth in me, and I in him, the same bringeth forth much fruit for without me ye can do nothing.

Study that relationship between the Father and the Son, and let that be your example to nourish your relationship with the Lord. He Desires to give of Himself to us, so that we may never have a lack in giving out to others in that same selfless divine nature that He is. In Him we live, because the Son lives of the Father, and we through Him can have life more abundantly.

There is no other way for us to BECOME the SON with Him, and Produce the FRUIT of the SON, but to eat of and go through the Son to the Father. Likewise, in order for HIS HEALING POWER to flow through us, the Power has to be in us... His Holy Spirit.

John 1:12 reveals that He gives us power to become sons... In Luke 24:49 Jesus tells them to wait until they are endued with power from on high, the promise of the Father.

So if the Holy Spirit is doing the work of the Father & Son IN you, and you are abiding in Him, then He will flow through you, as He desires. Just be ready ... and willing.

Has He made you one of His Gifts to the Body of Christ? Then work that gift for the edification of the body in love, but never forget that the Gift is Jesus Christ in You working.... Allow HIM to flow through You, yet You always acknowledging within yourself, that it is HIM, the Holy Spirit, the Lord from Heaven that enables you and causes you to be one with His Son as Co-Heirs, and as HIS SON in this world.

We are His habitation. That body. That help-mate. And we are so, only through His Son, Jesus Christ, which is the power of God.... now in us so creation can be set free. Romans 8:14-23

Amen.
RPJ

REVELATION 34
Abundant Life

Revelation 1:18 Jesus has the keys of hell and death.

Romans 6:9-11, 14, 18 Knowing that Christ being raised form the dead dieth no more; death hath no more dominion over him. For in that he died, he died unto sin once: but in that he liveth, he liveth unto God.
Likewise reckon ye also yourselves to be dead indeed unto sin, but alive unto God through Jesus Christ our Lord.
v 14 For sin shall not have dominion over you: for you are not under the law, but under grace.
v 18 Being then made free from sin, ye became the servants of righteousness.

Romans 8:9-11 But ye are not in the flesh, but in the Spirit, if so be that the Spirit of God dwell in you. Now if any man have not the Spirit of Christ, he is none of his. And if Christ be in you, the body is dead because of sin; but the Spirit is life because of righteousness. But if the Spirit of him that raised up Jesus from the dead dwell in you, he that raised up Christ from the dead shall also quicken your mortal bodies by his Spirit that dwelleth in you.

Jesus Christ is our Sufficiency to be Righteous. That Spirit of Life that was in Christ Jesus, is the Father. And it is that One that made Jesus sufficient, and able to Finish the Work that the Father had sent Him to do.

It was by This Spirit, that Jesus was able to present himself without spot to God..... And it is by This Spirit in us that we are able to be without spot before God.

By the blood of Jesus Christ that was shed, our conscience can now be cleansed from dead works (the works of the flesh), so that we can serve the living God without fear, but with Reverence and Love. For in Jesus Christ and by Jesus Christ... by That Spirit of Life in Him – The Father in Him.... are we now SANCTIFIED, and JUSTIFIED and FREED from ALL SIN AND DEATH.

Can you believe this?

HE holds the keys of hell and death, and has become the ABILITY for US to be released from their hold. And that ABILITY (Jesus Christ) Working In Us – POWER – is ABLE TO SUSTAIN US NO MATTER WHAT. He is our Security of Right Standing before GOD and IN God always.

By God's Own Will, or could say by His Own Arm He has brought us to Himself, spotless, and unblameable..... He Has Become Our Way..... to the Abundant Life.

Amen.
RPJ

REVELATION 35
We ask for God's help.... but will You help God? 

Where were you when He needed help? Help God First.... then when you call, He will help you.

The businesses and the people should be supporting God financially first.... Not God or the Church supplying the "people" for "monies" for businesses to profit. This is wrong.

Nothing is wrong with owning a business and profiting. But if you are using the body of Christ to make your profits.... this is wrong.

Give to the Body of Christ. Give to true Ministers and Ministries of God.

Where is the understanding, and the reverence to God? No wonder the USA is in a financial poverty.

Tell the businesses to start giving to the body of Christ, and to "true" ministers and ministries of God, and there will be a turnaround in the finances.

Ask God to show you who to give to, not by logic or reason, but by the Spirit of the Lord and His peace within... giving cheerfully. The one that outwardly looks defeated may be the one that needs it most; or the one that looks completed is actually the one that needs it most..... in other words, don't choose by looks or by the best asker, but ASK GOD and LISTEN for the peace in your heart that says this one.

Let God tell you, and then give as He desires. He is the one to bless you, and keep His promise. Don't listen to ones that make you promises, but LISTEN to the confirmation in your spirit of what The Holy Spirit is telling you. Learn to Commune with the Father daily, in all your actions.

Pass this on.....

Amen.
RPJ

(Write your notes here)

REVELATION 36
Abundance – Equality for All
Or All things in Common

2 Corinthians 8:10-16
10 And herein I give my advice: for this is expedient for you, who have begun before, not only to do, but also to be forward a year ago.

11 Now therefore perform the doing of it; that as there was a readiness to will, so there may be a performance also out of that which ye have.

12 For if there be first a willing mind, it is accepted according to that a man hath, and not according to that he hath not.

13 For I mean not that other men be eased, and ye burdened:

14 But by an equality, that now at this time your abundance may be a supply for their want, that their abundance also may be a supply for your want: that there may be equality:

15 As it is written, He that had gathered much had nothing over; and he that had gathered little had no lack.

16 But thanks be to God, which put the same earnest care into the heart of Titus for you.

Thank you Father.

Amen.
RPJ

REVELATION 37
If You Say You are God's Habitation...

John 14:2
Ephesians 2:19-22
1 Corinthians 3:16-17
2 Corinthians 3:17
and many more scriptures.....

If You say you are God's Habitation, Then God Is Dwelling IN YOU. Make up your mind.

It is time to make up our mind... Are we God's Habitation or not? I say "yes" and I Know This Is So.

Father, please open the blind eyes, and heal the deaf ears, In Jesus Name Amen.

The scriptures clearly show and by the revealing of the Holy Spirit that is IN us *(if it is so that you have received the Lord 2 Corinthians 3:17)*, that we, that have received Jesus Christ as the Son of God, Saviour from separation from God/LIFE, Priest/King *(and soooo many other worthy names and purposes and benefits and blessings has He been made for us to reap of)* ... that we are the habitation of Him/God.

Wow. Seriously... Wow.... So declare Him, Your Righteousness... that HE is Abiding In You, Today.

But yet I continuously am hearing of those that say they are the children of God, but yet they confess that Jesus Christ is not abiding in them. I think it is time for them/you to Wake Up, and Receive the Lord Jesus Christ and let Him abide In you.....

John 14:2 In my Father's house are many mansions: if it were not so, I would have told you. I go to prepare a place for you. And if I go and prepare a place for you, I will come again, and receive you unto myself; that where I am, there ye may be also.

Ephesians 2:19-22 v21 In whom all the building fitly framed together growth unto an holy temple in the Lord: In whom ye also are builded together for an habitation of God through the Spirit.

1 Corinthians 3:16-17 Know ye not that **ye are the temple of God**, and that **the Spirit of God dwelleth in you?**

2 Corinthians 3:17 Now the **Lord is that Spirit**: and **where** the Spirit of the Lord **is**, there is liberty.

We are the habitation, the body, the visible image of the invisible God.... GOD HAS DESIRED THIS, and has caused the SPIRIT OF THE SON, WHICH IS THE FATHER, TO DWELL IN YOU. If you have received that Word of Truth, Jesus Christ, and have believed that Word of Truth, and have Received that Spirit of Promise, the Father, in your soul....

Then you are SEALED with that holy Spirit of promise... Ephesians 1:13-14. Romans 8:9-11 ...if so be that the **Spirit of God dwell in you**. **Now if any man have not the Spirit of Christ, he is none of his**. And **if Christ be in you**, the body is dead because of sin; but the Spirit is life because of righteousness. **But if the Spirit of him that raised up Jesus** from the dead **dwell in you**,.....

OHHHH Hear this....... "if **the Spirit of Him that raised up Jesus from the dead dwell IN YOU**,.....

This is the Spirit that IS GOD..... the Father was in Jesus Christ, and it was HIM that raised Him from the dead. YOU ARE DEAD because SIN was REVEALED. Sin was revealed when Jesus Christ was preached and your eyes were opened and YOU REALIZED you needed THE SAVIOUR. HIS Presence not only shined on your filthiness, but HIS LOVE pulled on you to COME to HIM. So you asked HIM into your Heart, so that HE COULD CAUSE YOU to be able to be received back in to LIFE ....

Now be awakened to WHY HE IS IN YOU.... (this has been preached in earlier days messages, but it will be spoken of again at another time).

Declare HIS RIGHTEOUSNESS, PRESENCE IN YOU.... Unless your righteousness exceeds that of the ("working of the flesh") scribes and Pharisees.... let's read Matthew 5:20:

Matthew 5:20 (Jesus talking) For I say unto you, That except your righteousness shall exceed the righteousness of the scribes and Pharisees, ye shall in no case enter into the kingdom of heaven.
Jesus Christ IS that Righteousness..... THAT Presence IN YOU Makes You Righteous. (period)

So declare HIM, That Righteousness... that is Abiding In You, Today. It is the only SECURITY we need, and the only JUSTIFICATION that declares us before the Father as holy, unblameable, and loved.

Amen.
RPJ

REVELATION 38
The Lord is My Shepherd

Psalm 23
The Lord is my Shepherd I shall not want.....
Amen. That settles it ... and all issues.

The Lord is My Shepherd, and I have no need of anything anymore. Why? Because the Lord is my Shepherd I shall not want. Any need that has been, He has fulfilled. Whatever "need" now appears, He is fulfilling. And whatever need or want may come in the future, He will fulfill and provide for.

Although at times, I am patiently waiting for certain things to be brought in to my hands and materialize, yet I now have become one with the Father and Son, who is Master and Creator of all things. He has made all things by His Word, His Son, for his pleasure and purpose, including me. What is His is mine and what is mine is His. There is still sooo much to learn of Him and His Kingdom, and How all things work together for good ... according to His good pleasure. So there is never a day of lack.

Romans 8:28 And we know that all things work together for good to them that love God, to them who are the called according to his purpose.

The only need I have is Him, and since I have Him, I have need of nothing anymore. I ask Him and receive from Him. Sometimes it may be through another person, or by an angel or by a miracle of another means. It is just the Divine Life I live in.

I lack nothing. I am complete. I am His Son/Daughter. He is my Everything – my All in All!

What a Family we have! Look forward to meeting many, many more members of this wonderful, like Mind & Spirit & Soul body.

(Note: As you are reading this, note that You are saying "I" - make it your confession and declaration of God's provision through Jesus Christ. And if you are one with the Son, then you are one with the Father, and there is no lack in you or for you... God will fulfill all voids.)
Mark 14:36 And he said, Abba, Father, all things are possible unto thee; take away this cup from me: nevertheless not what I will, but what thou wilt.

Mark 11:22-26 And Jesus answering saith unto them, Have faith in God. 23 For verily I say unto you, That whosoever shall say unto this mountain, Be thou removed, and be thou cast into the sea; and shall not doubt in his heart, but shall believe that those things which he saith shall come to pass; he shall have whatsoever he saith. 24 Therefore I say unto you, What things soever ye desire, when ye pray, believe that ye receive them, and ye shall have them. 25 And when ye stand praying, forgive, if ye have ought against any: that your Father also which is in heaven may forgive you your trespasses. 26 But if ye do not forgive, neither will your Father which is in heaven forgive your trespasses.

Amen.
RPJ

REVELATION 39
Household of God

Mark 11:17
Matthew 6:9
Romans 8:26-34

God's House is a:

House of Prayer
Mark 11:17 And he taught, saying unto them, Is it not written, My house shall be called of all nations the house of prayer? but ye have made it a den of thieves.

God knows our heart and mind and why we do what we do, but we need to be honest to ourselves, and sincere to the Lord, revealing why we are doing what we do. "Sincerity and truth"

*Jesus' Example to Pray: (Matthew 6:9) Jesus showed us to Give Reverence to the Father first, next praying for His Kingdom & Will, then our Provision, Forgiveness, Direction & Protection, and Honor back to Father. This is Jesus' example to us when the law of sin and death, the first covenant was still in effect. Yet it is still wise to review even as we are now in Grace, knowing our own sins are now forgiven and have been washed in His word and Spirit having been born again and established in His present Kingdom which is now come and is now reigning over all kingdoms.

Hmmm.... so that prayer of Jesus has come to pass! Pretty cool revelation and understanding! Thank you Father!

*Praying in and by the Holy Ghost/Spirit: It is the Lord in us that is the "Intercessor" praying for others and setting free. For those that are hearing His calling to Pray – Pray as the Holy Spirit is revealing His Will to be done. There's no way to 'teach' this except by the leading and teaching of the Holy Spirit.... Just as you hear and see what the Lord is telling you, speak and Intercede for your neighbor(hood), and nation(s), and fellow ministers in the field... as the Lord is revealing to you to do. Pray without ceasing, or rather in a continual, open mind to the Lord in every situation, for others and for yourselves.

Jude 20-21 20 But ye, beloved, building up yourselves on your most holy faith, praying in the Holy Ghost, Keep yourselves in the love of God, looking for the mercy of our Lord Jesus Christ unto eternal life.

Romans 8:26-34 Likewise the Spirit also helpeth our infirmities: for we know not what we should pray for as we ought: but the Spirit itself maketh intercession for us with groanings which cannot be uttered.
And he that searcheth the hearts knoweth what is the mind of the Spirit, because he maketh intercession for the saints according to the will of God.
And we know that all things work together for good to them that love God, to them who are the called according to his purpose.
For whom he did foreknow, he also did predestinate to be conformed to the image of his Son, that he might be the firstborn among many brethren.
Moreover whom he did predestinate, them he also called: and whom he called, them he also justified: and whom he justified, them he also glorified.
What shall we then say to these things? If God be for us, who can be against us?
He that spared not his own Son, but delivered him up for us all, how shall he not with him also freely give us all things?
Who shall lay any thing to the charge of God's elect? It is God that justifieth.
Who is he that condemneth? It is Christ that died, yea rather, that is risen again, who is even at the right hand of God, who also maketh intercession for us.

Conformed to the image of the Son… for it is the Spirit of the Son in us that makes us God's Son. And it is that Spirit that is Interceding for all…. through us, His many membered body… in this world. Stop looking for HIM to Come outside of yourself, ol' body of Christ. For HE is Desiring to APPEAR IN YOU, and THROUGH YOU to THIS GENERATION AND AGE. Not separate from Him, but Himself through You As HE Is…. to this world. We are (becoming) the visible appearing of the invisible God…. NOT BY OUR EFFORTS,…. But by HIS WILL and PURPOSE in and for THIS Age.

Galatians 2:20 I am crucified with Christ: nevertheless I live; yet not I, but Christ liveth in me and the life which I now live in the flesh I live by the faith of the Son of God, who loved me and gave himself for me.

Take the Next Step into the Revelation (revealing) of the Son of God, and God's purpose for you In His Son….

It is no longer You, but Christ…. YIELD to the Spirit of the Son, the Spirit of God, the Spirit which is the Lord & Saviour that you are now sealed with… Ephesians 1:13-14 Galatians 4:6-7

Looking unto the Christ, who is your Saviour, to appear….. 2 Tim 1:9-10

2 Timothy 1:9-10
9 who has saved us and called us to a holy life — not because of anything we have done but because of his own purpose and grace. This grace was given us in Christ Jesus before the beginning of time,

10 but it has **now** been **revealed** through the **appearing** of our Savior, Christ Jesus, who has destroyed death and has brought life and immortality to light through the gospel.

We need to talk on this more…. so you may understand exactly what was happening back then, in THAT GENERATION… so that you may understand where You are in God’s plan IN THIS AGE.

Amen.
RPJ

(Write your notes here)

REVELATION 40
A Sure Foundation

Judges 6:6-22 v20 And the angel of God said unto him, Take the flesh and the unleavened cakes, and lay them upon this rock , and pour out the broth. And he did so.

The Flesh and Body of Jesus Christ was laid on That Rock and the broth was symbolic of His Blood.... Can you hear and see God's Sign even then..... Gideon asked for a sign that he was really talking to God, so God's angel provided one... and I see the revelation of the Son here too. Our Sure Foundation.

Isaiah 28:14-16 v16 Therefore thus saith the Lord God, Behold, I lay in Zion for a foundation **a stone**, a tried stone, a precious corner stone, a sure foundation: he that believeth shall not make haste.

The foundation in this verse is A STONE.... not many but one tried, corner stone. Hmmmm....

Matthew 16:15-19 He saith unto them, But whom say ye that I am? And Simon Peter answered and said, Thou art the Christ, the Son of the living God. And Jesus answered and said unto him, Blessed art thou, Simon Barjona: for flesh and blood hath not revealed it unto thee, but my Father which is in heaven. And I say also unto thee, That thou art Peter, and upon this rock I will build my church; and the gates of hell shall not prevail against it. And I will give unto thee the keys of the kingdom of heaven: and whatsoever thou shalt bind on earth shall be bound in heaven: and whatsoever thou shalt loose on earth shall be loosed in heaven.

A Sure Foundation IS the STONE, the ROCK, which is Jesus Christ, the Son of the living God.

But if you'll notice that once a 'revelation' ... a revealing of truth is made known to you by the Father, then you are CHANGED, and become One with that revealing/revelation. That's why Jesus speaks to Simon Barjona and changes his name to Peter. A change took place within him.

Thus it is, in the renewing of our mind, by the Holy Spirit, for as He speaks and makes known God's word to us, We Are Changed INTO the Same Image. Where ever the Lord, that Spirit appears, a change takes place... a birthing of His Divine Nature.

Philippians 3:21 who shall change our vile body, that it may be fashioned like unto his glorious body, according to the working whereby he is able even to subdue all things unto himself.

2 Corinthians 3:18 But we all, with open face beholding as in a glass the glory of the Lord, are changed into the same image from glory to glory, even as by the Spirit of the Lord.

Now, back to the foundation, which is that Rock upon which we stand.... There are multitudes of revelations here if you will allow the Father to reveal the Son to you:

This Corner Stone is the first stone to set the structure of the building. Then the Apostles of the Lamb that are the 12 foundations of the wall of the city of God, were added to it. They became one with Him as the foundation. Now the church, His body, has a place to function through – a place to work from – a dwelling for the family of God in heaven and earth to tabernacle in.

Is God making you part of His Foundation? (Hear this with Spiritual ears of understanding or you'll go off balance.) Look at 1 Corinthians 3:3-16. Here Paul is telling them that we are all labourers together with God, being His building, and husbandry. Everyone has their God given place to stand and work to do.

Each are important and to be respected by one another.... knowing there is only one sure foundation – verse 11 For other foundation can no man lay than that is laid, which is Jesus Christ.

Yet all will be tried with fire... just like in verse above of Judges 6:20-22. !! Read 1 Corinthians 3:3-16. We are to stand upon that Foundation which is the TRIED STONE, CORNER STONE... THE ROCK that is our SURE PLACE to be, the Stone that Guides, Balances, Secures, Establishes the rest of the building. There, on that Rock, God's presence will meet us, commune with us, consume us, and reveal to us that truly we are encountering the Lord God face to face.

Amen.
RPJ

REVELATION 41
Jesus’ Appearing

Take the Next Step into the Revelation (revealing) of the Son of God, and God’s purpose for you In His Son....

It is no longer You, but Christ.... YIELD to the Spirit of the Son, the Spirit of God, the Spirit which is the Lord & Saviour that you are now sealed with... Ephesians 1:13-14 Galatians 4:5-7

Galatians 2:20 I am crucified with Christ: nevertheless I live; yet not I, **but Christ liveth in me**: and the life which I now live in the flesh I live by the faith of the Son of God, who loved me, and gave himself for me.

Ephesians 1:13-14 In whom ye also trusted, after that ye heard the word of truth, the gospel of your salvation: in whom also after that ye believed, ye were sealed with that holy Spirit of promise, Which is the earnest of our inheritance until the redemption of the purchased possession, unto the praise of his glory.

Galatians 4:5-7To redeem them that were under the law, that we might receive the adoption of sons. And because ye are sons, God hath sent forth the Spirit of his Son into your hearts, crying, Abba, Father. Wherefore thou art no more a servant, but a son: and if a son, then an heir of God through Christ.

Paul told them in Galatians 4:19
My little children, of whom I travail in birth again until Christ be formed in you....
Looking unto the Christ, who is your Saviour, to appear.....

2 Timothy 1:9-10 Who hath saved us, and called us with an holy calling, not according to our works, but according to his own purpose and grace, which was given us in Christ Jesus before the

world began, But is **now** made **manifest by the appearing** of our Saviour Jesus Christ, who hath abolished death, and hath brought life and immortality to light through the gospel:

So, here is scripture that speaks of Jesus Christ already come, revealed, manifest. BUT yet, in other scriptures we find there is a coming of Jesus Christ, "waiting for the appearing..." and other ways the scriptures in the New Testament speak of.
So what is happening? or Rather, what was happening back in the new testament Generation?

We need to talk on this more.... so all may understand exactly what was happening back then, in THAT GENERATION... so that all may understand where we/you are in God's plan in THIS Age and generation.

I'll touch only on a couple facts to reveal the truth of Jesus' appearing, but would hope you would join us in future meetings to complete the revealing of what was and is happening.

In Matthew 23:36 Jesus says: 'Verily I say unto you, All these things shall come upon this generation.'

Jesus was speaking and telling them of what was going to happen in THAT GENERATION. Not us, but to them.

Now look at Matthew 24:34 where Jesus says: 'Verily I say unto you, This generation shall not pass, till all these things be fulfilled.'

And in Luke 21 tells us also of that generation being the age that would experience all this.

Jesus was speaking to them and telling them that the great tribulation and white throne judgment was going to happen according to all that the law and prophets have said.

What was happening, was that the fulfilling of the law and prophets concerning Christ was being fulfilled, so that the first order could be completed and moved out of the way, so that the Blood Covenant of Jesus Christ, the New Priesthood, and King, and Kingdom, etc... could be established. A new heaven and earth where God dwells. And that is in His People... Hasn't He said we are His Temple, Dwelling Place? Yes.

In order for the law and prophets to be fulfilled, and every jot and tittle of the law fulfilled, then there had to be the appearing of Jesus Christ, God in the flesh, to be the Priest, King, and Lamb of God to fulfill the requirements of law of sin and death. Jesus Christ fulfilled all righteousness, and the debt of sin, and the judgment of sin under that law, overcoming death.

But there was one more event that had to be accomplished under that old law, before the new order of God could come in. Judgment of sin upon THAT GENERATION for the shedding of God's innocent blood:

Luke 11:49-52 (Jesus speaking)
49 Therefore also said the wisdom of God, I will send them prophets and apostles, and some of them they shall slay and persecute:

50 That the blood of all the prophets, which was shed from the foundation of the world, may be required of **this generation**;

51 From the blood of Abel unto the blood of Zacharias, which perished between the altar and the temple: verily I say unto you, **It shall be required of this generation**.

52 Woe unto you, lawyers! for ye have taken away the key of knowledge: ye entered not in yourselves, and them that were entering in ye hindered.

Are you seeing this yet? The great tribulation was to come to THAT Generation, not us.

It was prophesied concerning THAT generation, not us. And in about 70 AD this Great Tribulation came to completion, thus the New Heaven, and New Earth of God came forth, and is Established Today. So stop believing the lie that the tribulation is in the future, and that all the things happening in the world is a fulfillment of Matthew 24, etc.... It is not. Matthew 24 did happen as prophesied IN That Generation.
Once Done, it is done.

The Kingdom of God/Heaven is not an outward establishment, but it is Righteousness, Peace, and Joy IN THE HOLY GHOST (Romans 14:17).

The Kingdom of God/Heaven is In You, In the Holy Ghost/Spirit:
Luke 17:20-21 And when he was demanded of the Pharisees, when the kingdom of God should come, he answered them and said, The kingdom of God cometh not with observation: Neither shall they say, Lo here! or, lo there! for, behold, the kingdom of God is within you. KJV

And the Kingdom of God/Heaven is also God's dominion that we press in to, and enter as John 3:3-5 talks of being born again is the only way to 'enter' the kingdom of God. And Luke 16:16 tells us that the law and the prophets were until John, and since then we 'press' in to the Kingdom.

So what is to be for this Age and generation? Whatever the Lord has planned...Which a lot is happening today in God's Kingdom and outside His kingdom.

But Ephesians 2:7 tells us that **this age** we live in is a time for God to **reveal His Kindness and Love**.

Eph 2:4-9 But God, who is rich in mercy, for his great love wherewith he loved us, Even when we were dead in sins, hath quickened us together with Christ, (by grace ye are saved;) And hath raised us up together, and made us sit together in heavenly places in Christ Jesus: That **in the ages to come** he might shew the **exceeding riches of his grace in his kindness** toward us through Christ Jesus. For by grace are ye saved through faith; and that not of yourselves: it is the gift of God: Not of works, lest any man should boast.
So stop believing the lie that the tribulation is in the future, and that all the things happening in the world is a fulfillment of Matthew 24, etc.... It is not. Matthew 24 did happen as prophesied IN That Generation.

Once Done, it is done.

Now What? Be Redeemed by the Blood of the Lamb and ENTER and DWELL in God's Kingdom with the Son, the Lamb of God. DO and GO as the Father Desires You to. Set the creature free.... (See Romans 8:All * 19)

Rom 8:19 For the earnest expectation of the creature waiteth for the manifestation of the sons of God.

Be Born Again... Be Conformed to the image of the Son... for it is the Spirit of the Son in us that makes us God's Son. And it is that Spirit that is Interceding for all.... through us, His many membered body... in this world.

Stop looking for HIM to Come outside of yourself, ol' body of Christ. For HE is Desiring to APPEAR IN YOU, and THROUGH YOU to THIS GENERATION AND AGE. Not separate from Him, but Himself through You As HE Is.... to this world. We are (becoming) the visible appearing of the invisible God.... NOT BY OUR EFFORTS,.... But by HIS WILL and PURPOSE in and for THIS Age.

" 'My Life In You' by Jesus Christ"

Galatians 2:20 I am crucified with Christ: nevertheless I live; yet not I, but Christ liveth in me and the life which I now live in the flesh I live by the faith of the Son of God, who loved me and gave himself for me.

Amen
RPJ

(Write your notes here)

REVELATION 42
Strengthened In Love

Ephesians 3:14-19 For this cause I bow my knees unto the Father of our Lord Jesus Christ, Of whom the whole family in heaven and earth is named, That he would grant you, according to the riches of his glory, to be strengthened with might by his Spirit in the inner man; That Christ may dwell in your hearts by faith; that ye, being rooted and grounded in love, May be able to comprehend with all saints what is the breadth, and length, and depth, and height; And to know the love of Christ, which passeth knowledge, that ye might be filled with all the fulness of God.

This passage of scripture, like many others, is just so powerful and wonderful to eat! First we see we have a family that is not just in the earth, but in heaven too. It is a family with God as our Father, and we are named after Him. And you know how many names He has! Big Responsibility here.

Verse 16 – 19 is the focus for today, so look deep and allow the Lord to reveal Himself to you in a clearer way...

In verse 16 HE GRANTS YOU... now I know this is Paul speaking as if a prayer in his heart, but that's my point... Would Paul's prayer be unanswered? No. So RECEIVE from the Apostle of God today also.

So... God Grants to You ACCORDING to HIS RICHES of GLORY... now this is Deep! We are not talking of rubies, diamonds, dollars.... This is talking of God's Presence IN You and the Effects it has on you... the Benefits He is IN You. !!! LIBERTY! Oh Hallelujah to the King!

God to grant you according to the riches of His Glory so You Can Be STRENGTHENED with POWER BY HIS PRESENCE – SPIRIT.... God is Spirit. There's only one Spirit and that is the Lord, the Holy

One, Yeshua, God (Ephesians 4).... STRENGTHENED BY His Spirit IN YOUR INNER MAN.

Now the next verse though CONNECTS Jesus Christ AS THAT SPIRIT.... That Christ may dwell in your hearts by faith. Jesus Christ IS THAT Spirit. One Spirit – God.

Then it tells us why – so you may be AFFECTED BY LOVE, and ANCHORED – SECURED in HIS THOUGHTS towards you.

...that ye, being rooted and grounded in love.... May be able to comprehend (understand) with all saints what is the breadth, and length, and depth, and height;

19 And to know the love of Christ, which passeth knowledge, that ye might be filled with all the fulness of God.

Now, verse 19 is speaking of a love that *exceeds* head knowledge.... it is an EXPERIENCIAL Love. An Experience that goes beyond head knowledge... An Experience in His Love that creates and causes a Change in your nature (Fills You With God – removes all voids, lack, emptiness).

His Presence In You – Is His Riches of Glory... Giving You His Best which is Himself.

Amen.
RPJ

REVELATION 43
Foundation of Love (Rooted and Grounded in Love)

To stand and be secured in the sure foundation is to be "rooted and grounded in love."
Something to think on....

Look in to Ephesians 3:14-19, and we find that the family of God that is in heaven and earth is named after God the Father.

v 14-15 For this cause I bow my knees unto the Father of our Lord Jesus Christ, Of whom the whole family in heaven and earth is named,...

v 17 That Christ may dwell in your hearts by faith; that ye, being rooted and grounded in love, May be able to comprehend (understand) with all saints what is the breadth, and length, and depth, and height: And to know the love of Christ, which passeth knowledge *(it is an experience)*, that ye might be filled with all the fulness of God.

Here... Is the Purpose of God our Father in the working of Jesus Christ.... so He may have a Home. A Dwelling Place... and We may have a Father & Family... & Friends.

That Foundation of Jesus Christ, God's Son, God's Lamb... is our security and assurance to allow God to finish His Will in and through us.... to day.

To KNOW that Love: is to EXPERIENCE His Presence in our Soul and Body, which is that Spirit that Intercedes for ourselves, and for others through us...

To KNOW that Love that will assure us that HIS MIND TOWARDS US is to command His very best for us... IF we will let Him, and IF we will Obey Him.

" 'My Life In You' by Jesus Christ"

All of us make mistakes, and mess things up, yet HE IS ABLE to correct and fix our messes, and bring forth HIS PLAN and PURPOSE for each of our lives in this earth.

Be ROOTED and GROUNDED IN HIS LOVE.... Get to KNOW Jesus Christ, not in the letter, but in an ENCOUNTER OF GOD's WORD that is SPIRIT & LIFE! JESUS CHRIST is God's WILL and Purpose of Eternal Life WORKING and BREATHING IN YOU. This LIFE is RAISING YOU UP OUT OF YOUR DEATH of sin and the GRAVE... To DAY it is being DONE..... IF YOU will let Him.

Lay your Life down, and let the Lord BREATH His Son's Life Into You.... which will RAISE YOU UP and cause you to ENTER your New Life (heaven & earth)... now. This is receiving your Inheritance... now... today, and not having to wait until you are buried six feet down. You can receive and Enjoy HIS LIFE to day.

John 15:9-13 As the Father hath loved me, so have I loved you: continue ye in my love. If ye keep my commandments, ye shall abide in my love; even as I have kept my Father's commandments, and abide in his love.
These things have I spoken unto you, that my joy might remain in you, and that your joy might be full. This is my commandment, That ye love one another, as I have loved you.
Greater love hath no man than this, that a man lay down his life for his friends.

Amen.
RPJ

REVELATION 44
ENTER, then EXIT - Experience

Ezekiel 46:13, 10

Getting to the point of the message, here is what the Lord is revealing:

In Ezekiel 46 it is talking of the Princes' responsibilities. The Prince was allowed to enter by the way of one gate and return out of that same gate. But the People were to enter by way of the north gate, then return by the south gate. They had to GO FORWARD and not return the same way they came in.

Revelation Speaking: Today, enter in to the Lord to worship Him in one mind, but exit out by another mind. Enter in being depressed, needy, poor, and exit out of the gate/mind of Liberty and Thanksgiving!

The Prince had responsibility to VOLUNTARILY present the offering to the Lord DAILY, EVERY MORNING. And the Sacrifice was of the lamb of the first year without blemish, oil, some flour, and meat prepared.

DAILY Every Morning the Prince would VOLUNTARILY Enter the gate WITH THE BURNT OFFERING of the lamb, Oil, Flour, Meat. The door would be opened to him, and then shut after him.

Now that was under the Law of Sin and Death, the working of the flesh. But by Revelation, To Day it is showing us:

> To WILLINGLY and FREELY Enter in to the Presence of God BY THE BLOOD OF THE LAMB, and BY THE LAMB OF GOD (meat/eternal sacrifice), That Holy Spirit (Oil), That True Priest/King (Word/flour/Bread) who has gone before us and has entered in before us, and who is the Doorkeeper

and Door itself that determines who can enter or not unto His Father.

DAILY ENTER INTO THE THRONE OF THE KING, communing and receiving from Him ALL that He desires to Give, and above/beyond all that you could possibly think. And leave out by that same Gate, THE LORD JESUS CHRIST, YESHUA, LAMB OF GOD & BLOOD, because He Has Made Us Priests & Kings of Him.

GO FORWARD... NOT REPEATING the same actions of the old mind, but be TRANSFORMED in the MIND OF THE SON, while being in the PRESENCE OF THE ALMIGHTY LORD, as He Writes upon our hearts and Puts within our MINDS the New Blood Covenant: the Revealing of the Lamb and Son of God.

EXIT in the mind of THANKSGIVING.... DAILY.... WILLINGLY... GRATEFUL TO AND OF THE LIVING LAMB, OUR PRIEST & KING.

Amen.
RPJ

REVELATION 45
Are You Ready for More?

John 16:12-16
12 I have yet many things to say unto you, but ye cannot bear them now.

In John 1:18 and Luke 16:22-23 the Lord has confirmed what He is saying... "everyone has a Place"...to abide in. But as the verse below John 16:12 says, that sometimes the reason the Lord does not reveal things to you, could be because you are not ready to "handle" them.

John 1:18
18 No man hath seen God at any time; the only begotten Son, which is in the bosom of the Father, he hath declared him.

Luke 16:22-23
22 And it came to pass, that the beggar died, and was carried by the angels into Abraham's bosom: the rich man also died, and was buried;

23 And in hell he lift up his eyes, being in torments, and seeth Abraham afar off, and Lazarus in his bosom.
(Look deep in the verses above...there is a wonderful revelation of the Lord.... and ask the Lord to reveal More...)

WANTING MORE?... Then ALLOW the Lord to shake you in those areas that are hard and stubborn, and prepare your mind to be "renewed in Christ Jesus" so that He can tell you more of Himself, His Kingdom, which is Truth.

Today is your Day... Begin.... or for most... Continue the Journey of Eternal Life.

John 16:12-16

12 I have yet many things to say unto you, but ye cannot bear them now.

13 Howbeit when he, the Spirit of truth, is come, he will guide you into all truth: for he shall not speak of himself; but whatsoever he shall hear, that shall he speak: and he will shew you things to come.

14 He shall glorify me: for he shall receive of mine, and shall shew it unto you.

15 All things that the Father hath are mine: therefore said I, that he shall take of mine, and shall shew it unto you.

16 A little while, and ye shall not see me: and again, a little while, and ye shall see me, because I go to the Father.

Even here the Lord Jesus is revealing that That Holy Spirit Is The Father which will & does dwell in and with those souls that believe in the Son.

Our Father will reveal to us, today, many things. If we are willing to allow Him to condition us... rather transform our minds so that we can receive them. These things can cause a spiritual shaking within or all that we thought we knew, concerning Jesus, heaven, God, hell and so much more.

But this is what is exciting! LEARNING of the FATHER and SON! Sitting at His Feet, or Hugged in His Arms and allowing Him to show us and TEACH us of things concerning Him.
I say "Yes, Lord." "Cause I want to know YOU."

And THIS IS ETERNAL LIFE.... 1 John 5:20, JOHN 17:3

1 John 5:20
20 And we know that the Son of God is come, and hath given us an understanding, that we may know him that is true, and we are in him that is true, even in his Son Jesus Christ. This is the true God, and eternal life.

John 17:3
3 And this is life eternal, that they might **know** thee the only true God, and Jesus Christ, whom thou hast sent.

1 John 5:11-13
11 And this is the record, that God hath given to us eternal life, and this life is in his Son.

12 He that **hath the Son hath life**; and he that hath not the Son of God hath not life.

13 These things have I written unto you that believe on the name of the Son of God; that ye may know that ye have eternal life, and that ye may believe on the name of the Son of God.

So, it is that we that have received the Son, have received the Father also. And SEALED of Him.
AND it is so, that we that have been sealed of Him, Have Eternal Life, for Eternal Life is In the Son, and the Son is now In Us.

Unless you are a reject, which is a reprobate.... 2 Corinthians 13:5 Examine yourselves, whether ye be in the faith; prove your own selves. Know ye not your own selves, how that Jesus Christ is in you, except ye be reprobates?

John 16:12-16 I have yet many things to say unto you, but ye cannot bear them now.

Are You Ready for More? ..... Can You Receive Them? .... Or will you leave also, like the religious sects did, because the words Jesus Spoke to them, they could not receive them.

Ask, and Receive from the Father, because He desires to give you the Kingdom, and reveal Truth to you.

Amen.
RPJ

(Write your notes here)

REVELATION 46
When That Which Is PERFECT Is Come 

Perfect means Complete, or Mature

Maturity is Not Old Age

Some people grow old but never mature.
Some people become mature before they are old.

Maturity is a transformation of the mind.
Old Age is a transformation of the physical body.

Putting off the 'old' is not putting off your body, it is the Receiving of the Identity and person of Jesus Christ. Read on to understand more.

Growing up in Christ isn't about growing old in Christ. It's about having our mind renewed by the Holy Spirit washing and cleansing us by Jesus Christ, which is the Water and Blood... justifying and sanctifying us. It is Receiving Him, His Mind and being changed, born again in His character & divine nature which means our behavior will change. We start to walk and begin producing the Lord's full character in all that we do.

1 Corinthians 13:10-13 But when that which is ***perfect is come***, **then** that which is in part shall be done away. 11 When I was a child, I spake as a child, I understood as a child, I thought as a child: but when I became a man, I put away childish things. 12 For now we see through a glass, darkly; but **then** face to face: now I know in part; but **then** shall I know even as also I am known. 13 And now abideth faith, hope, charity , these three; but the greatest of these is charity .

All of 1 Corinthians 13 reveals true Fruit of the Mature One. So when that Perfect One, or could say Complete One, or Mature

One is Come… Revealed IN Your SOUL, then the old nature will fall away. Hear the word of the Lord. *A change in identity… the second man, the quickening spirit, the Lord from heaven, Eternal Life begins to Appear in this World … through HIS BODY … To those that have ears to hear, hear what the Lord is saying….*

It is time to let the Mature One, the Perfect One Appear…

Ephesians 4:11-16
11 And he gave some, apostles; and some, prophets; and some, evangelists; and some, pastors and teachers; 12 For the perfecting of the saints, for the work of the ministry, for the edifying of the body of Christ: 13 Till we all come in the unity of the faith, and of the knowledge of the Son of God, unto a perfect man, unto the measure of the stature of the fulness of Christ: 14 That we henceforth be no more children, tossed to and fro, and carried about with every wind of doctrine, by the sleight of men, and cunning craftiness, whereby they lie in wait to deceive; 15 But *speaking the truth in love*, may grow up into him in all things, which is the head, even Christ: 16 From whom the whole body fitly joined together and compacted by that which every joint supplieth, according to the effectual working in the measure of every part, maketh increase of the body unto the edifying of itself in love.

Galatians 5:19-26
19 Now the works of the flesh are manifest, which are these; Adultery, fornication, uncleanness, lasciviousness, 20 Idolatry, witchcraft, hatred, variance, emulations, wrath, strife, seditions, heresies, 21 Envyings, murders, drunkenness, revellings, and such like: of the which I tell you before, as I have also told you in time past, that *they which do such things shall not inherit the kingdom of God.*
22 But the fruit of the Spirit is love, joy, peace, longsuffering, gentleness, goodness, faith, 23 Meekness, temperance: against such there is no law. 24 And they that are Christ's have crucified

the flesh with the affections and lusts. 25 If we live in the Spirit, let us also walk in the Spirit.
26 Let us not be desirous of vain glory, provoking one another, envying one another.
Gal 6:1-2 Brethren, if a man be overtaken in a fault, ye which are spiritual, restore such an one in the spirit of meekness; considering thyself, lest thou also be tempted. 2 Bear ye one another's burdens, and so fulfil the law of Christ.

Grace and Mercy abounding in Faith and Hope as we all continue this journey – out of the mind of death/sin (the old law) and into the mind of Eternal Life and Righteousness (Jesus Christ – the New Law). ***A transformation of character due to the Appearing of the Mature & Complete & Perfect One In Your Soul***.

Let the FRUIT of that One Come Forth.

Amen.
RPJ

REVELATION 47
Occupy Till I Come

Luke 19:7-15 And Zacchaeus stood, and said unto the Lord; Behold, Lord, the half of my goods I give to the poor; and if I have taken any thing from any man by false accusation, I restore him fourfold. And Jesus said unto him, This day is salvation come to this house, forsomuch as he also is a son of Abraham. For the Son of man is come to seek and to save that which was lost. And as they heard these things, he added and spake a parable, because he was nigh to Jerusalem, and *because they thought that the kingdom of God should immediately appear*. He said therefore, A certain nobleman went into a far country to receive for himself a kingdom, and to return. And he called his ten servants, and delivered them ten pounds, and said unto them, Occupy till I come. But his citizens hated him, and sent a message after him, saying, We will not have this man to reign over us. And it came to pass, that when he was returned, having received the kingdom, then he commanded these servants to be called unto him, to whom he had given the money, that he might know how much every man had gained by trading.

They thought the kingdom of God was to appear immediately, but clearly in scriptures by the leading of the Holy Spirit, He has revealed to us that the Kingdom of God is Righteousness, Peace, and Joy IN the Holy Spirit (Romans 14:17). And the Kingdom of God was WITHIN YOU (Luke 17:21-22). And that we are PRESSING INTO THE KINGDOM too (Luke 16:16).

So the coming and receiving of HIS KINGDOM was a working that was taking place in the SOUL's of Mankind (male/female).

It was the removing of the Kingdom and statutes, ordinances of the old law of sin and death, which was the working of the flesh. It was the removing of the Kingdom in the natural sense, out of natural Jerusalem. And a bringing in, receiving, establishing of the Kingdom of God, in the New Order of God, in His TRUE Habitation which would be IN Souls, by His Holy Spirit in the working of the Son within each soul.

Ephesians 5:25-27 Husbands, love your wives, even as Christ also loved the church, and gave himself for it; That he might sanctify and cleanse it with the washing of water by the word, That he might present it to himself a glorious church, not having spot, or wrinkle, or any such thing; but that it should be holy and without blemish.

Who in this scripture is doing the "sanctifying and cleansing? Jesus Christ the Son. He receives us to Himself....

The Preparation of every Soul to the Receiving of the Son... the coming of the Son Jesus Christ ... within You. YET, in the very working of the Holy Spirit, it is revealed that it is the Father that is revealing the Son to us and drawing us to the Son! YET, in the very working

of the Father, we see the Son revealing the Father to us also! And in THIS... we find that there is ONE SPIRIT all along working within us to reveal to us and cause our Souls to KNOW HIM, the ETERNAL ONE... Eternal LIFE....

1 John 5:20 And we know that the Son of God is come, and hath given us an understanding, that we may know him that is true, and we are in him that is true, even in his Son Jesus Christ. This is the true God, and eternal life.

This Eternal Life is the One that has been working in us all along to BRING Us, REDEEM Us back in to the Garden, God's Kingdom & Habitation, His Soul & Body. (which we are!..... can you hear this... His Garden... His Habitation... His Kingdom's dwelling place! Wow.)

What took place THEN is all an example for us today. Those Prophecies and Psalms have been fulfilled, Jesus said. He came to be the fulfillment of them all. That white throne judgment is a fulfilling of them in THAT Generation. It was the removing of the natural kingdom in Jerusalem, to establish the TRUE kingdom of God, the new Jerusalem in the souls of man(kind).

So if you are feeling that there is a fire burning in you, or a "tribulation" working in you, or something of that sorts, know that you are in a good place, and to allow God, the consuming fire, to continue to the work of receiving you and you His Kingdom.

Heb 12:22-29 But ye are come unto mount Sion, and unto the city of the living God, the heavenly Jerusalem, and to an innumerable company of angels,
23 To the general assembly and church of the firstborn, which are written in heaven, and to God the Judge of all, and to the spirits of just men made perfect,

24 And to Jesus the mediator of the new covenant, and to the blood of sprinkling, that speaketh better things than that of Abel.

25 See that ye refuse not him that speaketh. For if they escaped not who refused him that spake on earth, much more shall not we escape, if we turn away from him that speaketh from heaven:

26 Whose voice then shook the earth: but now he hath promised, saying, Yet once more I shake not the earth only, but also heaven.

27 And this word, Yet once more, signifieth the removing of those things that are shaken, as of things that are made, that those things which cannot be shaken may remain.

28 Wherefore we receiving a kingdom which cannot be moved, let us have grace, whereby we may serve God acceptably with reverence and godly fear:

29 For our God is a consuming fire.

As the Lord is revealing Himself (TRUTH) to you, there will be a shaking of what you know, so to have all that is not of Him, purged and removed from your mind. Lies, Seductions, Deceptions, Traditions of men, religious theologies, etc... will be tried and burned in the Lord's Presence WITHIN YOU.

God will send His Word and you will hear, and may fight the truth at first, but Truth will win and the old will be no more.

Then you will find that where you once stood, you can't stand there anymore... it becomes quicksand. And those you once stood with, you find, your paths are now going in separate ways... you have to leave them and go the path of truth.

Yet, that will be a choice you will have to make.

Come out from among them....

2 Corinthians 6:16-18 And what agreement hath the temple of God with idols? for ye are the temple of the living God; as God hath said, I will dwell in them, and walk in them; and I will be their God, and they shall be my people.

17 <u>Wherefore come out from among them, and be ye separate, saith the Lord, and touch not the unclean thing; and I will receive you</u>, And will be a Father unto you, and ye shall be my sons and daughters, saith the Lord Almighty.

Now we worship God not in the natural mountain, but in our SPIRIT/SOUL/MIND and in TRUTH.

John 4:23-24 But the hour cometh, and now is, when the true worshippers shall worship the Father in spirit and in truth: for the Father seeketh such to worship him.
24 God is a Spirit: and they that worship him must worship him in spirit and in truth.

So, what is Poverty? Poverty is when you do not know who He is and not knowing His Will & Desire for your soul.

When you KNOW and have EXPERIENCED through an ENCOUNTER of the Son Jesus Christ, then you Understand that there is NO LACK when you are joined to and become one with the Father, through the Son Jesus Christ.

There first is a Preparing and cleaning and sanctifying of the Soul/Spirit... by the Prophetic Word of the Holy Spirit writing upon your heart and putting in your mind the covenant of the Lord Jesus Christ.

Then simultaneously working in you, as your soul/house is set up, the Saviour Appears.... a little at a time revealed, setting you free, and establishing Liberty to every area of you: spirit, soul, mind, & body.

You BECOME a new creature... You BECOME one with the Son... and begin walking like Him, and talking like Him, and behaving in all the fullness of His character....

And then... you realize.... THIS Is the FATHER too.... wow.!

The King and Kingdom is come in this place and is established.

Daily entering... Daily revealing.... Eternal Life appears. (1 John 5)

We are Rich and Wealthy in all ways. It IS done. It is Done.

The I AM THAT I AM has been here all along. Rest.

Amen.
RPJ

(Write your notes here)

REVELATION 48
Eyes on the Lord

Keep your eyes focused on the Lord... let Him direct your steps... especially in which meetings to go to. He wants to feed you what YOU are needing. Go because He is instructing you, and not according to the happenings or the persona that is there. Go by the leading of the Holy Spirit in you, so He can Feed you what You are needing, and so His Will can come forth through you and prosper more. It may not be a 'cushioned' seat but it will be the 'right' seat for His working in you.

Passover Feast has begun yet we don't celebrate the feasts of old anymore... Why? Because Jesus Christ has fulfilled all the ordinances and statues, which were a working of the flesh, that was under the law of sin and death.

YET... Because Jesus Christ Has Fulfilled all those feasts and requirements, it is clearly understood that HE HAS BECOME OUR FEASTS and WORTHY TO BE CELEBRATED!!

Jesus Christ is our Passover.
1 Corinthians 5:7-8 Purge out therefore the old leaven, that ye may be a new lump, as ye are unleavened. For even Christ our Passover is sacrificed for us: Therefore let us keep the feast, not with old leaven, neither with the leaven of malice and wickedness; but with the unleavened bread of sincerity and truth.

Purge out the old leaven, is talking of the ordinances of the old law, and traditions of man in religious ceremonies that were done for the saving of the soul. Allow the lies, and deceptions, and seductions of doctrine to be no more a part of your worship. Worship the Lord in Spirit and in Truth.
The Passover's key element is about The Blood that was shed. Without the shedding of blood there was no remission of sin. So, we celebrate the Passover that is about the human blood sacrifice

of the Perfect One: the Lamb of God Jesus Christ which commemorates the removing of the debt of sin which was death, the sin itself, and the effects of sin. Sure, I could have just said "sin," but let's get in to the real working of what is happening when we Receive the Lord Jesus Christ as our Saviour, Passover. Allow His Blood to be APPLIED in all areas of your life: spirit, soul, & body.

Jesus Christ, eating of His body, and drinking of His blood.... this is a sincere action of the heart. You become One with the sacrifice you eat of. That is why they were not to eat of sacrifices given to idols. In other words, don't participate with your mind or body, in the behaviors and rituals of the lies, seductions, and deceptions.... being a form of godliness but denying the true One and Power.

As a human sacrifice, the Lamb of God, He gave His Body and Soul to God so we can have LIBERTY. Now that is Power. What an action of will. He is our shield, cover, guard, purifier, etc...

and identity... so it is okay to let go of the old ways of thinking about yourself and others, and be renewed in the mind of Christ, being transformed and changed into the Perfect One: Jesus Christ the Lamb and Son of God. Married/Joined to the Eternal Living Sacrifice... Wow!! Walking with HIM in His daily actions.... oh I pray you hear this!

FREEDOM in His KINGDOM equals LIBERTY WALKING. In Sincerity and Truth of all that God Is and has Done for us all, we can..... CAN Walk in Freedom, Liberty from all Harm and Lack. His Power Provides.

From Death... we can Walk in Life
From Sickness... we can Walk in Health
From Mental... we can Walk in Peace and a Sound Mind

From Void... we can Walk in Fulfilment, Contentment, and Purpose and the list goes on, and on.....

Jesus Christ, in all that He did and all that He is..... Jesus Christ is God's Power... For Us to be Blessed by.
God's Will towards us.... So we can Walk in Liberty away from ALL Decay.

Receive... Receive God's Blessing, Jesus Christ. HEAR and RECEIVE as He Speaks and declares to your soul all that He has done to Save us. Let THAT WORD of God be engrafted in your Soul, and allow the Birthing of the Saviour Jesus Christ to wash and cleanse you: in spirit, mind, soul and body.

Keep Your Eyes on the Lord, and let that be why you do what you do... and go where you go.

Amen.
RPJ

REVELATION 49
FASTING

Isaiah 58:5-13
5 Is it such a fast that I have chosen? a day for a man to afflict his soul? is it to bow down his head as a bulrush, and to spread sackcloth and ashes under him? wilt thou call this a fast , and an acceptable day to the LORD?

6 Is not this **the fast that I have chosen**? to loose the bands of wickedness, to undo the heavy burdens, and to let the oppressed go free, and that ye break every yoke?

7 Is it not to deal thy bread to the hungry, and that thou bring the poor that are cast out to thy house? when thou seest the naked, that thou cover him; and that thou hide not thyself from thine own flesh?

8 Then shall thy light break forth as the morning, and thine health shall spring forth speedily: and thy righteousness shall go before thee; the glory of the LORD shall be thy rearward.

9 Then shalt thou call, and the LORD shall answer; thou shalt cry, and he shall say, Here I am. If thou take away from the midst of thee the yoke, the putting forth of the finger, and speaking vanity;

10 And if thou draw out thy soul to the hungry, and satisfy the afflicted soul; then shall thy light rise in obscurity, and thy darkness be as the noonday:

11 And the LORD shall guide thee continually, and satisfy thy soul in drought, and make fat thy bones: and thou shalt be like a watered garden, and like a spring of water, whose waters fail not.
12 And they that shall be of thee shall build the old waste places: thou shalt raise up the foundations of many generations; and

thou shalt be called, The repairer of the breach, The restorer of paths to dwell in.

13 If thou turn away thy foot from the sabbath, from doing thy pleasure on my holy day; and call the sabbath a delight, the holy of the LORD, honourable; and shalt honour him, not doing thine own ways, nor finding thine own pleasure, nor speaking thine own words:

14 Then shalt thou delight thyself in the LORD; and I will cause thee to ride upon the high places of the earth, and feed thee with the heritage of Jacob thy father: for the mouth of the LORD hath spoken it.

Even though this is from the old testament, we still see God's Desire for us towards others. In this is love. God's purpose through His Son Jesus Christ, and by His Son now, in and through us, His Visible Body that is moved by His Holy Spirit.

The Body without the Spirit is dead, so is Faith without works dead. Fast Daily in God's true fast.

Amen.
RPJ

REVELATION 50
Baker & Butler (Bread & Wine)

Genesis 40 tells us of this story and how Joseph interpreted their dreams that the Lord had given them. Yet this message is not about that story, but it is to share with you a revealing of what the Baker and Butler are in God's Kingdom.

Baker is symbolic of one that represents the Bread, which is symbolic of the BODY OF CHRIST, the nourishment to the body, the sacrifice of the body of Jesus Christ which was given for the life of the world.

Butler is symbolic of one that represents the Cup, which is symbolic of the Wine, BLOOD of Jesus Christ, and the Spirit of Life.

John 6:51 I am the living bread which came down from heaven: if any man eat of this bread, he shall live forever: and the bread that I will give is my flesh, which I will give for the life of the world.

John 6:53-58 Then Jesus said unto them, Verily, verily, I say unto you, Except ye eat the flesh of the Son of man, and drink his blood, ye have no life in you. Whoso eateth my flesh, and drinketh my blood, hath eternal life; and I will raise him up at the last day. For my flesh is meat indeed, and my blood is drink indeed. He that eateth my flesh, and drinketh my blood, dwelleth in me, and I in him. As the living Father hath sent me, and I live by the Father: so he that eateth me, even he shall live by me. This is that bread which came down from heaven: not as your fathers did eat manna, and are dead: he that eateth of this bread shall live for ever.

Luke 22:19-20 And he took bread, and gave thanks, and brake it, and gave unto them, saying, This is my body which is given for you: this do in remembrance of me. Likewise also the cup after supper, saying, This cup is the new testament in my blood, which is shed for you.

Even in the revealing of the Baker and the Butler, we see that Jesus Christ has restored even this relationship to the King. Just as He did concerning the fall of Adam and that nature, we see in this event, that Jesus Christ has become the Officer (the one who officiates the service to the King), and has become the substance (Bread and Wine, Basket and Cup, Body and Blood) the Eternal Sacrifice unto God for us Forever ... alive forevermore. THE Priest and Eternal Sacrifice that was alive, died, and lives forevermore. THE Resurrection & Eternal Life – Our Lord!

Amen.
RPJ

REVELATION 51
Resurrection & Life

John 11:22-27
22 But I know, that even now, whatsoever thou wilt ask of God, God will give it thee.

23 Jesus saith unto her, Thy brother shall rise again.

24 Martha saith unto him, I know that he shall rise again in the resurrection at the last day.

25 Jesus said unto her, I am the resurrection , and the life : he that believeth in me, though he were dead, yet shall he live:

26 And whosoever liveth and believeth in me shall never die. Believest thou this?

27 She saith unto him, Yea, Lord: I believe that thou art the Christ, the Son of God, which should come into the world.

RESURRECTION & LIFE

Martha was looking for the resurrection to come and He was right in front of her.

So it is with many today......

Amen
RPJ

REVELATION 52
The Ultimate Offering 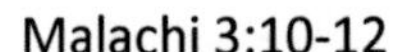

Malachi 3:10-12
It is more than money... in understanding we see that Jesus Christ has given Himself For Us, and In That Giving, That Offering unto the Lord, we too are blessed and able to say "In the Sacrifice and Offering of Jesus Christ... in This We Give to You Father Ourselves" Amen.... for All Your Desire. Amen.

In Abraham, it is said, that even his unborn offspring ... it was accounted unto them as giving to the Lord, even though they were not born yet.

So it is in Christ Jesus, it is accounted unto Righteousness towards us in His Giving of Himself.... and we reap of the ultimate sacrifice and offering unto our Lord, and Father.

This is intense, and deep, and I pray that the revelation of His word here will hit you like a ton of bricks, destroying all that is not God and Righteousness, and set you free,... running and rejoicing in the Lord Jesus Christ daily.! Amen.

Happy Resurrection Day!

Amen.
RPJ

REVELATION 53
House of Prayer

God's House is a House of Prayer. Yes, we know this, but today we are reminded that this is God's will concerning us.

In Isaiah 56:7 tells us this: *(read all 4-12 to hear God's heart)*
7 Even them will I bring to my holy mountain, and make them joyful in my house of prayer: their burnt offerings and their sacrifices shall be accepted upon mine altar; for mine house shall be called an house of prayer for all people.
In Matthew 21:13-14 And said unto them, It is written, My house shall be called the house of prayer; but ye have made it a den of thieves. And the blind and the lame came to him in the temple; and he healed them.
Also in Mark 11:17 and Luke 19:46 we see the same passage above.

God's House of Prayer. Prayer means a communion with God. It isn't a ritual or daily habit. It is about daily communing with God as we walk through our daily activities and talking to Him, and He to us, about His directives for this world. .... whether "world" means your own household or city or state or country or universe....

Prayer is Communing with God our Father daily, whether in talking to Him or listening to Him. Prayer is also just being available. How? By being open to Him at any moment to use us in a situation... Being in a heart of worship towards Him. True worship is an attitude of heart, not lots of songs and dance and noise, nor is it in Jerusalem... As Jesus said, "true worshippers shall worship the Father in spirit and in truth..."

John 4:23-24 But the hour cometh, and now is, when the true worshippers shall worship the Father in spirit and in truth: for the

Father seeketh such to worship him. God is a Spirit: and they that worship him must worship him in spirit and in truth.

John 14:17-20 Even the Spirit of truth; whom the world cannot receive, because it seeth him not, neither knoweth him: but ye know him; for he dwelleth with you, and shall be in you. I will not leave you comfortless: I will come to you. Yet a little while, and the world seeth me no more; but ye see me: because I live, ye shall live also. At that day ye shall know that I am in my Father, and ye in me, and I in you.

That is a wonderful scripture, even more so as we receive the Holy Spirit revealing it.... Then it is Life.

Being assembled as God's house of prayer is not to be grievous, even though He may have us at times be in heavy travail within our spirit. But it is His holy Spirit that is travailing/praying in us according to the Mind of God for each situation.

Romans 8:26-27 Likewise the Spirit also helpeth our infirmities: for we know not what we should pray for as we ought: but the Spirit itself maketh intercession for us with groanings which cannot be uttered. And he that searcheth the hearts knoweth what is the mind of the Spirit , because he maketh intercession for the saints according to the will of God.

So we need to learn to yield to the holy Spirit of truth and life that has made His home within us as He prays according to the need at hand. God's House of Prayer.

Amen.
RPJ

REVELATION 54
All God, All Man

Heaven and Earth brought together in One. Why? To redeem the "lack" of the lower realm: Earth. To "fix" the decaying realm: Earth. To Remove those things that were causing the destruction and decay of the lower realm: Earth.... Mankind..... Male and Female = Adam.

So God by His own arm, breathed forth His Will, and spoke His Word into existence..... Yeshua, Immanuel, Jesus Christ was made manifest in... IN the Earth... to Redeem it.... Man and all the creature in to a state of LIFE = restored existence in... IN God.

Is it Done in.... IN you, yet? Has all that Jesus Christ did for us ALL, been made understood in your own soul?

Until you can understand what He did and why, how then are you going to be able to WALK in Him... WALK in that Blessing? That is what is called being BLIND....

BUT, Once your EYES are OPENED (Luke 24) and you REALIZE that the One talking with you and walking with you (in you) IS Immanuel, the Risen One that was alive, was dead, but is RISEN from the dead and is ALIVE FOR EVER MORE.... THEN you are Changed and Transformed Out of DECAY AND DEATH, and IN TO ETERNAL LIFE.... That DIVINE NATURE (2 Peter 1) escaping the corruption that was in the world.

Romans 8 tells us that As Soon AS the sons of God mature and come forth ... *(BE REDEEMED, TRANSFORMED, CHANGED in to the SON= Put on Eternal Life – the DIVINE NATURE THAT HAS NO SIN or DEATH)*...THEN the Creature will ALSO BE LIBERATED from decay and death.
So, ALLOW the LORD, that Holy Spirit (2 Corinthians 3:17), to WASH you with the washing of the Water by the WORD (that is

spirit and life John 6:63), and bring you (present you) to Himself a glorious church (many membered Son of God = Jesus Christ appearing in the EARTH again yet it is through His many membered BODY – You) (Ephesians 5:26-27).

Let the Lord, that Holy Spirit, to write upon your heart and put in your mind the Blood Covenant, making manifest Jesus Christ In You, revealing Jesus Christ in you, appearing of Jesus Christ in you. And That Appearance (coming) of THE PERFECT ONE (1 Corinthians 13:12) Will Affect and Change and Release You From All Decay and Death. THE Perfect One appearing and making Himself known to you.... KNOWN TO YOU.... WILL affect you and cause your Soul to Manifest, Birth His Nature... DIVINE NATURE thru your Earthly Flesh.

Heaven and Earth now brought together In You.... By the Grace and Eternal Life making Himself Known to and In your soul.

For this cause, He is come into our world... your world... your soul..... Receive the Breath of the Father ... breathing His Son Eternal Life in you, today.

Heaven and Earth IS brought together, redeemed in and by the Son... so that Your Spirit (heaven) AND Body (earth) can REAP of the BLESSINGS of the SON .... TODAY. Let Faith Work and Receive Him.

Amen.
RPJ

REVELATION 55
When God Is Quiet

Out of my experience with our Father, when He gets quiet, that means He is working on something for us. I'm sure some of you could probably add to this, but for today's message, please read on...

If God is quiet it usually means He is working on something for you, and for you to Stand Fast in Faith, having the whole armor on, and continue in the heart/mind of worship and mouth of praise.

Ephesians 6:10-19
10 Finally, my brethren, be strong in the Lord, and in the power of his might.
11 Put on the whole armour of God, that ye may be able to stand against the wiles of the devil.
12 For we wrestle not against flesh and blood, but against principalities, against powers, against the rulers of the darkness of this world, against spiritual wickedness in high places.
13 Wherefore take unto you the whole armour of God, that ye may be able to withstand in the evil day, and <u>having done all, to stand</u>.
14 <u>Stand therefore</u>, having your loins girt about with **truth**, and having on the breastplate of **righteousness;**
15 And your feet shod with the **preparation of the gospel of peace**;
16 Above all, taking the shield of **faith**, wherewith ye shall be able to quench all the fiery darts of the wicked.
17 And take the helmet of **salvation**, and the sword of the Spirit, which is the **word of God**:
18 **Praying always** with all prayer and supplication **in the Spirit**, and watching thereunto with all perseverance and supplication for all saints;

19 And for me, that utterance may be given unto me, that I may open my mouth boldly, to make known the mystery of the gospel,
20 For which I am an ambassador in bonds: that therein I may speak boldly, as I ought to speak.

Philippians 1:27
27 Only let your conversation be as it becometh the gospel of Christ: that whether I come and see you, or else be absent, I may hear of your affairs, that ye stand fast in one spirit, with one mind striving together for the faith of the gospel;...

Galatians 5:1
1 Stand fast therefore in the liberty wherewith Christ hath made us free, and be not entangled again with the yoke of bondage.

So whatever "trial of your faith" you may be going through, know that the Lord Knows it and has established your steps. So Stand Fast in the liberty He provided, Stand Fast with each other in the faith of the gospel, put on and be secured in the full armor of the gospel of Jesus Christ, and help others do the same.

The Lord is taking you to the next step, level of maturity, so let your heart worship Him and your mouth praise Him along the way. His Love Never Fails.....

Amen.
RPJ

REVELATION 56
HEAR HIS VOICE
The SOUND of His VOICE

Mary was talking to the Gardner, but didn't know it was the Risen Lord until she HEARD HIS VOICE.

Our natural nature is affected... our inward man is changed... when we HEAR OUR LORD'S VOICE.

Listen for His Sound, His Voice. If you look after the outward person you may miss the appearing of the Lord to you. But if you look with the listening of your Heart/Spirit/Soul, then there is no way to miss Him.

He may speak to you via the form of a man, or woman, or an angel, or other minister, and as He has done before – thru a donkey. Whatever means He chooses to use to get to you, and to set you free, and to wash you and bring you in to Him, today.... REDEMPTION is REDEEMING.... Right Here, Right Now, Today if you will HEAR HIS VOICE, harden not your heart... don't be stubborn, like they were before and then had to wait 40 years before entering into the inheritance of God that He had for them.... yet "they" that began ended up not entering in because of unbelief and stubbornness.

Hebrews 3:7-15 (read all 3 and 4)
7 Wherefore (as the Holy Ghost saith, To day if ye will hear his voice, **Harden not your hearts**, as in the provocation, in the day of temptation in the wilderness: When your fathers tempted me, proved me, and saw my works forty years. Wherefore I was grieved with that generation, and said, They do alway err in their heart; and they have not known my ways. So I sware in my wrath, They shall not enter into my rest.) Take heed, brethren, lest there be in any of you an evil heart of unbelief, in departing from the living God. But exhort one another daily, while it is called To

day; lest any of you be hardened through the deceitfulness of sin. **For we are made partakers of Christ**, if we hold the beginning of our confidence stedfast unto the end; While it is said, **To day if ye will hear his voice, harden not your hearts,** as in the provocation,...

Today... not to wait till you die and are buried, but Today... If you will HEAR HIS VOICE.... ENTER into His Rest prepared for you.

That Rest is IN Jesus Christ. By Faith Of Him and In Him. ENTER in to your rest from Religious rituals, and habits of self righteousness which is only a form of godliness, denying His power.

Enter into the Kingdom of God which is also the same as the Kingdom of Heaven, by being born again as Jesus instructs in John 3:3-5, Ephesians 5:26-27, 1 Peter 1:23 and many other places.
HEAR HIS VOICE
John 3:3-8
3 Jesus answered and said unto him, Verily, verily, I say unto thee, **Except a man be born again , he cannot see** the kingdom of God. Nicodemus saith unto him, How can a man be born when he is old? can he enter the second time into his mother's womb, and be born?

Jesus answered, Verily, verily, I say unto thee, **Except a man be born of water and of the Spirit, he cannot enter** into the kingdom of God. That which is born of the flesh is flesh; and that which is born of the Spirit is spirit. Marvel not that **I said unto thee, Ye must be born again**.
The wind bloweth where it listeth, and thou **hearest the sound thereof**, but canst not tell whence it cometh, and whither it goeth: so is every one that is born of the Spirit.

Listen, Listen, Listen for His Sound..... and say Here Am I Lord, come and teach me of all Truth. Reveal yourself to me, and cause me to be changed into the image of the Son. (John 14:21-23; Philippians 3:21; 2 Corinthians 3:16-18)

Amen.
RPJ

(Write your notes here)

REVELATION 57
HEAR HIS VOICE: Water AND Spirit

Enter into the Kingdom of God which is also the same as the Kingdom of Heaven, by being born again as Jesus instructs in John 3:3-5, Ephesians 5:26-27 and many other places.

John 3:3-8
3 Jesus answered and said unto him, Verily, verily, I say unto thee, **Except a man be born again, he cannot see** the kingdom of God. Nicodemus saith unto him, How can a man be born when he is old? can he enter the second time into his mother's womb, and be born?

Jesus answered, Verily, verily, I say unto thee, **Except a man be born of water and of the Spirit, he cannot enter** into the kingdom of God. That which is born of the flesh is flesh; and that which is born of the Spirit is spirit. Marvel not that **I said unto thee, Ye must be born again**.
The wind bloweth where it listeth, and **<u>thou hearest the sound thereof</u>**, but canst not tell whence it cometh, and whither it goeth: so is every one that is born of the Spirit.

He instructs us to be born of the Water AND Spirit…. now go with me here and see something…

John came baptizing in the water unto repentance, but Jesus came in the fulness of God, the Spirit, the Lord from Heaven to replace all authority, for our benefit. (yes and amen!)

Now watch this though….
John came in the Spirit of Elijah, as the one to wash, prepare the people to receive the Lamb of God, and to make known to Israel The Lamb of God, and to fulfill the works of the flesh under the law of sin and death, thus fulfilling ALL Righteousness concerning the working of the flesh.

JESUS, then takes over, having fulfilled all righteousness, and now sealed by GOD, Holy Spirit, and begins where John ended.

Thus the fulfillment of one prophecy that John said "I (John) must decrease and He (Jesus) must increase."

John came in the Spirit of Elijah as prophetically was said, and it was fulfilled. But then Jesus took over. Jesus began birthing in the New Order and Covenant of God that was a working of Faith, by Grace, through His own Righteousness... for us all to be benefited by, and become co-heirs with Him. God wanted a place to Inhabit... so the Son became that place.

Now having ascended, He is subduing each member completely unto the Father, and for the Father's dwelling.... !!!

So, Jesus took over in all areas that we needed. HE is our Lord, King, Priest, and the Prophet, the Spirit of Elijah that Speaks and Reveals the Son to us... This Word is the WATER that WASHES US, PREPARES US, causes us to RECEIVE the benefits of the LAMB of God that takes away our sin. This is the only WAY TO BE BORN AGAIN.

By allowing Jesus Christ, the Holy Spirit which is the Father & Son, to wash and cleanse us through that testimony of Jesus Christ, which is the spirit of prophecy. (Revelation 19:10)

**That Testimony of Jesus is the spirit of prophecy. That sure word of the Father, as HE WRITES IT UPON YOUR HEARTS and PUTS IT IN YOUR MIND.... the SURETY, ASSURANCE given to us by the FATHER, and done as He reveals to Us His Son.... He gives Us Eternal Life.... Marks Us and SEALS Us by His Word and Spirit.

In the Prophets of old, it was God's Word (Spirit) that was spoken through them. He did not inhabit them, as the Father has purposed to do in us... those that have received His Son.

So, Today, God our Father, through His Son, washes us and sanctifies us by His own testimony of the Son, that HE IS SPEAKING TO US.... HE IS WRITING HIS COVENANT IN OUR HEART AND MIND... our Seal of Liberty and Life. Preparing us as HIS HABITATION. (2 Corinthians 6:16; Hebrews 8:10-13)

Jesus Christ, the Lamb of God, that Holy Spirit is now BAPTIZING (washing & cleansing) US IN THE WATER, HIS SPOKEN WORD THAT IS SPIRIT AND LIFE. (John 15:3, John 6:63,...)

That Comforter, Spirit of Truth, Holy Spirit of the Father & Son that raised Jesus from the grave and the dead, is the One that Prepares us by the washing of the WATER BY THE WORD, and RAISES US up also. (Ephesians 5:26-27, James 1:18, 1 Peter 1:23....)

Then HE is the One that RECEIVES US unto HIMSELF as a glorious church (member). AND simultaneously is Redeeming Us in to the FATHER... Now ALL AS ONE VESSEL, many members, one church, one body joined by His Spirit ... Holy Spirit in us.

Then Us too, ENTER Into the Kingdom which is IN the Holy Spirit... He Swallows Us Up...

Oh, the Wisdom of the working of God!!! Only those that have ears to Hear Him, have any hope of Understanding such Wisdom. And Only by His Grace may any of See His Kingdom. To You Father All Honor and Praise!.

Now the world can Experience HIM.... yet through - humble minded us. He has made us His Body.

All Flesh, Soul, Spirit, and Mind are caught up until the Father and there will WE ALL BE TOGETHER, In the Son, In the Father... victorious... ruling and reigning... as the Kingdom of God is come.

“ ‘My Life In You’ by Jesus Christ”

To God Be All Glory… in All His Will…. Done.

Amen.
RPJ

(Write your notes here)

REVELATION 58
A Perfect Heart (To Body of Christ)

When You know that your sin(s) are forgiven,
And you Forgive the sin(s) of others,
Then.... I Will.

We don't have to "do" something to receive the blessings of the Lord and healing and forgiveness...etc...
He did it... Provision is Done... Faith Receives... and We are One with Jesus Christ in the Inheritance of Life, Co-Heirs with Him. So there is No lack in provision, whether the need is in the natural, physical or spiritual.

So, why then is it that sometimes the healing, or provision doesn't come?

Answer: There is a block in your own soul and mind, preventing His Blessing & Benefit from coming.

Ask the Lord to reveal to you what it is in your own soul that is hindering or getting in the way of HIS LIFE FLOWING THROUGH YOU.

HE has done everything necessary for All Provision. HE desires You to Share and Have All of Him and Kingdom. So the problem or issue is usually in us; as the Reason for "not having" or "lacking."

So how do we get rid of the hindrance? First ask of the Lord what it is. Second, BE WILLING to be OBEDIENT to Him. Third Keep a Humble Mind & THANK the Lord always.

Most of the time it is as simple as FORGIVING others and a Willing Mind of God's LOVE towards others. That means you desire God's best for them. Not for "evil mind" to prosper, but that God's righteous mind/spirit will work in them. Not holding a grudge or wishing them harm or pay back. Let it go... giving it to the Lord to rectify in Righteousness. Matter fact, let that be your prayer for them... *"Father I wish Your Life and Righteousness to rule in their minds so they may know you, but protect me and keep all evil and harm away from me."* See Jesus' example of prayer below...

Luke 11:2-4 Jesus' example of prayer:
And he said unto them, When ye pray, say, Our Father which art in heaven, Hallowed be thy name. Thy kingdom come. Thy will be done, as in heaven, so in earth. Give us day by day our daily bread.
**4 And <u>forgive us our sins; for we also forgive every one</u> that is indebted to us. And lead us not into temptation; but deliver us from evil.

Remember, Jesus on the cross... He prayed "Father forgive them for they know not what they do." But even after praying that, judgment still came on that generation for their unrepented wickedness. Hear what the Lord is saying.

Give to Him to "fix," by asking the Lord to forgive them... that is the mind of Love working in you towards them. And that makes way for God's forgiveness (healing, provision, etc) to flow in your life. Our Father will deal with all that are out to hurt us, but we need to get out of the way, so He can work. Then they will come forth, in God's Glorious working to produce His Righteousness in that situation. ! . It's so wonderful to see God's working in our own lives and others!

Take a look here in Matthew 5:44-48
But I say unto you, Love your enemies , bless them that curse you, do good to them that hate you, and pray for them which despitefully use you, and persecute you; That ye may be the children of your Father which is in heaven: *for he maketh his sun to rise on the evil and on the good, and sendeth rain on the just*

and on the unjust. For if ye love them which love you, what reward have ye? do not even the publicans the same? And if ye salute your brethren only, what do ye more than others? do not even the publicans so? Be ye therefore perfect, even as your Father which is in heaven is perfect.

And Matthew6:14-15 For if ye forgive men their trespasses, your heavenly Father will also forgive you: But if ye forgive **not** men their trespasses, **neither** will your Father **forgive your** trespasses.

So, as it says above... **Be ye therefore perfect, even as your Father which is in heaven is perfect**

Remove and let go of your hindrances of unforgiveness or hatred or self righteousness. That just keeps God's love and healing and restoration from PROSPERING in your own soul (3 John verse2). Let Your hurt be healed. Walk in His Provision, and Abundant Life Today: Jesus Christ Is With You and Now In You, if it is so that you have received the Spirit of Son, which is the Father. (Secret: Father was the one in Jesus doing all the work through Jesus, and raising Him from the dead).

Allow the Father to work that **Perfect Heart in You**...
Be Blessed ... exceeding abundantly.

Amen.
RPJ

REVELATION 59
Born of God – Can Not Sin

It is time to understand this scripture:

1 John 1:4-10 And these things write we unto you, that your joy may be full. This then is the message which we have heard of him, and declare unto you, that God is light, and in him is no darkness at all. If we say that we have fellowship with him, and walk in darkness, we lie, and do not the truth:

But if we walk in the light, as he is in the light, we have fellowship one with another, and the blood of Jesus Christ his Son cleanseth us from all sin. If we say that we have no sin, we deceive ourselves, and the truth is not in us. If we confess our sins, he is faithful and just to forgive us our sins, and to cleanse us from all unrighteousness. If we say that we have not sinned, we make him a liar, and his word is not in us.

This scripture is Not telling us that we are stuck in sin, but rather is saying, that we all were in sin at one time, but when you receive Jesus Christ as your Saviour, He sets up house IN YOU.

2 Corinthians 3:16-18 v17 THE LORD is THAT SPIRIT: and where the Spirit of the Lord is, there is liberty. Now IN You, right?

THEN YOU REAP OF HIM, and ARE WITHOUT SIN ALSO…. How? It is all about The New Law….Continue reading….

Have fellowship with TRUTH, not Wickedness or evil or lies. Have fellowship with God's LOVE, not man's manipulation, deceptions, greed, envies, jealousies. Even God gets jealous and uses jealousy for His purpose, but in this we see that THERE IS A DIFFERENCE between GOD'S MIND vs Man's Carnal Thinking.
And the ONLY way to be free and changed, transformed, renewed is BY THE HOLY SPIRIT AND TRUTH in the BLOOD Covenant of

JESUS CHRIST…. If you are WASHED and CLEANSED by THIS WORD, then YOU ARE CLEAN AND FREED INDEED!

And if you are FREE by the SON OF GOD, then you will understand that YOU CAN NOT SIN ANYMORE.

WHY? Jesus Christ is the Lord, that Holy Spirit, which we have received of the Father. HE then begins to plant or impregnate our Soul with the SEED (word that is Spirit and Life) which is the gospel of Jesus Christ and His Kingdom – Salvation of God – Good Will of God to all. **Christ IN US, is now having relationship with our Soul to produce**….. **give birth** to HIS MIND, CHARACTER, THINKING, DIVINE NATURE ….IN our Soul… Then to be manifested through us, because we will have BEEN CHANGED INTO THE SAME IMAGE.

This is REDEMPTION of GOD complete. His Process of creating His family, children. Being Born of God, by His word of Truth.

Now, going back to the beginning of today's message…..
Our Saviour Jesus Christ, God gives us HIS Spirit… the Spirit of the Son (Galatians 4).

Jesus Christ is God's Power and Wisdom and Righteousness dwelling within our Soul before God. Jesus Christ OBTAINED SANCTIFICATION, JUSTIFICATION, VICTORY from sin for us. We were not able to obtain PEACE with God by our own fleshly efforts, right? Right. So we needed a Saviour that could fulfill all fleshly efforts under the Law of Sin and Death, so to complete that for us. He did that. He became our Priest, King, and Lamb to fulfill all requirements of the old law of sin and death, the works of flesh toward God.

Then God through the man Jesus Christ ESTABLISHED a BETTER Covenant and Better Promises, and a Better and New Law, by which we are now Freed from the old law, if so we have received the Risen Lord. The Risen Lord has Established the new Law of the Spirit of Life in Christ Jesus (Romans 8:1-2) This law of the Spirit of Life in Christ Jesus has made us free from the law of sin and death, because what the law of sin and death could not do according to the flesh, Jesus Christ has accomplished ... and accomplished it for us.

Now we that have received Jesus Christ, are married to Him... Joined unto Him by that Blood Covenant. Not of our effort, right? Right. All because of what HE HAS DONE, we now are freed.

Jesus overcame death and sin. Sin no longer dwells in Christ Jesus the flesh man that walked on the earth after the resurrection. He had to do that.... in and as the second Man, Last Adam... so that WE in the natural can Also BE FREE FROM SIN AND DEATH, in our mind, spirit, soul, AND BODY.

Catch a hold.... Grasp this TRUTH!! Because we REAP where we did not sow.... We REAP of the benefits of Jesus Christ the Resurrection. HE OVERCAME SIN AND REMOVED IT.... REMOVED IT OUT OF THE WAY.

So, if there is no more sin working or abiding in the flesh man Jesus Christ, then THOSE THAT PARTAKE OF HIS BODY AND DRINK OF HIS BLOOD are ALSO WITHOUT SIN.

A NEW LAW IS WORKING WITHIN THE LAND! GRACE ABOUNDS... WHERE SIN ONCE WAS (Romans 5:20-21) Where DEATH WAS... ETERNAL LIFE IS EVIDENT, through the presence of RIGHTEOUSNESS.

Is HE COME IN YOU? If RIGHTEOUSNESS IS COME IN YOUR SPIRIT, THEN SIN CAN NO LONGER WORK IN YOU.... NOR DEATH.

Let your Faith Receive Him today, and UNDERSTAND what our Lord and Saviour have truly done for us.

REAP where you have not Sowed. Eat of Him daily and ENTER in to the Kingdom of God, Eternal Life.

James 1:8 A double minded man is unstable in all his ways.
NOTE: This is talking of asking and receiving. So do not walk in the mindset of the old law of Sin, and the new law of Grace.

Romans 7:23-25 But I see another law in my members, warring against the law of my mind, and bringing me into captivity to the law of sin which is in my members.
24 O wretched man that I am! who shall deliver me from the body of this death?
25 I thank God through Jesus Christ our Lord. So then with the mind I myself serve the law of God; but with the flesh the law of sin.

NOTE: As you are being washed in His Truth/Word/Spirit, it is as a two-edged sword is used to cut away that body of sin that is that carnal mind. (Hebrews 4:12)

Eat of Him Daily. Be renewed. Allow Him to birth HIS MIND in you. It IS a working. (....work out your own salvation through fear and trembling...Philippians 2:12)

Romans 6:6-14 v6 Knowing this, that our old man is crucified with him, that the body of sin might be destroyed, that henceforth we should not serve sin. For he that is dead is freed from sin.
14 For sin shall not have dominion over you: for ye are not under the law, but under grace.

Romans 8:1-4 There is therefore now no condemnation to them which are in Christ Jesus, who walk not after the flesh, but after the Spirit. For the law of the Spirit of life in Christ Jesus hath made me free from the law of sin and death.

3 For what the law could not do, in that it was weak through the flesh, God sending his own Son in the likeness of sinful flesh, and for sin, condemned sin in the flesh:
4 That the righteousness of the law might be fulfilled in us, who walk not after the flesh, but after the Spirit.

Lamb of God that taketh away the sin of the world... It is done for all, and to all that receive Him HE BENEFITS THEM UNTO LIFE AND LIBERTY.

So, to those that are in Christ Jesus, you no longer can sin, but you can mess up and still be corrected of God. If it is not of FAITH, then it is of Sin. Aren't you walking in Faith of His Presence in you? Isn't it Grace we run to in all situations, looking for that mercy? BUT be willing to ALLOW the Holy Spirit to WASH YOU, and RENEW YOU. GRACE Abounds, and so does His CORRECTION. But Sin no longer can separate us from God or "sting" us. HIS FAITH overcame, and HIS Love Never Fails.

1 John 3:8-9 He that committeth sin is of the devil; for the devil sinneth from the beginning. For this purpose the Son of God was manifested, that he might destroy the works of the devil.
9 **Whosoever is born of God doth not commit sin; for his seed remaineth in him: and he cannot sin, because he is born of God**.

1 John 5:18
18 We know that whosoever is born of God sinneth not; but he that is begotten of God keepeth himself, and that wicked one toucheth him not.

It is all for the working of REDEMPTION and RECONCILIATION...

Receiving Us unto our Father and God. The King and Kingdom has already been birthed forth by Jesus Christ a long time ago.... It is Come..... Hebrews 12:22-29... From age to age Redemption is working.

Now every man presses INTO the kingdom... Luke 16:16 The law and the prophets were until John: since that time the kingdom of God is preached, and every man presseth into it. But all have to go through The Door – Jesus Christ. The Way and Truth and Life.

Sure you can stand outside Him if you want. But you need to know that you are judged according to your works, and by His Word. So you are judged of sin still, which results in death eternal, because you have not received your liberation from sin, which is being preached to you...

Hey, it is God's FREE Gift of Liberty and a more abundant LIFE. Jesus Christ.

Can you hear His Love yet?

He paid the price of sin and made it EASY for you to come to the Father... just as you are.

Don't let the carnal mind CHEAT you out of the BEST GIFT Ever. Just start talking to the Father and ASK HIM to REVEAL His Son to you more.

Are You Hearing His Liberty Ringing In your spirit and soul!? Awaken and Rejoice for our Liberty is Come... and is Received here.

Allow the Righteousness of God to appear... be awakened unto Righteousness.... Continue to walk in HOPE by Grace through Faith of this very thing. And, if it has not awakened or been made evident to you yet, then continue to Listen for His Voice in Revealing the Righteous One that is the Righteousness of God for us.

IN HIM YOU CAN NOT SIN… HE IS STANDING WITHIN YOUR SOUL, UPHOLDING YOU IN JUSTIFICATION BEFORE ALL THAT WISH TO CONDEMN. GRACE IS SUSTAINING.

In This New Law of the Spirit of Life in Christ Jesus DIFFERENT RULES apply. The Same God, the same Lord, but the rules and administration has changed! It is of a better promises, and produces a greater Glory. Oh so Exciting. Come on In!

Amen.
RPJ

REVELATION 60
To All The Souls that God Produces His Son Through

Be at peace and know God's plan... the trying of your Faith works much, but the end result is You in His Greater Glory.

GRACE is the Path and Provides the Time to Walk Properly....

GRACE does not mean we can stay in the misbehaving thinking.

GOD's Correction does Work in Grace

Yet His Correction is to bring you in to Obedience and
More of His Life and Glory Flowing.

Not to destroy your Soul, but to Give It LIFE ETERNAL .... THE PATH.

Jesus Christ IS the Way, the Truth, and the LIFE
Way = Path and Provision
Truth = God's Power to Sustain and Provide and Set Free
Life = Eternal Life our New Nature (Jesus Christ became the first of that New Divine Nature to walk on the earth after the resurrection, thus we too become without sin/death, and Walk in and as This New Divine Life and Nature Today, because we have been Brought Into and Redeemed/Reconciled IN Him and birthed forth ...born again!)

Let RIGHTEOUSNESS Bring you to this New Divine Existence in This Earth.

"Flesh" cannot inherit Eternal Life, but your natural nature CAN BE CHANGED as it is affected by the Risen Lord, and Exist without Sin and death... It is said that our spirit and BODY belong to God, not just the soul. That is why we CAN be Healed in all areas... the natural nature, our Body too.

When the Spirit of God takes possession of you, the old carnal spirit/mind is defeated and goes through a 'cutting away of the flesh' process. You could say experience, because that old flesh mind puts up a fight, yet, Jesus Christ has already declared its defeat and departure from your Soul. And this is done through the the Word of God being breathed within you and cutting it away.

Also during this process, we are communing with God, and in that communion with The Lord, His Purpose for acquiring you is made known even more. He wants to Birth His Son through You. Not a natural birth, but a Spiritual/Soul birthing that literally AFFECTS and CHANGES you: spirit, soul and body. Yet, He processes this a little at a time, so we are not overwhelmed in His appearing... Ephesians 3:19-20... that ye might be filled with all the fulness of God. Now unto Him that is able... Reconciliation and Redemption at its fullness.

We see this in the Resurrection of Jesus Christ... His flesh man walked in the earth and was without sin, no more death, and He did this as our example, being the FIRST FRUIT of the SPIRIT, as the SPIRIT (GOD) created a New Thing in the Earth!!! Yes We Are Hearing You Lord... THANK YOU. So continue the journey and allow God to Redeem the Whole Vessel: spirit, soul, and body.

WHY is this possible? and HOW can this be possible?

Why – because Jesus took all sin out of the way, and condemned sin in His own flesh and natural nature for all mankind and creature... so we can receive the Risen Lord and UNDERSTAND What He did, and Be Free.

How – because Jesus was the first one to come forth Victorious from the grave, death, and sin... having Defeated it all, and Overcame its bondage... for us all. He is the NEW MAN, SECOND MAN, LAST ADAM, The Lord from Heaven, Quickening Spirit ...

and He did so for Our EXAMPLE to follow Him IN HIS VICTORY and step out of our bondage(s).
To WALK without sin and with death destroyed... to show us that by and through HIS EFFORTS and WORKS we can have the DIVINE NATURE too.... and have it today, walking upon the earth as He did AFTER the Resurrection.

In this REGENERATION of this new era of God, God came as Jesus Christ to "fix" and make anew what the first Adam could not do. He was the First of this NEW DIVINE Man of God... the SECOND MAN that is the LORD from HEAVEN, and is the QUICKENING SPIRIT dwelling IN the Last Adam.

Allow The Redeemer and Reconciler to AFFECT you, and Birth His Nature through your soul.

Now, the only way this transformation can come forth In Us is through Him and by Him, the Lord which is the Holy Spirit working that redemptive plan in our own spirit, soul, mind and Body.

A little at a time.... processing us .... to be born again... renewed mind... transformed... after the image of the Son for it is THAT Seed being birthed, being raised up out of our soul/mind. !

The Spirit of the Son, which is the Father, now in us to impregnate our soul with the TRUTH, God's SEED, God's Word which is the gospel of Jesus Christ, God's Power.

Now, God's WILL, WORD, SEED of salvation (the gospel of Jesus Christ which is the power of God Romans 1:16-17) is working in our souls, to produce His Divine Nature in & thru us: born again experience.

THE Divine One in our souls is creating (speaking, writing, producing) HIS Nature/SEED which IS THE SON OF GOD – JESUS

CHRIST. Redemption and Reconciliation Working. God's family manifested in Heaven & Earth.

John 1:12-13 But as man as received him, to them gave he power to become the sons of God, even to them that believe on his name: Which were born, not of blood, nor of the will of the flesh, nor of the will of man, but of God,...

James 1:18 Of his own will begat he us with the word of truth, that we should be a kind of firstfruits of his creatures.

As 1 Corinthians 15 tells us that each seed brings forth after its kind. And that this is like and is the resurrection, which is the on-going redemptive working of the reconciliation of God, which is working from one age to the next, producing and working in us THIS GRACE that is now our sufficiency unto the completion of the revealing of HIS FINISHED work in us: spirit, soul, and body.

The MIND of Christ ruling and reigning in us and through us as LORD to all the world: God's Government and Kingdom Increasing.

Allow God's working to swallow you up more today, and allow HIS MIND to produce In You His Son.

God/Jesus Christ comes and appears in your Soul to Plant His Seed which is Jesus Christ/God's Word in your Soul, to Produce His Son/Jesus Christ THROUGH your earthen vessel.

Yet appearing as He Is, for many to experience Him through us, as us, yet HIM we become, our identity changed when we married Him and gave birth of His Son.... we became One Flesh, One Body, which is the Lord from Heaven, the Quickening Spirit.
Galatians 2:20-21
I am crucified with Christ: nevertheless I live; yet not I, but Christ liveth in me, and the life which I now live in the flesh I live by the

faith of the Son of God, who loved me, and gave himself for me. I do not frustrate the grace of God:...
Amen.
RPJ

(Write your notes here)

REVELATION 61
Forgiveness Is Come….

"Forgiveness is come… yet in order to receive it and reap of it, there is need of a repentive mind that conditions the heart so you can receive and reap of all the benefits of forgiveness."

So true. Jesus Christ has provided ALL forgiveness and release of debt, yet why are there so many still in bondage, sickness, and messed up lives without peace?

Because there must first be a Preaching of the Gospel of Jesus Christ, and a Repentive Mind or Heart in order to RECEIVE of Jesus Christ and all His Benefits.

This is a message that really could go on and on and on cause the Good News of Jesus Christ is just that wonderful. But for now this will just be the shorter version….

If you find that you have been in a situation, dis-ease, or messed up life, a life of plenty but a feeling of void within, or just going in circles … or worse… then TALK TO THE LORD. Ask Him about His Son Jesus Christ, and seek the Lord with all your heart, and know that the one true God has provided for all of mankind the Perfect Solution and Remedy for our lives: His Son Jesus Christ.

His son Jesus Christ came to forgive us of our sin and deliver us from death.

1 Corinthians 15:51-58 (Read all this later, when you can. It will bless your soul)
v55-57 O death, where is thy sting? O grave, where is thy victory? The sting of death is sin; and the strength of sin is the law. But thanks be to God, which giveth us the victory through our Lord Jesus Christ.

" 'My Life In You' by Jesus Christ"

2 Corinthians 5:20-21
... be ye reconciled to God. For he hath made him to be sin for us, who knew no sin; that we might be made the righteousness of God in Him.

He has fulfilled the old covenant of God which was a working of the flesh and animal sacrifice in order to be sanctified and found righteous in God's eyes. It was a burdensome law. Jesus Christ came in the flesh nature of sinful man, and as the spiritual nature in the fullness of God to fulfill all fleshly requirements of that first covenant and fulfill all Spiritual requirements of the new order.

Now the new order is established on better promises, and better testimony, and surety by His own blood that was shed for sin, rather than animal blood. After the order of Melchisedec, God has ordained and established the second order through the blood covenant, so that the law of the Spirit of Life in Christ Jesus is the only law we walk by.

It is a working by Faith of Christ Jesus, and in Faith of Christ Jesus. Grace replaces sin, and through His Righteousness we obtain Eternal Life.

So, as you hear this message today, if you find within yourself a tugging at your heart to Receive the Lord Jesus Christ for the forgiveness of sin, then say a prayer and tell the Lord you know you are a sinner, and all though you don't understand it all, you feel you need HIM to come into your heart for the forgiveness of all sin.

Lord, I agree with them now, to let the journey begin of their new born again life in You. Let there be healing from all that sin has done to them, and restore to them that perfect relationship with you by your Spirit that is holy, now to dwell in them forever. Protect them and set them in that perfect place of fellowship with other like minded members of the body of Christ that will love them, and the leadership will be of You their Shepherd, to nurture them and cause the birthing to come forth to full term. To You Father be all Glory and Honor. Amen.

Amen.
RPJ

(Write your notes here)

REVELATION 62
Taking the Next Step...

Understanding...
When you Understand what God is doing, then Faith can go forward in assurance that you are on the right path and not being mislead.

But what about when God doesn't show you or let you know what is up, but just shows enough for the next step...

Then FAITH walks in TRUST of God's thoughts toward you ... HOPE and LOVE...

KNOWING that God Loves you and desires His GOOD WILL and JOY and GLORY to be yours too... and sooooo much more of the Life of His Son Jesus Christ, does He desire for you to share today in this age, and all ages to come.

FAITH, HOPE, TRUST, LOVE.... WALKING in the Security of God's Heart towards us. His Will (GRACE) for us is to prosper in HIS RIGHTEOUSNESS and LIFE.

God, our Father, wills us out of sin and death, decay and misery, sickness and dis-ease, and all forms of unrighteousness... and into His Abundant Life of Love, Liberty, Justice, Purity, Wholeness, Completeness, Contentment, Joy, Success, Wealth..... Abundance, Abundance, Abundance In & Of & By His Eternal Life (Spirit) that is working in our inner man. (Ephesians 3:16-17)

Through the Righteousness of Jesus Christ, we enter into Eternal Life... Grace abounding instead of sin and Life abundance instead of death and separation from God.

As God is Receiving us, and every son that is in Christ Jesus, He corrects along the path, as we enter into His Kingdom. Yet HIS

Correction is to bring forth more of His Life, and not to destroy our souls. He desires HIS VERY BEST FOR US. !!! And that is what He Gave Us in Christ Jesus.

God has given His very best for us, so even though we don't have to give back to receive His blessing, why don't we do that anyway... out of love.

Besides, He has bought us with His Son's blood, so He Owns Us. So submitting to Him in Love will nurture that relationship with our Hero and Saviour and allow Him to interact with us, for the benefits of others.

Yes, we are His Vessel to work through, but more than that. Why not allow His Will to be done in us, which is John 3:3-5 ... Being Born Again of His Water & Spirit, so that we are Family for Him to commune in Love with. Not the kind of dysfunctional family in earth that most of us have, but the one that is made out of the Son Jesus Christ.

Jesus even says that His true family is the ones that do His Father's Will. Look at this verse ...

Matthew 12:48-50 But he answered and said unto him that told him, Who is my mother? and who are my brethren?
49 And he stretched forth his hand toward his disciples, and said, Behold my mother and my brethren!
50 For whosoever shall do the will of my Father which is in heaven, the same is my brother, and sister, and mother.

That's intense! He wasn't rejecting His earthen family, but He was making a point, and it is a lesson to learn.

So, just love God with all your heart, soul, and body, submitting to Him and letting His fruit come forth in our lives to each other.

Galatians 5 is worth reading here:
Galatians 5: all *22 But the fruit of the Spirit is love, joy, peace, longsuffering, gentleness, goodness, faith, meekness, temperance: against such there is no law. 24 And they that are Christ's have crucified the flesh with the affections and lusts. 25 If we live in the Spirit, let us also walk in the Spirit. 26 Let us not be desirous of vain glory, provoking one another, envying one another....

If a family member is misbehaving, you don't have to stay around them or deal with them, but you do need to love and pray for them.

Let them go, and let the Father intervene in that situation so they can have His Righteousness affect them and bring forth a change.

Meanwhile, you don't have to interact with them, and get hurt, and bruised, etc...

Go enjoy your life in the Lord, and be strong in His Love... then you will be better strengthened to handle them that are still in their unregenerate state. Some you can't be around at all, but the Lord will instruct you along the way. Meanwhile, go forward and let the Lord have His way through you.

Seek the Kingdom of God, let His Life be revealed to you as you commune with the Holy Spirit. Enjoy your time and life in Him.

Allow the Lord to take you to the next step of His Glory, so that more of His Life will swallow up your mortality, and the "birthing" of more of His Abundant Life can come forth in and through each one of us.... unto thanksgiving to God from us all.

Taking the Next Step....

Hang on to His Love for you, and know that there is His reason for you being here, and even though you may not understand it.... He will work it to completion.

Meanwhile, nourish your relationship with Him. Spend time with Him alone.... Allow Him to make a Difference in Your life.

Amen.
RPJ

(Write your notes here)

REVELATION 63
A Word from the Lord to State of Israel, and Jews

Recently the Lord spoke about Old Israel, Jerusalem, and those that dwell there... and those that want to go there..

On May 21, 2011 the Lord gave a short message for them, that went like this:

"Again... if they will Turn from Their Ways and Receive Mine, I will save."

A vision accompanied this that revealed the understanding:..
The state of Israel is most definitely heading for more troubles. Yet, God is desiring for them to once AGAIN come in to His Will that He has ordained for This Day. Again, the people are attempting to "rebuild" what He has removed, and Again He will bring it down. The Lord, Yeshua, Immanuel, Jesus Christ is the Head of God's Family and that New Law which is the law of the Spirit of Life in Christ Jesus, has done away with the old laws of sin & death. There is a remnant, again, that will be preserved, and that is why there are those that have Received His Son Immanuel, which are dwelling there.

The Lord revealed that He is like a Step Parent or Parent of a broken home, in which the children of the old marriage do not desire the new family head (Jesus Christ) so much. Yet, HE desires for them to be blessed above and beyond what they once had... But they will have to turn from doing it their way. Only IF They TURN from their ways, and DESIRE HIS WAY THROUGH HIS SON IMMANUEL JESUS CHRIST to be the Head of their state, can they Then once again Become part of His Promised Seed that is the Blessing for all and the inheritor of the Blessings and promises of God.
(Isaiah 50:1)

A New Zion and a New Jerusalem has come forth... God's Kingdom Is Come. A new order and new laws, along with a new blood covenant ... all that is better than what it once was.

There is a New Zion and a New Jerusalem. If New then it is not the old.

John 4:21-24 tells us Where we worship God...
Hebrews 12:22-29 tells us of this current Zion and habitation of God...
Hebrews 11:10, 14-16 tells us the place they came out of was not the place they were heading to, but the one they were walking in faith towards was the "better" place.

John 4:20-24 20 Our fathers worshipped in this mountain; and ye say, that in Jerusalem is the place where men ought to worship. 21 Jesus saith unto her, Woman, believe me, the hour cometh, when ye shall neither in this mountain, nor yet at Jerusalem, worship the Father. 22 Ye worship ye know not what: we know what we worship: for salvation is of the Jews. 23 But the hour cometh, and now is, when the true worshippers shall worship the Father in spirit and in truth: for the Father seeketh such to worship him. 24 God is a Spirit: and they that worship him must worship him in spirit and in truth.

A Word from the Lord to State of Israel, and Jews CONTINUED...
Hebrews 12:22 But ye are come unto mount Zion, and unto the city of the living God, the heavenly Jerusalem, and to an innumerable company of angels....

Don't rebuild the old... HE will only bring it down... But hear His Love and Declare His Son within your land.... His Righteousness and Peace will sustain. He is the King and Lord of all lands and nations. His Government is ruling and reigning.

(Romans 14:17, Luke 17:20-21, Luke 16:16, 2 Corinthians 13:5, Galatians 4:1-7, Romans 2:28-29, Romans 4 & 5, and many other scriptures)
May the revelation of God's Son be more evident within you today, increasing ever more every day, To God Be All Glory and Thanksgiving!

Amen.
RPJ

REVELATION 64
The Lord is That Spirit

2 Corinthians 3:17 Now the Lord is that Spirit, and where the Spirit of the Lord is, there is liberty.

There is one Spirit, one Lord, one Father..... Ephesians 4:4-7

Romans 8:9-11 But ye are not in the flesh, but in the Spirit, if so be that the Spirit of God dwell in you. Now if any man have not the Spirit of Christ, he is none of his.
10 And if Christ be in you, the body is dead because of sin; but the Spirit is life because of righteousness.
11 But if the Spirit of him that raised up Jesus from the dead dwell in you, he that raised up Christ from the dead shall also quicken your mortal bodies by his Spirit that dwelleth in you.

Romans 8:14-15 For as many as are led by the Spirit of God, they are the sons of God.
15 For ye have not received the spirit of bondage again to fear; but ye have received the Spirit of adoption, whereby we cry, Abba, Father.
16-17 The Spirit itself beareth witness with our spirit, that we are the children of God; And if children, then heirs; heirs of God, and joint-heirs with Christ; if so be that we suffer with him, that we may be also glorified together....

The Spirit is the Intercessor -- Christ is our Intercessor

Romans 8:26-27, 34
26-27Likwise the Spirit also helpeth our infirmities; for we know not what we should pray for as we ought: but the Spirit itself maketh intercession for us with groanings which cannot be uttered. And he that searcheth the hearts knoweth what is the mind of the Spirit, because he maketh intercession for the saints according to the will of God.

v 34 Who is he that condemneth? It is Christ that died, yea rather, that is risen again, who is even at the right hand of God, who also maketh intercession for us.

So the Lord is that Spirit.... and He dwells In You and Me... and our spirit cries out Abba Father... for it is the same Spirit in us that was in Jesus... the same Spirit that raised Him from the grave, and is quickening us daily out of death and into Eternal Life.

Amen.
RPJ

REVELATION 65
Power of God

1 Corinthians 4:19-20 But I will come to you shortly, if the Lord will, and will know, not the speech of them which are puffed up, but the power. For the **kingdom of God is not in word, but in power**.

Kingdom of God is in power, not in the wisdom and speech of man. Not in the appearance of "who" is speaking, but rather if God is speaking through that one. If God is, then the anointing and love of God will be evident. People will be set free. If this is not happening, without gimmicks, then it is just the hot air of the empty man.

Romans 1:16-19 For I am not ashamed of the **gospel of Christ: for it is the power of God** unto salvation to every one that believeth; to the Jew first, and also to the Greek. For **therein is** the righteousness of God revealed from faith to faith: as it is written, The just shall live by faith. For the wrath of God is revealed from heaven against all ungodliness and unrighteousness of men, who hold the truth in unrighteousness; Because that which may be known of God is manifest in them; for God hath shewed it unto them.

The Gospel of Jesus Christ is POWER of God towards us and for us, in attaining Liberty and Victory over all evil, harm, wickedness, and all unrighteousness of that carnal mind of man. THAT POWER frees us from all the works of satan and satan himself. That devil sinned from the beginning and Jesus Christ has destroyed the devil (satan) and the works of the devil (sin) (Hebrews 2:14, 1 John 3:8-10, Rev 20:10).

This wonderful Power of God: Jesus Christ.... is God's OATH.... The Father's Word and Breath towards us... is being breathed (spoken) in our ears and hearts with understanding, to liberate us from the filth of the fleshly mind of the first Adam. So as God ministers and preaches to us of HIS TESTIMONY of HIS SON, and WE RECEIVE HIM – that Testimony of Jesus Christ... Then we are receiving the WASHING of the WATER by His Word – Testimony – His Son Jesus Christ revealed to us and we receive that Word that is Spirit and LIFE in our hearts and souls. THIS engrafted Word RELEASES US from sickness, decay, death, sin, and all unrighteousness! And delivers our Soul unto the Father in the King's domain, even as we are still alive and remain in the earth – the visible realm.

To God is all Glory for all that He has Done! Praise the Lord!

So by the simplicity of Preaching ... the spoken word of the Holy Spirit, as He reveals the Son by the gospel of Jesus Christ.... we are changed into the Son... yet He is always the Head and Leader and King and Priest and All Authority we are yielded to always.... without Him we can be no kind of minister... But with Him we can do all things that He wills to be done. Co-Heirs. Amen.

1 Corinthians 1:17-18 For Christ sent me not to baptize, but **to preach the gospel: <u>not</u> with wisdom of words**, <u>lest the cross of Christ should be made of none effect</u>. For the **preaching of the cross** is to them that perish foolishness; but unto us which are saved it **is the power of God**.

1 Corinthians 1:19-24 For it is written, I will destroy the wisdom of the wise, and will bring to nothing the understanding of the prudent. Where is the wise? where is the scribe? where is the disputer of this world? hath not God made foolish the wisdom of this world?

21 For after that **in the wisdom of God** the world by wisdom knew not God, **it pleased God by the foolishness of preaching to save them that believe**. For the Jews require a sign, and the Greeks seek after wisdom: But **we preach Christ crucified**, unto

the Jews a stumblingblock, and unto the Greeks foolishness; <u>But unto them which are called</u>, both Jews and Greeks, **Christ the power of God, and the wisdom of God**.

Amen.
RPJ

REVELATION 66
Reaping and Sowing: Faith Working

Works of the Spirit or Works of Flesh, either way We Must Work... yet we Rest in the Works of the Son.

Faith without works is dead... Faith with Works is alive and producing Eternal Life.

Body without the Spirit is dead... If one has not the Spirit of Son, then they are dead, and the Spirit of Eternal Life is not in them.

Flesh with works is dead... produces corruption.

So anyway you look at it, we must work. BUT HOW we work and by WHAT we work ...MATTERS.

Galatians 6:10 shows us that if we sow to the flesh (Gal 5:16-21) we reap or produce the flesh which is corruption. But if sow to the Spirit, we will of the Spirit reap or produce of the Spirit which is Eternal Life... Fruit of the Spirit: Love, Joy, Peace, Longsuffering, Gentleness, Faith, Meekness, Temperance
Gal 5:22-23.

So how to SOW to the Spirit is **By Faith Working**. **Works of the Spirit ARE Works of Faith**.

If our Works are of the Spirit, then we Reap Eternal Life.

If our Works are of the Flesh, then we Reap Corruption.

If we by the Spirit sow into the Spirit, we will reap of that Spirit the Fruit of the Spirit.
If we by the Flesh sow into the Flesh, we will reap of that Flesh the Fruit of the flesh.

So what are you Producing? What is your life giving back to you? This answer will reveal to you what you are sowing.

If you are sowing RIGHTEOUSNESS through FAITH by GRACE into the hearts of others and yourself, then you Will produce PEACE and the Life of Jesus Christ with all His benefits of that life. Galatians 5:22-23

Likewise, yet in the opposite, if you are sowing carnal thinking, and behavior to others and yourself, then you Will produce corruption, destruction, decay, and the benefits of corruption. Galatians 5:16-21

Read Galatians 5:16-26 for the effects of the fruit of the Spirit, and the flesh. So which do you see being produced in your life? You have a choice. You have the controls to change direction.

Sow into your garden (life) the SEED of Eternal Life which is Jesus Christ. Feed yourself daily of His Spirit, so you may have Seed to Sow to others, and let the cycle of harvest produce His Life in and through you daily. That is what is meant of "If we live in the Spirit, let us also walk in the Spirit" Galatians 5:25. If you live, or could say, abide in the Spirit by Faith, then walk in, or could say produce of the Spirit.

Galatians 6:6-10 *v8 For he that soweth to his flesh shall of the flesh reap corruption; but he that soweth to the Spirit shall of the Spirit reap life everlasting.
v10 As we have therefore opportunity, let us do good unto all men, especially unto them who are of the household of faith.

So, even though we can REST in Jesus Christ, Yet, We still Work, but by FAITH WORKING, and thus, WALKING in GRACE ... seeing that He has obtained salvation Thru Works of His own Spirit, having overcome His flesh for all flesh...

... for in THIS RIGHTEOUSNESS of Jesus Christ we are sanctified, justified, and liberated daily, knowing that because He has obtained salvation and victory and liberty from that sinful flesh nature FOR US, that WE TOO can WALK in HIS WORK that has been accomplished, and BY FAITH we can Walk in the Spirit of Life, and by the Spirit of Life produce His Fruit and the Character of the Resurrected One – Jesus Christ our Lord.

Walking Now, in the Divine Nature of the Perfect One, who is liberated from all sin and death of the flesh, soul, and spirit.... Now that's a mouth full to say... but it is right and fruitful.

Sooooo SOW to the Spirit .... **Walk in Faith of the Works of the Son**, and Then your Faith will be alive, and not dead... because your Faith will be working, and it will be accounted unto you for righteousness also... for Believing all that the Father has done.

John 6:28-29 Then said they unto him, What shall we do, that we might work the works of God ?
Jesus answered and said unto them,
This is the work of God, that ye believe on him whom he hath sent.

Thank You Father!

Amen.
RPJ

REVELATION 67
Face To Face

Psalm 27:7-8 Hear, O Lord, when I cry with my voice: have mercy also upon me, and answer me.
When thou saidst, Seek ye my face; my heart said unto thee, Thy face, Lord, will I seek.

The Lord is calling certain ones to Seek His Face and to have a Face to Face moment with Him.
If that is You, then continue forward and approach the Father in His Throne.... or wherever He wants s to meet you face to face.

Proverbs 27:19
As in water face answereth to face, so the heart of man to man.

Note the "in water".... this is symbolic of God's Word. So In His Word, we Meet Him Face to Face.

Note that HIS WORD IS Jesus Christ.... so in the Gospel – Blood Covenant – Testament of Salvation Jesus Christ – Lamb of God .... God's Word and Oath to us of Salvation & Liberty is being spoken by Him in our Soul, then He is Revealing within our Earthen Vessel, and Writing upon our Hearts and Putting in our Minds THAT Covenant and His Witness/Testament of the Son. That is God's Power Dwelling in Us, for it is not a letter, but it is the very presence and revealing of His Son and Lamb that Washes Us, and Cleanses Us.... Justifies and Sanctifies Us for HIS Good Pleasure. He Seals Us by His own Spirit... the same one that dwelled in Jesus when He was on the earth, and did the work through him... He is making us His habitation of His Glory by raising us from our own graves and grave clothes. Transforming and Changing us in to the image of His Son. See scriptures below:
Hebrews 8:10 For this is the covenant that I will make with the hours of Israel after those days, saith the Lord; I will put my laws

into their mind, and write them in their hearts: and I will be to them a God, and they shall be to me a people.

2 Corinthians 4:6-7 For God, who commanded the light to shine out of darkness, **hath shined in our hearts**, to give **the light of the knowledge** of the glory of God **in the FACE** of Jesus Christ.
But **we** have this treasure **in earthen vessels**, that **the excellency of the power may be of God**, and not of us.

1 Corinthians 13:10-12
But **when** that which is **perfect is come**, **then** that which is **in part shall be done away**.

This is speaking of the law of sin and death which was the covenant that was of the things that were only a shadow of the true, being replaced with that which is the True Covenant and Law: The Law of the Spirit of Life in Christ Jesus.... He that IS the Perfect One Is Come and has fulfilled the old, in every jot, and tittle; and has birthed forth the New Jerusalem that is not of this earth, nor in that mountain, but a new heaven and earth in the hearts and souls of man has God our Father desired to dwell.... BUT UNTIL YOU SEE and AWAKEN TO HIM – YOUR RIGHTEOUSNESS ... YOU ARE STILL DEAD AND IN YOUR GRAVES OF DEATH. BECAUSE YOU HAVE NOT RECEVIED THE PERFECT ONE – THE RESURRECTION AND LIFE WHO HAS OVERCOME ALL THINGS, AND HAS APPEARED THE SECOND TIME WITHOUT SIN UNTO YOUR SALVATION. BUT UNTIL YOU SEE THIS, YOU CAN NOT ENTER INTO IT... AND BE FREE OF SIN. ONLY BY RECEIVING THE SON, YESHUA, IMMANUEL, LAMB OF GOD, JESUS CHRIST... CAN YOU BE SET FREE AND OBTAIN YOUR REDEMPTION. ALL BLESSINGS ABIDE IN THE SON, AND ONLY THOSE THAT RECEIVE THE SON, CAN RECEIVE HIS BENEFITS.
Hebrews 9:26-28 So Christ was once offered to bear the sins of many; and unto them that look for him shall he appear the second time without sin unto salvation.

The Spirit of the Son is come in you, and you cry "Abba Father"? Have you received that WORD of God that was preached? The testament of that Holy Spirit, the Father that was in Jesus when on the earth, is the SAME Spirit that raised Jesus from the grave after having taken on our sin and death.

Galatians 4:1-7 ....to redeem them that were under the law, that we might receive the adoption of sons. And because ye are sons, God hath sent forth the **Spirit of his Son into your hearts**, crying, **Abba, Father**. Wherefore thou art **no more a servant, but a son**; and **if a son, then an heir of God through Christ**.

Romans 1:16-17 For I am not ashamed of the gospel of Christ: for **it is the power of God** unto salvation to every one that believeth: to the Jew first, and also to the Greek....

John 1:12 But as many as **received him**, to them gave he **power to become the sons of God**, even to them that believe on his name:..... which were born,... of God.

So we must Grow Up, Mature... How? Continuing daily in His Spirit, and allow the Teacher to teach, ground, preach the Word of God that is Eternal Life... AND You Must Receive and Believe by the working of your Faith IN the Son of God.

1 Corinthians 13:11-12 When I was a child, I spake as a child, I understood as a child, I thought as a child: but **when** I became a man, I put away childish things. For now we see through a glass, darkly; but **then face to face**: now I know in part; but **then shall I know even as also I am known**.
John 10:15 **As the Father knoweth me, even so know I the Father:** and I lay down my life for the sheep.

Take Your Next Step in God's Plan for your maturing in the Son, and allow The Son to be revealed through you, as His New Heaven and Earth: God's habitation.

" 'My Life In You' by Jesus Christ"

Galatians 2:20 I am crucified with Christ: nevertheless I live; yet not I, but **Christ liveth in me** and the life which I now live in the flesh I live by the faith of the Son of God, who loved me, and gave himself for me.

2 Corinthians 3:16-18 ...Now the Lord is that Spirit: and where the Spirit of the Lord is, there is liberty.
But we all, with open FACE beholding as in a glass the glory of the Lord, are changed into the same image from glory to glory, even as by the Spirit of the Lord.

Now back to Proverbs 17:19 As in water face answereth to face, so the heart of man to man.

Deep calleth unto the deep: God is The Deep calling unto our souls to allow Him to make your well deeper of His Water for others to come to.

Amen.
RPJ

REVELATION 68
It Happened In That Generation

Many scriptures are on this and the other topics, so they will be displayed and noted a little at a time. Enjoy.

One of the first things to note is that in Matthew 23-24, Luke 11:46-52 and other places Jesus tells us that all the tribulation and end of the world will take place IN THAT GENERATION. Not us or a future generation, but THAT Generation. It it happened as the prophets of God had prophesied.

Luke 11:49-51 (Jesus spoke this) There fore also said the wisdom of God, I will send them prophets and apostles, and some of them they shall slay and persecute: That the blood of all the prophets, which was shed from the foundation of the world, may be **required of this generation**; From the blood of Abel unto the blood of Zacharias, which perished between the altar and the temple: verily I say unto you, **It shall be required of this generation**.

Matthew 23:33-36 (all through these two chapters are "awakening moments") (Jesus speaking here) Ye serpents, ye generation of vipers, how can ye escape the damnation of hell? Wherefore, behold, I send unto you prophets, and wise men, and scribes: and some of them ye shall kill and crucify; and some of them shall ye scourge in your synagogues, and persecute them from city to city: That upon you may come all the righteous blood shed upon the earth, from the blood of righteous Abel unto the blood of Zacharias son of Barachias, whom ye slew between the temple and the altar. Verily I say unto you, **All these things shall come upon this generation**.

So how many times does Jesus need to say this to that generation, before You in this generation of 2011 will understand that Jesus was telling them back in the New Testament days that all this tribulation was going to come on their generation.

Now, hang on to Christ Jesus your foundation and surety, and read more as you are able to digest and be free from lies of the traditions and doctrines of man.

Amen.
RPJ

REVELATION 69
Kingdom of God: From Basics 101 and beyond

The basic who, what, when, where and how of God's Kingdom and then looking deeper to what the Lord is revealing.

Let's start with WHAT is the Kingdom of God?
Romans 14:17 For the kingdom of God is not meat and drink; but **righteousness, and peace, and joy in the Holy Ghost**.

The Kingdom of God (kingdom of heaven) is Righteousness, Peace, and Joy..... located in the Holy Ghost.
And when the Holy Ghost came upon and in Jesus Christ, the Kingdom of God was upon and in the earth... In Jesus Christ.

People that were healed and received miracles, Jesus would tell some that the Kingdom of God was nigh or near you. It was IN Him.

Now that brings us to the next questions of WHO and WHERE and WHEN?

The Kingdom of God was IN Jesus Christ.

Luke 17:20-21 says "And when he was demanded of the Pharisees, **when the kingdom of God should come**, he answered them and said, The kingdom of God cometh **not** with observation: Neither shall they say, Lo here! or, lo there! for, behold, **the kingdom of God is within you**."

And He told them this too...
Luke 11:52
52 Woe unto you, lawyers! for ye have taken away the key of knowledge: ye entered not in yourselves, and them that were entering in ye hindered.

They held the key to ENTER the Kingdom but would not enter, and hindered others that were trying to enter in. The KEY is TRUTH

WHERE is the Kingdom of God? IN YOU.... IN THE HOLY GHOST. So was the Holy Ghost in the Pharisees too???? Hmmm. Was it that they had polluted the Kingdom???? Hmmmm. But what was the whole concept here.....???? Hmmmm
Pause.....

Jesus had to take over the Kingdom of God that was in the old order and Priesthood.... they had polluted it. Jesus had to take over the dominion and set things in its proper order. They had not been good stewards. Vipers, Foxes Jesus called them. The change had begun.... a new heaven and earth where GOD was to DWELL had begun to be birthed (regeneration).... a change for the better....

Matthew 19:28 "And Jesus said unto them (disciples), Verily I say unto you, That ye which have followed me, **in the regeneration** when the Son of man shall sit in the throne of his glory, ye also shall sit upon twelve thrones, judging the twelve tribes of Israel." Regeneration here means "REBIRTH". ALL creation... Heaven and Earth, THAT WORLD was about to be done away, and the NEW HEAVEN AND EARTH was about to be birthed forth and established. Wow! Amen.

The Great Tribulation and Judgment was about to commence on that world. That generation. That age. Things were changing...

The NEW WINE could not be put into the OLD WINE SKIN!!! Hear this. The Old order and priesthood was not to minister the things of the New Heaven and Earth: The Law and ALL the elements were going to be after a different order. The Order of FAITH and GRACE. A Priest after the order of Melchesdec. After the power of an endless life (Eternal Life).

Even that was a shadow of what was to be created, but the first became the last. The beginning became the end.

See what the Lord is showing.

In the beginning was the word, ... in the end the Word became King and His Kingdom and Government there is no end. It is completed and set ... throughout all eternity... A complete work for all ages. It is Finished. It is done. Hallelujah and Amen Father Amen.!!!!

Now for the HOW question:... HOW did Jesus bring in the New Heaven and Earth: God's Kingdom?

God's Kingdom was within in them, the elect ones. But they, nor the elements and ordinances, could make the conscience CLEAN... non polluted. So Jesus Christ had to come through the creature that was made of the dust, Adamic mankind, and be birthed as in the natural like we all were. Then Jesus had to overcome EVERY OBSTACLE and HINDERANCE of man. SIN was the obstacle and hinderance, which separated MANKIND (male/female) from the ETERNAL LIFE - GOD.

WHO was ABLE to REDEEM ALL THINGS? Someone that was separate from but yet produced out of the sinful nature, but YET, was bigger and BETTER than it all. There was only ONE – God himself.

Soooo He sent... produced His only begotten Son... all man and all God, in ONE PERFECT Vessel. Tempted in every way as a man, faced every downfall and lack of man, yet overcame it all as man YET all the Power of Liberty: God.

Jesus Christ was re-establishing God's habitation IN man... the place where He desires His Kingdom to dwell... in the souls of man. This is His Garden, Field, dwelling place, secret place in some... Yet our souls are swallowed up in Him as we enter His Kingdom... full redemption...

THIS IS BIG!!!! Hear what the Lord is saying that words can not express.!

I hope you are seeing what I am seeing. This is intense. Deeper into the whole working of God through Jesus Christ.... Maybe this is only for me to see... but I don't think so. I hope you are rejoicing with me too.

Now... WHEN? .... NOW TODAY is the day of Salvation. Today is your day to ENTER into HIS KINGDOM of Righteousness, Peace, and JOY IN THE HOLY GHOST...... GOD IN YOU.

Every man has the measure of faith, but not every man is AWAKENED unto the Righteousness they are in need of, which is the PERFECT ONE "IMMANUEL".

God already owns EVERY SOUL. BUT not every soul has allowed HIM to implant His Seed, WORD OF THE SON – WORD OF LIFE in them. THEY HAVE NOT PRODUCED AFTER HIS SEED.

Jesus said "You say 'you did this for me and that for me... but I know you not". How can He not know everyone? What He is saying is that you never produced ("born again") after my seed... the eternal life, Jesus Christ. You just showed off in the gifts.

You have to have intimate time with God and allow Him to BREATH HIS WORD of ETERNAL LIFE in you, and produce HIS Spirit and Divine Nature through you, and become you. Your Mortality swallowed up of LIFE. ONLY THROUGH JESUS CHRIST, YESHUA, IMMANUEL can we ENTER in to God's Kingdom, and ONLY THROUGH BEING BORN of His Spirit, and Water: HIS WORD engrafted in our souls and washed of His word can we SEE AND ENTER HIS KINGDOM.

John 3:3-5 v3 Jesus answered and said unto him, Verily, verily, I say unto thee, Except a man be born again, he cannot see the kingdom of God.... v5 Jesus answered, Verily, verily, I say unto thee, Except a man be born of water and of the Spirit, he cannot enter into the kingdom of God.

Ephesians 5:26-27 That he might sanctify and cleanse it (the church) with the washing of water by the word, That he might present it to himself a glorious church, not having spot, or wrinkle, or any such thing; but that it should be holy and without blemish.

He will clean you up as you allow Him to. Give Him your time and know that He is the rewarded of those that diligently seek Him. Allow Him to take the veil off your face so you may behold Him as He is and be changed into the same image which is the Son of God.

John 1:12 But as many as received him, to them gave he power to become the sons of God, even to them that believe on his name: which were born, not of blood, nor of the will of the flesh, nor of the will of man, but of God....

Galatians 2:20 I am crucified with Christ: nevertheless I live; yet not I, but Christ liveth in me: and the life which I now live in the flesh I live by the faith of the Son of God, who loved me, and gave himself for me.

Jesus Christ is the Power of God in you, the Word that was made flesh, and we now know as the Spirit of God that is Holy.

Now, Enter into His Kingdom .... for His Presence in you is Righteousness and is Power. Put on the Second Man's life that is

without sin and death, for He has made you to be Co-Heirs with Him in His Kingdom.
Hallelujah! Rejoice!

Amen.
RPJ

(Write your notes here)

REVELATION 70
God is Able

Some areas of the Body of Christ are "out of balance"...
Here is an understanding and clarification for the Body of Christ, which is God's Habitation, to bring back "balance"...

The assembling of the body in local churches are not to be for the prospering of the "leader" and the body going without. This is a body out of "balance".

Titus 1:11 says... Whose mouths must be stopped, who subvert whole house, teaching things which they ought not, for filthy lucre's sake.

There are other scriptures on this that rebuke those that are using lies and doctrines of the traditions of men for their selfish gains, rather than declaring Truth and Life for the prospering of God's people and family into eternal Life and Liberty. They are without power. Yet our Father God will set them free in His way and time.

Clearly God is transforming new Shepherds that are after His own heart; those that will protect His people, which are His possessions. Shepherds that will not use them for selfish gain, but rather prosper and build them in the Spiritual riches and wealth of God through Jesus Christ, AND.... will also build them, God's people, to be God's house that will be prosperous in the material means too. The riches of material means are not the problem.... it is the MIND of the person that pollutes God's blessings.

So, let your mind be renewed in TRUTH. Allow God's Power – His Word to be breathed within your Soul and mind, so that you may be a transformed, changed individual that is walking BY THE MIND OF CHRIST in all your works. Producing His fruit and helping to Prosper Others, as the Lord prospers you: whether in the spiritual wealth or the material wealth or all means.

2 Corinthians 4:4-7; Revelation 21:24; 2 Corinthians 3:7, 18
chpt 4:6 For God, who commanded the light to shine out of darkness, hath shined in our hearts, to give the light of the knowledge of the glory of God in the face of Jesus Christ.
chpt 3:18 But we all, with open face beholding as in a glass the glory of the Lord, are changed into the same image from glory to glory, even as by the Spirit of the Lord.

These verses sum up the purpose of God, the Holy Spirit in us.... changing us into that Divine Nature that is no longer in sin and death or decay. His Heavenly Body – His fullness- revealed and abiding in His Church to all that are in heaven and earth. This is THE Prosperity that the world is in need of ... not just spiritual, but materially as well....

You see,... God is Able. God owns all things and lacks nothing. As the Head of all, and from which all blessings flow, if the Head is prosperous, then the field (people) will be prosperous.

The problem in many churches today is that they have it backwards: The leaders are lacking or rich because they are using the people. OR it is the leaders are prospering from the people and leaving the people lacking. IT IS OUT OF BALANCE.

Let's allow the Lord to FIX THIS within each of us today, and cause us to unite in God's Mind of how His Church should be run.... no matter where it is being assembled or how many people are there.

God is our head... from Him only should each member of the body seek HIS DIRECTION and instructions for the day's necessities. And as He prospers you, prosper others too. Whether it is spiritual giving, material giving, or other... however the Lord has prospered you, nourish the body too... This is what is meant by all things common, so there is no lack in the body of Christ, nor is there any greed or envy or jealousies. Instead, Provision is provided through the sincerity of the Lord in all Purity and Love in the Power of His Holy Spirit... flowing and providing for His Habitation, His body.... so there is no lack.

2 Corinthians 4:1-2 Therefore seeing we have this ministry, as we have received mercy, we faint not; But have renounced the hidden things of dishonesty, not walking in craftiness, nor handling the word of God deceitfully; but by manifestation of the truth commending ourselves to every man's conscience in the sight of God.

God is Able. If each member of the Body will seek Him daily, and give daily to the Body of Christ, according to what God has made them able, then there will be no lack in any member of the body of Christ.

AMEN.
RPJ

REVELATION 71
Testimony of Grace – Liberation is Sounding

After studying and digging deep into 1 Peter 1:1-25, my heart and soul rejoice of the revealing of Jesus Christ! Yet for time sake, I'm pulling a couple of scriptures from there to touch on for today....

1 Peter 1:10-11
10 Of which salvation the prophets have inquired and searched diligently, who prophesied of the grace that should come unto you:
11 Searching what, or what manner of time the Spirit of Christ which was in them did signify, when it testified beforehand the sufferings of Christ, and the glory that should follow.

1 Peter 1:13
13 Wherefore gird up the loins of your mind, be sober, and hope to the end for the grace that is to be brought unto you at the revelation of Jesus Christ;

Awwwww... "the grace that is to be brought unto you at the revelation of Jesus Christ" !! Hallelujah! For He is come unto this age!

Open your eyes and behold Him in His Glory and Receive the Lord Jesus Christ into your world, so that He may bring you into His place that He has prepared for you. He is the Author and Finisher of your faith: the beginning and the end. (Hebrews 12:2)

Hebrews 12:2 Looking unto Jesus **the author and finisher of our faith**; who for the joy that was set before him endured the cross, despising the shame, and is set down at the right hand of the throne of God.
1 Peter 1:8-10
8 Whom having not seen, ye love; in whom, though now ye see him not, yet believing, ye rejoice with joy unspeakable and full of

glory: **Receiving the end of your faith, even the salvation of your souls.**
10 Of which salvation the prophets have inquired and searched diligently, who **prophesied of the grace that should come unto you**:

Such Sufficiency Grace Is... to us all.

God's Blood Testimony: New Law and Order for which HE can CONNECT with US, and US with HIM.... as ONE BODY connected to the HEAD, governing heaven and earth and all things. !!! wow.

All things in heaven and earth are His. Every knee bows and confesses that Jesus Christ is Lord. And if there are any that do not confess yet.... they will.

All is being subdued unto the Son, then to Father... from age to age... through that same Word and Knowledge of His Son, Jesus Christ. His Power is over the whole world and ruling and reigning all things. So this is.

This Grace and Presence is welcome to swallow me up, so that all that I am is subdued to the Father. Does life stop once the earthen vessel goes back to the dust? NO. Heaven and Earth ARE one in Jesus Christ. The visible realm and invisible realm are the Lord's. Jesus Christ has destroyed and defeated the devil, satan, and its works of sin. It has been accomplished and all things are now the Lord's property. His authority is ruling.

He has clothed us in His own body: flesh & blood, and skin (identity of last adam) that covers our nakedness. The Robe of Righteousness & Garment of Salvation is His authority & identity which we are clothed in. The Eternal Sacrifice that causes us to be Born Again. Which causes of to become and be known as His visible body and church which is seen by all principalities and dominions, in both the earth and heaven. wow! Hear what the Holy Spirit is saying…

So why are any of us allowing any carnality mindset to spoil our joy? In the Power of the Son, this too stops. Father, these people are your people, and you have bought their soul by the blood of your Son. You have purchased them for your dwelling place and heritage. Flow in them more and more. Set up your sanctuary in the way that pleases you. So be it, that your Son, Yeshua Messiah, may appear in the full stature of His character, and to your joy, moving about in this world as you please. You are our blessing… in all thanksgiving of Your Son, our Saviour Jesus Christ, Thank you.

That's the key…. Receive Him – the Blessing & allow Him to flow freeing by faith working in you. The Intercessor is abiding in you. He alone knows exactly what is needed for the situation and moment. So, fellowship with the Father and allow Him to flow through you, the many membered Son.

The World is waiting for their deliverance which comes as the Son appears. (Romans 8:18-23) Be awakened unto what is Done, and step into it. The body that is without sin…. Romans 8:23, Heb 9:28.

Set the motion of the day according to His Will of Peace and Provision. He has already provided His Sufficiency for our Day… so set the course of your day in the blessing He has anchored us in.

Psalm 23 The Lord is my Shepherd, I shall not want… Thank you Father.

He maketh me to lie down in green pastures…provision is provided.

He leadeth me beside still waters... peace abounds in His righteousness.

He restores my soul...rest.

Psalm 103 Bless the Lord o my soul: and all that is within me, bless his holy name.

Bless the Lord, O my soul, and forget not all his benefits: ...

... Oh what Grace He Is, dwelling within our souls. (John 14)

You might have to walk through some valleys that have the appearance of death, but YOU are ABIDING In Christ....the heavenly kingdom swallows you up. And if it hasn't swallowed you up yet... then continue your journey out of death, and enter LIFE which is the place that has been prepared for you, which is in the Son of God. Then allow Him to appear within your soul, and give you peace in your daily walk.

John 14 you say Lord, that you will make yourself manifest to them/us.... and in verse 23 you even say that you and the Father will make your abode within us.... Thank you for it is so in me and many that are reading this, but please Appear within those others that are waiting for future appearing of you... they are hindered by the lie from doctrines of man and do not understand yet. Allow them to hear and see you Lord, and open the blind eyes and deaf ears to hear... for You are the GRACE that was and is come and have been Received in this place, and I pray that they too can experience You also and encounter the True Living Lord of all Souls. Thank you for rescuing us all, and setting us in heavenly places in Christ Jesus, today.

Ephesians 2:4-8
4 But God, who is rich in mercy, for his great love wherewith he loved us,

5 Even when we were dead in sins, hath quickened us together with Christ, (by grace ye are saved;)
6 And hath raised us up together, and made us sit together in heavenly places in Christ Jesus:
7 That in the ages to come he might shew the exceeding riches of his grace in his kindness toward us through Christ Jesus.
8 For by grace are ye saved through faith; and that not of yourselves: it is the gift of God:

GRACE appears, and is sufficient for each day. This is God's daily love and forgiveness, which is the Power that sets free the repented soul, and births forth every member of the body of Christ. Liberation is Sounding.

Amen.
RPJ

REVELATION 72
Whatsoever is Not of Faith, Is Sin

Anything or Action that is Not a working of "faith" IS sin.

Romans 14:23 And he that doubteth is damned if he eat, because he eateth not of faith:
for whatsoever is **not of faith is sin**.

Galatians 3:11-12 But that no man is justified by the law in the sight of God, it is evident: for,
The just shall live by faith.
12 And the **law is not of faith**: but, the man that doeth them shall live in them.

You are not sanctified by the working of the old law of sin and death, the ten commandments, ordinances and festivals of rituals and rules, etc.... These were all produced to reveal how much man was in need of the Lamb of God, and Saviour of the World.... of our own selves we can do nothing. (John 15:1-5)

We needed someone Greater than man, greater than ourselves to work God's Righteousness for us.... We needed **God In Man** to redeem man... so God sent His Only Begotten Son......

Acts 26:18 ... that they may receive forgiveness of sins, and inheritance among them **which are *sanctified* by *faith* that is in me**.

And those that Believe and Walk in those Works of the Son, can Rest by Faith in the Son for all that He has Done and Completed..... For all generations to be blessed by.

Once Born of God... You Can Not Sin... Because Christ Jesus is the Word/Seed of God IN YOU that has SANCTIFIED YOU and daily Sanctifies you. HE only Anchors us all in Righteousness and Love.

YET.... if you willingly after knowing the Truth & LOVE of God and have tasted of this GRACE decided to walk in hatred, envy, jealousies, grudges, vindictiveness, and other workings of the carnal mind.....

IF you willingly do this, THEN disobedience begins to PRESS and Darken your soul's vision.... Misery sets in.

AND UNTIL you Turn and "repent" or rather Come To The Father in mercy and do not want to walk in that mind set any more, You will continue to walk in that "dark" place and misery of your soul..... the place of disobedience.

BUT ONCE you have told the Father you do not want to walk in that mindset towards "so-n-so" or whatever the situation was that got you in that mess,...

THEN HE WILL SET YOU FREE once again, and Restore Your Vision.... so you may behold His Glory, and be clothed in His Liberty EVEN MORE THAN BEFORE.

But if you choose to be stubborn, then hang on for some turbulence,... because that Glorious Seed in you will not return void... IT Will Set You Free. God is not mocked. The Consuming Fire will remove the adversary in you, one means or another... for His Seed In You has made You His property and Inheritance. Hebrews 12:29 God is a consuming fire. Read Hebrews 12:22-29 for full effect.

The Process of Being Born again is a journey through the Son of God, as we eat and partake of Him as the Father reveals Him to us:
Hebrews 10:16-26 This is the covenant that I will make with them after those days, saith the Lord, I will put my laws into their hearts, and in their minds will I write them; And their sins and iniquities will I remember no more .

18 Now where remission of these is, there is no more offering for sin.
19 Having therefore, brethren, **boldness to enter** into the holiest **by the blood of Jesus,**
20 **By a new and living way**, which he hath consecrated for us, **through the veil, that is to say, his flesh**;
21 And **having a high priest over the house of God**;
22 Let us draw near with a true heart in **full assurance of faith**, **having our hearts sprinkled from an evil conscience, and our bodies washed with pure water**.
23 Let us hold fast the profession of our faith without wavering; (for he is faithful that promised;)
24 And let us consider one another to **provoke unto love and to good works**:
25 Not forsaking the assembling of ourselves together, as the manner of some is; but exhorting one another: and so much the more, as ye see the day approaching.
26 For if we sin wilfully after that we have received the knowledge of the truth, there remaineth no more sacrifice for sins,...

Yet, the Process of Being Born again is also taking us from one revealing of that man of sin, to the other. And each time it reveals its head --- GOD ABOUNDS WITH GRACE AND FIRE TO Purge us more and deliver and strip us of that old nature, revealing MORE and MORE of His Son in us! (Hebrews 12: 5-11)

Yet, He does not leave us naked... He Clothes us In More and More and MORE of HIS GLORY... mortality swallowed up of Life! Amen. Hallelujah! (Romans 5; Romans 6:22-23; 2 Cor 5: 1-5, 4:14-15; Romans 8:9-11, 18-23; 1 Corinthians 15:27-28,53-57, and many more...)
Awwww.... Freedom.... Health... Liberty in Christ is LIFE!

God's New Blood Covenant of Jesus Christ is a NEW Covenant of LOVE.... with NEW regulations and rules to go by. They are not burdensome as before, and we can find REST for our souls. Yet the COMMANDMENT is to LOVE ONE ANOTHER..... in the Strong Love of the Father which delivers all from all forms of decay.

If after you have tasted of God's love towards yourself, you decide to walk "out of this love" towards others in hatred, jealousies, strife, revenge, etc... , then His Corrective Hand will work on you. Not to destroy YOU, but DESTROY THE ADVERSARY, THAT ALWAYS SINS, AND DISOBEYS GOD. Separation ... not of you and the Father anymore... but separation of you and the adversary that does not walk in LOVE.

So, Can You Sin if you are Born of God? NO. But if WHILE YOU ARE <u>BEING</u> BORN of God you, or rather while you are being stripped of that old carnal skin/nature.... while your mind is being renewed and transformed, and regenerated (this means 'born again')..... and You Allow that old nature to produce fruit through you.... then the corrective hand of God will purge out the one in you that is causing the problem.... Yet your soul is preserved by His Seed that is righteous. God will not destroy your soul, but He WILL REMOVE from you that ADVERSARY THAT HAS BEEN WORKING IN YOU....

So BEING BORN AGAIN is a process... a little here and a little there... delivering you until there is nothing left in you but HIS OWN IMAGE and FRUIT... His Kingdom Established and the King ruling and reigning IN YOU. Allllll that you are Redeemed. (Ephesians 1:13-14; 2 Corinthians 3:16-18, Philippians 3:21, 12-14, ...)

How is this to take place.... BY a daily washing and cleansing in the Son & Lamb of God.......
Washed in God's Word (Water) and Cleansed by His Blood (Spirit) we become Born Again and can not sin. (John 3:3-5; Ephesians 5:26-27; 1 Peter 1:23 (22-23), 1 John 3:8-9, Romans 8:9-11, 1 Corinthians 15:51-58, and many other confirmations....)

But we can be Corrected during this manifestation of the Son. Hebrews 12: 1-29 clearly reveals that God Will correct us, but unto LIBERTY and more of HIS Righteousness and Glory for us! Not to destroy us.

This New Law and Order of Grace: the Law of the Spirit of Life in Christ Jesus... is the Law of LOVE working.... through Faith and Hope we are to Choose to Walk in LOVE... GOD's LOVE Towards You... always. Then You will be able to Give out of His Mind to those around you. But you have to have His Mind Set in You first, then He will SET You in HIS MIND... Live in the Spirit, and Walk in the Spirit (Gal 5:16-26). To Know God's Love is an Experience, that is a result of an Encounter of Him. You Will be affected ... and Changed in to the body of Christ that is without sin. (Ephesians 3:14-21).

Galatians 5:6 For in Jesus Christ neither circumcision availeth anything, nor uncircumcision;
but faith which worketh by love.

SEEK, ASK, and KNOCK after His Love. He Will Fill Your Soul (house) with His Glory (presence).

... And You Will Be Changed... in the twinkling of an eye.... for you will have heard His Voice (trumpet) sounding and declaring Salvation (Jesus Christ) and making Him known to you....

The Last Trumpet has Sounded. It is Finished. Now allow all that you are to be "subdued" unto the Father through the Son Jesus Christ.
And if you have not heard the last trumpet sounding in victory, then continue your journey out of death and into His Life.... Until You HEAR the Trumpet (message/voice) of the Finished Work of Jesus Christ sound within you, that It Is Finished in you too.

Many are still crossing over the Red Sea experience within themselves. Enter Into the Promised Land which is Jesus Christ and the Father: God's Kingdom.... The Eternal Life that Never Ends.... and in FAITH of His Works, REST with Him where He is. (Eph 2:5-7; John 17:21-24,....)

Amen.
RPJ

REVELATION 73
God's Operation of Hope

HOPE Secures our Steps in His Righteousness... Our Security and Guarantee of His Righteousness... as we are Walking in the Faith of the Son of God who is abiding within.... to bring us to and into His Glory. Therein is the place that HE has prepared for us to inhabit (John 14:2-3).

TODAY... WE ARE WALKING IN FAITH AND HOPE as we are GOING WHERE?????? We are taking a walk in the Son. He is being revealed to us in every experience of His Glory... transforming and changing us into the same image.

Hebrews 6:19-20 Which **hope** we have as an **anchor of the soul**, both sure and stedfast, and which entereth into that within the veil; Whither the forerunner is for us entered, even Jesus, made an high priest for ever after the order of Melchisedec.

So, we are Entering through the Veil which is the flesh of the Son, the Sacrifice, and it leads us to the Father in the most holy place.

EVERY Step is a step of faith that is revealing the Son of God to us... His Righteousness, His Character, His Power, His Presence being made manifest to us in our daily walk, as we ENTER INTO HIS KINGDOM.

Romans 1:16-17 For therein is the righteousness of God revealed, from faith to faith.... Now, for some of you this is enough to take in... but for those that are desiring to see the deeper understanding of God's Operation, please feel free to continue on with me....
In John 14, again, we hear Jesus speaking to tell us that He and the Father will "dwell" in us, and Jesus says that He will make himself "**manifest**" to us, then **He and the Father** will **dwell within us**.

John 14:20-23 **At that day** …. Some of you are still waiting for "that day" to come to you, yet if today you should HEAR His Voice, then Today Is Your Day…. Receive His Word and RISE out of your grave…..

…. At that day ye shall know that I **am in my Father, and ye in me, and I in you**. He that hath my commandments, and keepeth them, he it is that loveth me: and he that loveth me shall be loved of my Father, and I will love him, and **will manifest myself to him**. Judas saith unto him, not Iscariot, Lord, how is it that thou wilt manifest thyself unto us, and not unto the world? Jesus answered and said unto him, If a man love me, he will keep my words: and my Father will love him, and **we will come unto him, and make our abode with him**.

John 17:22-26 (Jesus Praying to the Father)
22 And the **glory** which thou gavest me **I have given them**; that they may **be one**, even **as we are one**:
23 **I in them, and thou in me**, that they may be made perfect in one; and that the world may know that thou hast sent me, and hast loved them, as thou hast loved me.
24 Father, I will that they also, whom thou hast given me, **be with me where I am**; **that they may behold my glory, which thou hast given me**: for thou lovedst me before the foundation of the world.
25 O righteous Father, the world hath not known thee: but I have known thee, and these have known that thou hast sent me. And I have declared unto them thy name, and will declare it: that **the love** wherewith **thou hast loved me may be in them, and I in them**.
He is talking of coming (appearing) in His elect as The Holy Spirit, which Is the Lord (2 Corinthians 3:17), to make them One with the Lord. They with Him, walking in this earthen realm again, yet through the many member body that have become joined unto the Him, the Son.

The complete work of the Father, in and through His Son, is being written in your hearts by the Spirit, which is the Lord, and put in your mind (Hebrews 8:10; Ephesians 1:13-14)that you are sealed by His Spirit.... Marked by His Spirit.... Secured and Guaranteed by His Spirit to enter His Kingdom and Abide for ever more in that Place which is now prepared and ready for you to dwell in... in the Son of God.

Those that are predestined must be born again.... birthed by the Spirit and Water: the baptism of Jesus Christ. Jesus was the first to come forth of the Spirit, and dwell in the earth after the resurrection. Preeminence. Firstfruits of the Spirit.

1 Corinthians 15:21-23 For since by man came death, by man came also the resurrection of the dead.
For as in Adam all die, even so in Christ shall all be made alive.
But every man in his own order : **Christ the firstfruits**; afterward they that are Christ's at his coming.

Hebrews 6:19-20 Which **hope** we have as an **anchor of the soul**, both sure and stedfast, and which **entereth into that within the veil**; Whither the **forerunner is for us entered, even Jesus**, made an high priest for ever after the order of Melchisedec.

No more sin in His earthen nature. His Earthen vessel which had been sacrificed, has experienced Liberty of the sinful nature! He was without sin. He was/is all Righteousness. He obtained our Liberty. He obtained our Salvation. He obtained our Redemption – Releasing from all sin, decay, and death. The Divine Nature had come forth. And we that receive HIM, can experience the same, and be changed in the same way. Hallelujah!
2 Corinthians 3:16-18
Nevertheless when it shall turn to the Lord, the veil shall be taken away.
Now the Lord is that Spirit: and where the Spirit of the Lord is, there is liberty.

But we all, with open face beholding as in a glass the glory of the Lord, are changed into the same image from glory to glory, even as by the Spirit of the Lord.

Turn to the Lord in His Glory and Victory, and you too, can be freed the body of the sins of the flesh. He Is The Power that can do just that. Grasp a hold of His Strength, as His Strength grabs a hold of you to set you free. (Romans 6:6, 5-11)
Romans 6:6 Knowing this, that our old man is crucified with him, that the body of sin might be destroyed, that henceforth we should not serve sin. ... v11 Likewise, reckon ye also yourselves to be dead indeed unto sin, but alive unto God through Jesus Christ our Lord.

All sin and death was conquered and removed. Jesus was/is the Last Adam.... the eternal sacrifice... which came into the world to redeem all mankind, and creation from sin and death. But the only way for man to receive liberty, was to receive HIM THAT HAD OBTAINED IT. His Government IS ruling and reigning.

The sinful flesh was overcome by the sinful flesh that sinned not: the Lamb of God that came in the form of the seed of Abraham. First Adam redeemed by the Last Adam. Jesus experienced all temptation of sin yet defeated its pull and overcame it... Now in His Strength and Success, He liberates each of us, when it is our appointed time to enter His glory (1 Cor 15:22-23). We are changed. We are free from that sinful body too. He liberates us forevermore. ALL THINGS have been destroyed and put under His feet... even death (2 Timothy 1:10). It Is Done.

Now this is what is happening today.... Now from age to age, HE is continuously REDEEMING and RECONCILING all by HIS KNOWLEDGE and WORD (that is Spirit & Life). By the simplicity of Holy Spirit Preaching the Good News. So, HE sends His Son: His many member body that has been joined to the Head, to preach THIS TESTIMONY as the Father speaks through them. Those that are hearing His Voice and hearing His Good News, and hearing the declaration of His Righteousness & Blood that was shed for the continual Reconciliation & Redemption of all mankind.... are also joining them which are alive and remain, and with those that have gone on before them.... from age to age, world without end... (Ephesians 3:14-21).

For we all that have received the Lord are together with HIM Today...
John 17:22-26 (Jesus Praying to the Father)
22 And the **glory** which thou gavest me **I have given them**; that they may **be one**, even **as we are one**:
23 **I in them, and thou in me**, that they may **be made perfect in one**; and that the world may know that thou hast sent me, and hast loved them, as thou hast loved me.
24 Father, I will that they also, whom thou hast given me, **be with me where I am**; **that they may behold my glory, which thou hast given me**: for thou lovedst me before the foundation of the world.
25 O righteous Father, the world hath not known thee: but I have known thee, and these have known that thou hast sent me. And I have declared unto them thy name, and will declare it: that **the love** wherewith **thou hast loved me may be in them**, **and I in them**.

John 14:20-23 At that day ye shall know that I **am in my Father, and ye in me, and I in you**. He that hath my commandments, and keepeth them, he it is that loveth me: and he that loveth me shall be loved of my Father, and I will love him, and **will manifest myself to him**. ..... Jesus answered and said unto him, If a man love me, he will keep my words: and my Father will love him, and **we will come unto him, and make our abode with him**.

Wow... Can You Believe This: Heaven and Earth having been brought together as one, in The One – Jesus Christ.

Ephesians 1:10 That in the dispensation of the fulness of times he might **gather together in one all things in Christ, both which are in heaven , and which are on earth** ; even in him:
Galatians 4:4-5 **Tells us this dispensation of the fulness of times came....** Read it here:
v4 But when the fulness of the time was come, God sent forth his Son, made of a woman, made under the law, To redeem them that were under the law, that we might receive the adoption of son.....
v6 And because ye are sons, God hath sent forth the Spirit of his Son into your hearts, crying , Abba, Father.
Oh Hallelujah!!! TODAY if you are Hearing His Voice... Receive His Word/Him and Press on in!!!

HE has accomplished all this in past ages.... and IS Continuously Administering This from age to age: the Ministry of Reconciliation ...

2 Corinthians 5:17-19
17 Therefore if any man be in Christ, he is a new creature: old things are passed away; behold, all things are become new.
18 And all things are of God, **who hath reconciled us to himself by Jesus Christ, and hath given to us the ministry of reconciliation;**
19 **To wit, that God was in Christ, reconciling the world unto himself, not imputing their trespasses unto them; and hath committed unto us the word of reconciliation.**

Those that are alive and remain have and are joining those that have already gone on in.... **TODAY is the Day to allow God's fullness to bring your Earth and Heaven into the victory of the Son.** Allow all that you are: in spirit, soul, mind, emotions, character, and body be "redeemed" by the Blood of the Lamb of God. Experience the fullness of your redemption.

Allow your spirit, soul, & body to enter into the kingdom of God and be reconciled to the Father. Allow the Lord to appear in & through you.

The creation is waiting for the manifestation of the sons of God…. as THE SON OF GOD IMMANUEL appears through YOU ….. for you are the temple of God (many scriptures on this).

Continue the Journey of pressing in to His Kingdom…. Spirit, Soul, Mind and Body. Jesus Christ, Yeshua Messiah is appearing through His Many Member Body.

Don't allow traditions, lies, seductions, tickling of ears… keep you from the Father's purpose of His Son fully working IN You.

Romans 5: 1-5 Therefore being justified by faith, we have peace with God through our Lord Jesus Christ:
2 **By whom also we have access by faith into this grace wherein we stand, and rejoice in hope of the glory of God.**
3 And not only so, but we glory in tribulations also: knowing that tribulation worketh patience;
4 And patience, experience; and experience, **hope:**
5 And hope maketh not ashamed; because the love of God is shed abroad in our hearts by the Holy Ghost which is given unto us.

HOPE of Glory…. JESUS CHRIST IN YOU… Your security and anchor so that YOU TOO can ENTER INTO His Father's presence, and be changed in to His Divine Nature, as He had intended from the foundation of the world.
Colossians 1:27
27 To whom God would make known what is the riches of the glory of this mystery among the Gentiles; which is **Christ in you, the hope of glory**:

John 17:22-26 (Jesus Praying to the Father)

22 And the glory which thou gavest me **I have given them**; that they may **be one**, even **as we are one**:
23 **I in them, and thou in me**, that they may be made perfect in one; and that the world may know that thou hast sent me, and hast loved them, as thou hast loved me.
24 Father, I will that they also, whom thou hast given me, **be with me where I am**; **that they may behold my glory, which thou hast given me**: for thou lovedst me before the foundation of the world.
25 O righteous Father, the world hath not known thee: but I have known thee, and these have known that thou hast sent me. And I have declared unto them thy name, and will declare it: that **the love** wherewith **thou hast loved me may be in them, and I in them**.

Christ in You is Your HOPE of GLORY. Entering into Perfection & being made "Whole" ... God's Glory is swallowing us up. LOOK into His Face... SEE His Glory... and be CHANGED..... into His Same Image. Behold Your Victory.
(2 Corinthians 3:18)
But we all, with open face beholding as in a glass the glory of the Lord, are changed into the same image from glory to glory, even as by the Spirit of the Lord.

Today is your day to take the next step of Glory.... Faith, Hope and Love has established your steps in His Operation of raising you from the dead. Every day that you take a new step in Him, a new experience of His Glory is swallowing you up into His Presence... Being reconciled to the Father.

Be Free from the carnal adamic garments. God's Word is removing the old Adam by revealing the Last Adam, and producing the new man, the Second Man which is the Lord from Heaven, the Quickening Spirit. Jesus Christ is appearing through His many-member body!

" 'My Life In You' by Jesus Christ"

To those that are chosen of Him, Rejoicing! To those that are called, answer, rise from your grave and let go of your grave clothes, which is the first Adam. If you Hear His Voice, Rise Up out of your carnal grave and put on the Garments of the Son.

Amen.
RPJ

REVELATION 74
The "Birthing" is Complete

John 16:20-21 speaks of the women in travail and Jesus is explaining to the disciples that once the birthing is complete, then the sorrow will turn to joy. What was he talking about? He was telling them that the bringing in of God's new order... (Grace through Righteousness - Blood of Jesus Christ Covenant - New Priest Order - after the order of Melchesidec - judgment of that generation - fulfillment of the Law of Sin & Death, and more) ...God's order of Grace was about to be "finished." The Church in that age was experiencing the great tribulation, the regeneration that Jesus spoke of in Matthew 19:28.

So Today is after those days and that generation, yet the blessings of our Saviour expanded not only to us that are beyond then, but all those before.

What are we looking for Today, if it was "then" that all is complete?

YOUR BIRTHING (your realization & EXPERIENCE of His Presence to you and In You - pressing into) INTO WHAT ALREADY IS - The Kingdom of God has arrived and it happened in that generation. Oh Hallelujah!!!

Luke 16:16 tells us "The law and the prophets were until John: since that time the kingdom of God is preached, and every man presseth into it."

1 Corinthians 15:22-23 tells us "....so in Christ shall all be made alive. But every man in his own order: Christ the firstfruits; afterward they that are Christ's at his coming." And that he did, he came to that generation in the fulfillment of all that the Prophets had prophesied. And He is still coming (appearing, making himself manifest) in the Hearts of those the Father are

drawing unto and through the Son for Himself. (Read John 14:20-24)

John 16:22-23 Jesus says he will see them again... telling THEM that He will see Them again.

Then in verse 23 says that "in that day", and we see His instructions afterward of a wonderful "joyous" blessing for them when the birthing and tribulation is over.... Now look at John 14:20 and Jesus says "At that day...." and He declares that after it is over (at that day) they THEY ('ye' meaning them) shall know that I am in my Father, and ye in me, and I in you." Oh Hallelujah!

Now, for us Today, as HE draws us to himself and washes us in His Word (which is Spirit and Life – the living Word that is Jesus Christ – the Testimony/Witness/Record of the Father in us), we too are raptured up with all of them that were before us, and even though we too are alive and remain**, WE TOO are together with the Lord and BIRTHED into the Presence of the Lord and His Kingdom (**the scriptures in 1 Thessalonians are speaking of 'THEN' which is that generation, but we Today that are alive and remain are pressing in to Him... but it is after the fulfillment of all concerning Christ Jesus and that old order & law of sin and death).

Oh, there are such facets to see in this One Truth! Jesus Christ has provided such Liberty and JOY! for all of us to partake of. But in looking and understanding what THEY went thru with HIM in the birthing and regeneration of the Lord's New Order and Priesthood (Hebrews), we find Ephesians 2:7 telling it like it is for us.

Sure, we will and WILL go through the trying of our Faith in Jesus Christ, and will go from Faith to Faith and Glory to Glory as we are being placed in HIM (adoption of sons means "placing"), but as Ephesians 2:7 and other verses tell us...

Ephesians 2:7 That in the ages to come *(that is us),* he might show the exceeding riches of his grace (*wow - exceeding riches of grace!)* in his kindness toward us through Christ Jesus. *(Oh WOW WOW - His KINDNESS towards them after the consummation of that first order and the bringing in of the second; and HIS Kindness Towards US!!)*

Wow, and Thank you Father for your Understanding and Vision that all may See You without sin within their own soul (& world) and be changed into that same, same body!!! (without sin) !!!!

Oh glory to YOU oh Lord and Father!!! Thank You, Amen.

So you see, the "Birthing" or "Regeneration" that the scriptures spoke of, and what our Lord and Saviour Jesus Christ spoke of was to happen in that generation. Look at Matthew 23 & 24.

And even though it is fulfilled, Completed and FINISHED, just as Jesus had said, there is still the "pressing into the Kingdom" for every age afterward, and each person in their own order as the Father has determined.

Faith coming alive in you.... as His Word is spoken and you receive Him...

The Washing by His Word and Blood/Spirit within your Soul and Body, transforming & renewing your mind in Christ.

The Trying of your faith to continue in HIS faith (the Faith of the Son) as you exit death & sin, and enter into Eternal Life which is our Lord and Saviour and God (1 John 5:20).

Continue your journey....
Seek Him....

We will not have to be whipped & crucified on the Cross as He did (oh Thank YOU Father)...

But we do get to enjoy the Benefits of what He suffered for Us. What a humbling Blessing!

(THANK YOU FATHER for THIS FREE GIFT !!!!!!!!!!!!!!)

We will not have to go through the great tribulation that was prophesied and was done & completed in that generation... It was terrible what the apostles, disciples, and all of that generation had to endure in the birthing of God's new order. Matthew 24:21 Jesus says "For then shall be great tribulation, such as was not since the beginning of the world to this time, no, nor ever shall be."

Can you hear this yet? (Wow Lord! No words can express the gratitude of this!!! !!!)

But through the completion of God's plan: .... removing of the first, to establish the second... Hebrews 10:7-10 He has provided a New Covenant, New Priesthood, New Law, New Government that is Better than the Old. Through the Free Gift of the Father, His Son Jesus Christ, He wants Us to RECEIVE HIM AND ALL THE BENEFITS PROVIDED BY HIM.

(This is such a humbling Gift to be given.... The Blessings just keep coming... You can Never Repay, so just Enjoy Having a Divine Life and Relationship With Him for He Desires for Us to be Co-Heirs of all with Him... OH Hallelujah! HE is the Head.)

Sure, we will have our own trying of faith (I say again), and we will have to endure situations and be overcomers of obstacles in our situations, because these are placed there of the Lord, our Father who loves us much. And placed there to LEARN of HIM - HIS WAY to handle all situations... HIS Way to administer HIS Life to others....

So our responsibility, in whatever "place" we have been placed in Him, is to LISTEN to Him and be OBEDIENT to Him. That will settle all issues.

Oh glory to YOU oh Lord and Father!!! Thank You, Amen.

There are soooo many more scriptures to reveal this "setting free" Truth, and we can show them to you. Meet us at one of our services and lets dig in more.

Amen.
RPJ

REVELATION 75
God's Provision of Liberty (From Adam's Rib to Women's Lib Takes On a New Meaning)

My husband was making this comment on Facebook the other day, and it stirred up the fact that many people have not realized the TRUTH of the liberation of women AND men from the Curse of the Lord after the fall. It is worth Knowing. So here is a comment I had written concerning God's Liberation to man and woman.....

From Adam's Rib to Women's Lib is what my husband wrote..... of course the Women's lib here is speaking of those women that burned the bras and were in "fight" mode for their freedom to do things that man was not letting them do.... But the fight isn't necessary, and this article is Not concerning That Movement.

IT IS ABOUT THE MOVEMENT OF GOD to Liberate ALL SOULS.

When man listened to the women instead of being obedient to God, all mankind fell and God put a curse on the serpent who started the whole mess, on the woman, and on the man.

Read Genesis 3:14-19. This WAS the Curse. Here is what the curse was to each:

To the Serpent, God said: Because thou hast done this, thou art cursed above all cattle, and above every beast of the field: upon thy belly shalt thou go, and dust shalt thou eat all the days of thy life...

To the Woman, God said: I will greatly multiply thy sorrow and thy conception; in sorrow thou shall bring forth children; and thy desire shall be to thy husband, and he shall rule over thee...

To the Man, God said: cursed is the ground for thy sake; in sorrow shalt thou eat of it all the days of thy life; Thorns also and thistles shall it bring forth to thee; and thou shall eat the herb of the field; In the sweat of thy face shalt thou eat bread, till thou return unto the ground; for out of it wast thou taken: for dust thou art, and unto dust shalt thou return.

Wow.... THIS was the Curse of God on Man and Woman.... THIS .... WAS THE CURSE.

NOW **IN CHRIST JESUS THE** CURSE IS REMOVED! You Are LIBERATED by His Blood that was shed on that cross. HE took that curse on Himself to pay the price of liberation for all Souls. !!! He being the LAST ADAM corrected all that the First Adam had done.

NOW we that have Received HIM – the Son of God – LAST ADAM..... We REAP OF HIS OBEDIENCE! Hallelujah! And Are Married To The King and Priest of All! Glory Lord, Hallelujah!

From the curse of God, to His Glorious Liberty, only to be made HIS WIFE of Glory, Righteousness, Peace, and Joy.... Where His Rule is Forever... and we are Faithful and Loyal to Him only... GRACE abounding in His Righteousness unto Eternal Life... We are Restored, Redeemed, Reconciled to the Head of the Family. Reaping of His Actions Forever.

Oh, How can or could anyone turn away from such a Salvation and Gift! This Is the Marriage of the Son... That Soul that is the Eternal Sacrifice now has a Soul that is His Wife... so the two can work as One in both Heaven And Earth... as the Son – One Identity!!!

The earth is the Lord's and the fullness thereof, and all the inhabitants... Oh Souls, we have a magnificent King... He is the Lord from Heaven, the quickening Spirit.... Abiding within our Souls. He has not only redeemed us, and reconciled us, but has CONSECRATED US for His own purpose and Glory.

Here is the comment noted in facebook:

"Actually women has been liberated... freed from the Curse that God put on women at the fall of man. Read Genesis 3:16 this is verse that shows the curse to the woman was that her desire would be to the man and he would rule over her. But Now In Christ Jesus the Curse has been removed, so now the Women, just like the Men, are to Submit to The Head which is Christ Jesus. So if the Lord has given you a Woman/Wife then if All Souls (male or female) are to Submit to the Lord, then LOVE and HONOR will abound between man and woman and Harmony will be the produce of that relationship. And if one goes off in the carnal mind, then the other is to HELP them come back to the Head by praying in the Holy Spirit's instructions for that situation. Submit to The Head of the Family all you Souls.... then Harmony and Peace in His Love will flow. Be Blessed.! And Free! Liberty of Christ and In Christ is SWEET SMELLING SAVOR!!!! God gave this and more to me a long time ago to set and make me free from the traditions that I had been taught as a child. xoxo"

So to the Women that God has joined to a Man, submit to the Lord your Head, and allow the Lord's Love and Character (Fruit of the Spirit) to flow towards that man: Honor, Respect, and the Special times too. Also the Man that God has joined to a Woman, submit to the Lord who is your Head, and also allow the Lord's Love and Character (Fruit of the Spirit) to flow towards that woman: Honor,Respect, and the Special times too. If one of you acts out in the carnal mind's character or actions, then the other should deal with this by the leading of the Lord who is in you, so to bring that harmony back again... Team Work in the Lord. Each of you has a mind that the Lord is in the process of RENEWING... so be in prayer, and submit to the PERFECT One that will give you the victory every time.

The Woman is Not to Lord over the Man; and Man is Not to Lord over the Woman... But as Christ Jesus as the Head of both, let

LOVE be the guide and basis for ALL actions to each. Then your relationship will also Prosper. Desire God’s Best for Each Other.

Not Only is Women liberated from the curse, but Men too... So that they, who are in Christ Jesus, should not have to labor in this earth so hard anymore. Enter into His Rest. But if they will submit to the Head of the Household and ask of Him how and where, etc to provide the provision for His household, then it would be provided for them...

Does this mean Man or Woman should be “lazy”? NO. But we all should seek the Lord in ALL our doings, submitting to Him in ALL the areas of our life. The Lord will give the direction needed, and make provision as needed, just as Jesus did in the earth too.

All Souls submit to the Head: our Lord and Saviour Jesus Christ and Ask of the Father for the next step.

He knows what you have need of (Matthew 6:33; Matthew 11:28-30) and will make provision. Watch and See. By miracle or an Angel or by a tool in the earth (job, business idea, etc)... His Provision(Grace) is Sufficient. Whether it is Spiritually, or in the Natural realm, or even monetary area that is needing the Lord’s provision, **He Loves us and is able to take care of His Family**.

Jesus, by miracles, made provision for a wedding feast by turning water to wine.... by multiplying what fish and bread was available to feed thousands,... by paying the tax bill by the miracle of a coin in the first fish.... So brothers and sisters, look to the Head of our family and REST in His LOVE and Care for you.
Be free from the traditions of the world and mankind and religion.... Let the Lord Show You, Teach You, and Send His Provision to you in whatever way He chooses. He may send His Chosen to you for your miracle, as the Prophet in the old testament was sent to the prophet’s widow and gave her instructions on how to have her bill provided for and paid. He

gave her instructions, she followed them, and the miracle was performed. Provision was made. Always submit only to the Lord and His Word.

The Curse is Removed.... Be free in God's Provision of Liberty!!!

Amen.
RPJ

REVELATION 76
God's Clean Up Vessels

Are you in need of a Spiritual Vacuum cleaner or a weed (debris) blower?

Is it time to be a spiritual vacuum cleaner that sucks up the dirt from the feet of those that have trampled into your "living room"? Then discards it in the garbage.

or Is it time to be that weed and debris blower that blows the path clean before you?

Ask the Holy Spirit to be your vacuum cleaner and weed blower to clean up your living space and path He has you on, so your journey can be more "in joy-able". Of course, you will have to participate in that cleanup....

The Holy Spirit In you Is The Only Power that will do the job perfectly.

You have become (and some are becoming) the Lord's Word, that vacuum cleaner or weed blower, that will affect your dwelling and the dwelling of others, as the Lord moves in their lives...

Thank you Father!

Amen.
RPJ

REVELATION 77
His Perfect One

The Lord knows what you need to go through and what you have to go through, to cause you to become the vessel, the instrument, that member of the Son that He needs you to be. You have submitted all and surrendered all…. now hold on…. don't give up.

Stand fast in Christ. Don't let go of the first stone, the corner stone that holds it all together.

The reward, of His Presence and You as One, is most precious and cost a great price. Victory Is. Follow the Lord's lead……

One Voice, One Heart, One Spirit……..

Consecrated, set apart for His good pleasure and purpose. All that you are Is His. Surrendered. All that you have Is His. Given Up.

The reward of giving up your life, Is His. Hallelujah!

To Those that Have Ears to hear, hear what the ending of this Is……………

Amen.
RPJ

" 'My Life In You' by Jesus Christ"

REVELATION 78
"You are greater than me"

"You are greater than me" an Angel could say.

Yet he was sent to help you get what you needed and where you needed to go.

Jesus needed them in all ways: provide strength, deliverance, provision, etc....

Miracles are performed by God's spoken word and thought, and angels help to administer some of those actions.

Many years ago at the beach,God gave me a heart for valentine day, and it was made of sandstone.... First, He or someone had to have made it. Second, someone had to have delivered it. And third, it was God that spoke in my soul that day and resolved all issues.

On another day, there were angel hands carrying that birthday cake with flickering candles on it, and angels that sang "Happy Birthday" to me. God's Holy Angels are all around, for our good.

The Comforter has appeared for many people and myself. He is here. The Spirit of Truth, the Spirit of the Son, the One and only Spirit that raised Jesus from the grave is come for you and me, and is in us. He has made us His dwelling place. And by Him we are joined to a many-membered body: Body of the Son, Jesus Christ. For those that have not encountered the Lord and have not been sealed with that Holy Spirit, then ask of the Lord. A change for the better will occur.

That in its self is a miracle. Miracles and Provision.....
Miracles and Provision. God has been speaking that. His people are needing His help and He is sending and has sent His help.

Don’t refuse your help from the Lord.

You are greater than angels..... And angels are sent to help you. It was for Your sake that Jesus was sent to die on the cross and be raised again.... You are of much value... The value and price of His only begotten Son. All souls belong to God, scripture tells us. All souls does the Lord desires to redeem and reconcile back to Him. So speak all you that are of the Son, speak and declare the Righteousness of the Son. The dead can only rise when THAT VOICE is speaking: The Voice of the Son. Then the dead Hear His Voice and begin to Rise from their graves of death, and enter in through the Son to the Father.

Scripture tells us that all were dead, if so that Jesus died for all. Now through the Son, can all be made alive. But until they “hear His Voice” they will not know to come forth.

Don’t be weary doing the work of the Lord, for a plan is unfolding, and the mystery is being revealed. And the saints and witnesses are gathering around as one more soul is entering in through the Son.

Rejoice and Hallelujah!!! Miracles and Provision is Here.

Amen.
RPJ

REVELATION 79
Righteousness Is Come

Are you waiting for Righteousness? Then continue in Hope until you HEAR the Voice of the Lord declaring HIS RIGHTEOUSNESS for you, and Receive Him that has obtained all Salvation for Us.... now be Free having obtained His Righteousness and your Liberty.

He that is Perfect Is Come – Receive Him... and be Perfect too.

Hosea 10:12 Sow to yourselves in righteousness, reap in mercy; break up your fallow ground: for it is time to seek the Lord, till he come and rain righteousness upon you.

Then, Romans 3:20-22
Therefore by the deeds of the law there shall no flesh be justified in his sight: for by the law is the knowledge of sin. But now the righteousness of God without the law is manifested, being witnessed by the law and the prophets; Even **the righteousness of God which is by faith of Jesus Christ unto all and *upon all them that believe***: for there is no difference:

Now the Righteousness of God through Jesus Christ has come and is manifested. It is manifested TO ALL, but it is not applied to the benefit of each one until they Believe - "upon all them that believe." Although God's new order of Grace, Righteousness and Authority of His Son is over all, those that have not believed are yet still in their sin and judged so, yet so under Grace.

So how will they believe unless the ones that God has sent speaks and preaches by that Holy Spirit the testimony of the Father concerning the Son ....

Then they Hear, and Faith comes alive and they Receive Him that has obtained our Liberty and Provision which causes us to be ReJoined Unto The Father in the Kingdom.... ministry of

Reconciliation continuing to work from age to age, yet by that same Spirit that raised Jesus from the grave, now raising each and every one of us, yet in the appointed order. Hallelujah! Amen! Righteousness working..... and setting all free.

In Jeremiah 4:2-4 the word of the Lord is commanding them to stop being so hard hearted (break up fallow ground) and free themselves from the flesh of the heart (carnal spirit; unregenerated mind; disobedience; unrighteousness). This is so symbolic of what the Lord requires of us, yet it is through hearing of Jesus Christ, receiving Him, and allowing His Spirit and Presence to circumcise our hearts by the His word washing and cleansing us (John 6:63; Ephesians 5:26-27; John 15:3, James 1:18-21; and many more verses of confirmation).

Colossians 2:11 says it best...
11 In whom also ye are circumcised with the circumcision made without hands, in putting off the body of the sins of the flesh by the circumcision of Christ:
Coming out of duality, and becoming One in Christ.

By God's Word being spoken (written) in your heart and mind, will you be delivered and set you free... For it is Life Eternal abiding In You.... delivering to you all Provisions necessary for the earthen living, and spiritual living. (2 Peter 1:3)
Here are a couple other scriptures on this...

Rom 2:28-29 But he is not a Jew, which is one outwardly; neither is that circumcision, which is outward in the flesh: But he is a Jew, which is one inwardly; and circumcision is that of the heart, in the spirit, and not in the letter; whose praise is not of men, but of God.

Rom 4:11 And he received the sign of circumcision, a seal of therighteousness of the faith which he had yet being uncircumcised: that he might be the father of all them that believe, though they be not circumcised; that righteousness might be imputed unto them also:

The Word of God received within your heart By Faith.... This Word is the water you are baptized in by the Holy Spirit, and works in you as a two-edged sword that cuts away the carnal mind and spirit. ... sealed by the Holy Spirit and confirming that you belong to the Lord.

Now you are "marked" with the markings of the Lord Jesus Christ. His Death is Testament abiding in your Soul, and declaring His Righteousness as your right to His Blessings and Benefits. Resurrection and Life abiding in You.... An Eternal Right(standing) and Inheritance.

This is God's Will for us.

Amen.
RPJ

REVELATION 80
"Devil Destroyed" or can be called "Success" 

If you have the death of Jesus Christ declared within your soul, then the devil is destroyed in you and his works too.

And if you have the death of Jesus Christ in you, then you must have the Resurrection abiding in you and seated in His throne, your mind, and you have the Victory over every adversary.

Hebrews 2:14-15 Forasmuch then as the children are partakers of flesh and blood, he also himself likewise took part of the same; **that through death** he might destroy him that had the power of death, that is, the devil; And deliver them who through fear of death were all their lifetime subject to bondage.

1 John 3:8 He that committeth sin is of the devil; for the devil sinneth from the beginning. **For this purpose** the Son of God was manifested, that he might destroy the works of the devil.

1 John 4:4 ye are of God, little children, and have overcome them: because greater is he that is in you, than he that is in the world.

And the prince that was of the world IS ALREADY JUDGED. Jesus took care of that too.

John 12:31-32 Now is the judgment of this world: now shall the prince of this world be cast out. And I, if I be lifted up from the earth, will draw all men unto me. (This already took place back then)

John 16:11 Of judgment, because the prince of this world is judged.

Your Faith causes you to overcome all obstacles. As in 1 John 5:4-5...

1 John 5:4-5 For whatsoever is born of God overcometh the world: and this is the victory that overcometh the world, even our faith. Who is he that overcometh the world, but he that believeth that Jesus is the Son of God? This is he that came by water and blood, even Jesus Christ; not by water only, but by water and blood. And it is the Spirit that beareth witness, because the Spirit is truth. (awww the Father in the Son)

So, if you have that TESTIMONY ... That Witness and Record of the Father concerning the Son written within your mind and soul, then the devil, satan is destroyed and his works are destroyed.

You are Sealed by the Spirit of Truth, declaring the work of the Son **successful** in you and for you.

Now that is SUCCESS.

Now Jesus Christ, who lived, and died, and lives forevermore is alive and living and working in you to bring you in to His Perfect Place in Himself. Causing you to be "born again" and "resurrected" with Him in His Glory. (John 17)

Stand in the liberty of Jesus Christ.... Galatians 5:1 Stand fast therefore in the liberty wherewith Christ hath made us free, and be not entangled again with the yoke of bondage.

Amen.
RPJ

REVELATION 81
Sanctified by the Father and Son – Spirit of Truth

2 Thessalonians 2:11-14
11 And for this cause God shall send them strong delusion, that they should believe a lie:
12 That they all might be damned who believed not the truth, but had pleasure in unrighteousness.
13 But we are bound to give thanks alway to God for you, brethren beloved of the Lord, because God hath from the beginning chosen you to salvation **through sanctification of the Spirit and belief of the truth**:
14 Whereunto he called you by our gospel, to the obtaining of the glory of our Lord Jesus Christ.

Simply put..... Sanctified by the Spirit of Truth... He will guide you... through the WAY... into the Kingdom of God.

Jesus is the Way, the Truth, and the Life, right? Right. John 14:6 Jesus saith unto him, I am the way, the truth, and the life: no man cometh unto the Father, but by me.

By TRUTH we come to the Father: The Spirit of Truth. To take you through all the scriptures may be too much so here is the condensed version of today's message.

The Spirit within the Son was the Father. It was the Father that spoke in the Son, then the Son spoke what the Father said. It was the Father that drew you or any to the Son, and only through the Son could any of us come to the Father and enter His Kingdom. Teamwork. They understood each other, the goal, and how to achieve it. How? They are ONE. Their MIND (Spirit) that moved each of its members was the SAME SINGLE MIND. There was One SOUL that was to become the Eternal Soul, and One Head and Body: all working and flowing by that SAME SPIRIT in Harmony of God's plan.

John 14:10 Believest thou not that I am in the Father, and the Father in me? the words that I speak unto you I speak not of myself: but the Father that dwelleth in me, he doeth the works.

The Father was not out somewhere separate from the Son, who was man. This man was all man yet the one and only God was fully in this man. Thus making the Son. The visible image of the invisible God.

The Son, and Father were abiding together and the Father was working His operation through the Son to cause US to be one with them.... In heaven AND Earth... God's Family abiding in the SAME SPIRIT OF TRUTH... the SAME MIND.

The Plan was made, His purpose revealed and manifested... a complete work was done. NOW this work of the operation of the Father in the Son is now causing us to be REUNITED REDEEMED back with the Father , yet we must go Through the Son.

The WAY. The Spirit of Truth washes us, prepares us by the salvation of God which is the Word that is spirit and life... which is God's testament of His Son engraved in our souls... the Blood Covenant of the Eternal Sacrifice... God's promises... God's Word. He gave His Word and Sealed our Souls with the Word of Truth. Now That Spirit is Power working in us to bring us and secure us in the Father and Son in Kingdom.

HE has caused us to become One with His Son, and with Him. We are God's inheritance, redeemed by the price of much value. We... are... that... desirable to the Father.... His Holy Habitation. The Life of His Son for the Redemption of ours from the grave of death, so HE can LIVE IN and THROUGH Us. The visible image of the invisible God. !!!

“ ‘My Life In You’ by Jesus Christ”

John 14:17 Even the Spirit of truth; whom the world cannot receive, because it seeth him not, neither knoweth him: but ye know him; for he dwelleth with you, and shall be in you.

John 15:26 But when the Comforter is come, who I will send unto you from the Father, even the Spirit of truth, which proceedeth from the Father, he shall testify of me: ...

John 16:13-16 Howbeit when he, the Spirit of truth, is come, he will guide you into all truth: for he shall not speak of himself; but whatsoever he shall hear, that shall he speak: and he will show you things to come....

John 17:17-19 Sanctify them through thy truth: thy word is truth. As thou hast sent me into the world, even so have I also sent them into the world. And for their sakes I sanctify myself, that they also might be sanctified through the truth.

James 1:18-21 Of his own will begat he us with the word of truth, that we should be a kind of firstfruits of his creatures.... Wherefore lay apart all filthiness and superfluity of naughtiness, and receive with meekness the engrafted word, which is able to save your souls.

.... death is in the tongue.... God has spoken... Receive Truth and Live.

Amen.
RPJ

REVELATION 82
Joined unto the Lord Only

In reading Luke 16:18, verse 18 the Lord began talking and revealing truth. Then moved me to verse 13. Then verse 9.

Luke 16:18 Whosoever putteth away his wife, and marrieth another, committeth adultery: and whosoever marrieth her that is put away from her husband committeth adultery.

We all have heard and read this and understood it. But then the Lord moved me to verse 13 which states:

Luke 16:13 No servant can serve two masters: for either he will hate the one, and love the other; or else he will hold to the one, and despise the other. Ye cannot serve God and mammon.

Then HE connected them... Verse 18 that talks of adultery, is talking of those that serve mammon instead of God. Or those that are trying to serve God, while having money control them (lack of or abundance of).

God alone must be all that controls our every move. In Him we live, and move, and have our being. So, God alone should we give place to... in setting up how our lives should be lived. What work we do in the earth to do for His glory... where to live... church to go to or start up... etc...... HE alone is our supplier, and source of everything. Not money or job or entrepreneurship.

Don't let mammon and greed or riches or goals cheat out God from being the head of your passion. Let God Be Your Passion and REASON for doing what you do. Allow Him to be head of all in our lives to direct us in the way we should go. Not Him following our lead, but us following His lead. Giving back our life, for His... and for His purpose. (Galatians 2:20)

So, Luke 16 verse 18 is speaking of verse 13. Then He took me to verse 9 which balances this all out....
Luke 16:9 And I say unto you, Make to yourselves friends of the mammon of unrighteousness: that, when ye fail, they may receive you into everlasting habitations.

I have taken this step of yielding to God in all things, and it has not always been easy. Yet, it is rewarding in my soul to know that He is my source and supply for all things: in heaven and earth. He blessed His Kings with much material wealth etc..... He does not want us to be without, but He does desire us to trust Him for all. All spiritual and natural blessings are for us... The earth is the Lords and the fullness thereof, etc... so it is for us too, those that have received Him. Seek God.... He will provide.

Matthew 6:32-34 v33 But seek ye first the kingdom of God, and his righteousness; and all these things shall be added unto you.

Wisdom is the principal thing. Understanding establishes the house, and knowledge fills it. (Proverbs 24:3-4; Prov 9:1; Prov 4:7)

Let God speak in you by the Voice of Wisdom, Understanding, and Knowledge... and abide in His Comfort.

Amen.
RPJ

REVELATION 83
End Time Message is a Past Tense Occurrence 

Before reading this you will need the Holy Spirit guiding you within your mind... or you will not be able to see or hear with the Lord's understanding. So ask the Lord to open your understanding to His will and plan.

First, when you read the bible you need to read with the understanding that it was written to them in that age and generation. Then with the Holy Spirit you can understand how it applies to you in this age and generation.

Read in this book the following Revelations:
Revelation 47
Revelation 68
Revelation 69
Revelation 74
Revelation 85
Revelation 101

Now as you read Luke 24:44 you will see that Jesus, having risen from the grave, was appearing to the disciples/apostles a little at a time. But they wouldn't know that it was him until he opened up their understanding, yet their spirit burned within them of the Lord.

Luke 24:44 And he said unto them, These are the words which I spake unto you, while I was yet with you, that all things must be fulfilled, which were written in the law of Moses, and in the prophets, and in the psalms, concerning me.

Note in Luke 24:44 Jesus just told them in that generation, that all things must be fulfilled concerning him and that it was being accomplished then... in that moment of time.

Everything in the Law of Moses, in the prophets, and in the psalms that was written of him had then and was being fulfilled.

So it is not for our future, for it was in that generation and age that all things that were written concerning Jesus Christ in the law and prophets and psalms, were fulfilled back in that time.... not in our future.

Matthew 23:36 and 24:34 says
23:36 Verily I say unto you, All these things shall come upon this generation.
24:34 Verily I say unto you, This generation shall not pass, till all these things be fulfilled.

Jesus was speaking and these are the things he spoke to them of that Luke 24:44 talks of that were to be fulfilled, and then was... in that generation.

Also in Matthew 24:21 Jesus tells them
24:21 For then shall be great tribulation, such as was not since the beginning of the world to this time, no, nor ever shall be.

Jesus said to them that the Great Tribulation was going to come on that generation. Not us now but back then... and IT DID. It was terrible! And that is putting it lightly! Read Josephus and other historical documents written of all that happened back then. Too horrible to write here.

And JESUS SAYS For then.... that generation and age and time... will be great tribulation, such as was not since the beginning of the world ... to this time (that generation not us), and no, nor ever shall be.... which is speaking of every age and generation after that time... which includes us today.

So those waiting for a great tribulation to come in our future is in error of the scriptures.

It already happened as Jesus said it would... concerning him and that generation.

And Our age will not have to endure such great tribulation as that age did... Praise the Lord and Thank the Lord!!! amen.

So what for us today? ENTER His Kingdom which is Righteousness, Peace, and Joy that is in the Holy Spirit (Romans 14:17, Luke 17:21; John 3:3-5; Luke 16:16)

So what is for us today? Ephesians 2:7
That in the ages to come (that is us and every age after that generation)... That in the ages to come he might show the exceeding riches of his grace in his kindness toward us through Christ Jesus.

IN HIS KINDNESS toward us THROUGH CHRIST JESUS. AMEN.

Praise the Lord! for all that had to endure that generation's judgment, so that we may walk in the newness of the Spirit and not in the oldness of the letter.

One more scripture.... I was asking the Lord for a scripture on his coming during that age to judge them in that generation and He gave me Matthew 10:23.... to those that have His Spirit to understand... be Free and Walk in the Liberty of the Lord!

Matthew 10:19-23 *23 But when they persecute you in this city, flee ye into another: for verily I say unto you, Ye shall not have gone over the cities of Israel, till the Son of man be come.

Jesus was returning <u>in that generation</u> in power and glory and with the cloud of witnesses to judge That Generation and Age.

Jesus told them that they would not have time to go over the cities of Israel, because He would come back to judge before they would have time to do that.... in that generation and age.

Praise the Lord! for all that had to endure the changing of garments of the world... being freed from the working of the flesh order and law of sin and death...... translated into the regeneration of the kingdom of God that was then and is now a working of the Spirit in the law of the Spirit of life in Christ Jesus.

Praise to the Lamb of God and Son for the Father's work is Done.

Grace abounds now, where sin once was.

Righteousness reigns now, where Corruption once was.

Mercy is evident now, where Judgment once was.

Eternal Life is flowing and sustaining us, where death once was destroying us.

For the Blood of Jesus Christ, the Lamb of God who was alive, yet died in our place, and now is alive forever more.

Now we can abide In Him, in the Life that is more abundant.
To God Be The Glory and Honor forever.

Amen.
RPJ

REVELATION 84
Armor of God: For the Mature Ones

The other night I had a dream and in the dream there was a corn field with high stalks, and then people appeared in midst of the field and began walking out of the field to enter an open door. More was done in the dream, but when I woke I asked the Lord if this was just one of those “funky” dreams or was there a meaning to it from Him. Then the understanding began to come:

Understanding is that the high stalks of corn were mature.... the people were those people of the Lord, His saints that had come to some maturity. And God wants them to put on the Armor of God.

So in further obedience to the Lord, here is the understanding of the armor of God for you that may not know or understand; and for those that do know and understand, here is a refreshing of the armor of God:

Ephesians 6:10-20 Finally, my brethren, be strong in the Lord, and in the power of his might. Put on the whole armour of God, that ye may be able to stand against the wiles of the devil. For we wrestle not against flesh and blood, but against principalities, against powers, against the rulers of the darkness of this world, against spiritual wickedness in high places. Wherefore take unto you the **whole armour of God**, that ye may be able to withstand in the evil day, and **having done all, to stand**. Stand therefore, having your loins girt about with truth, and having on the breastplate of righteousness; And your feet shod with the preparation of the gospel of peace; Above all, taking the shield of faith, wherewith ye shall be able to quench all the fiery darts of the wicked.

And take the helmet of salvation, and the sword of the Spirit, which is the word of God: Praying always with all prayer and supplication in the Spirit, and watching thereunto with all perseverance and supplication for all saints; And for me, that utterance may be given unto me, that I may open my mouth boldly, to make known the mystery of the gospel, For which I am an ambassador in bonds: that therein I may speak boldly, as I ought to speak.

Armor of God

Stand In and having...

1. Your Mind Established in Truth
2. Anchored in The Righteousness of Jesus Christ
3. Your Walk bathed in Peace of Jesus Christ towards all as much as possible (Forgiveness) "Preparation" means "to make ready" – Jesus washed their feet (See notes below)
4. Shield yourself in and by FAITH

Knowing that GOD's LOVE towards you never fails

Knowing that God's Love towards them will overcome all evil.

Faith is the substance of things hoped for, the evidence of things not seen: God is with you, In you, and surrounds you... for your protection in every situation He sends you.

5. "Have Faith in God" Mark 11:22-26

Helmet of Salvation: All Grace Abounds in Righteousness unto Eternal Life... Remember You Have the Victory and have overcome the enemy, for greater is Christ IN you than he that is in the world.... Overcame by the Blood of the Lamb and the Word of His Testimony. Joined unto the head which is Christ Jesus.

(1 John 4:4; Rev 12:10-11)

6. Sword of the Spirit – God's Word (God's word, not man's or religion)
7. Praying always in the Spirit with all manner of prayer and with all supplication

8. Watching with "perseverance and supplication" for all saints

I am directed by the Lord to express the 3rd point the most here.
<u>your feet shod with the preparation of the gospel of peace</u>

First, the Lord says that the word preparation means to wash. So I looked it up in Strongs and it says there "to make ready".

TO MAKE READY to walk in the right manner and mind. So have your feet, the thoughts you think on that cause you to walk in a certain manner and behavior, made ready – prepared - to go... This is the birthing that has come forth by the "preparation and washing" by Jesus Christ – God's Truth – God's Word. (John 3:3-5; Ephesians 5:25-27; 1 Peter 1:22-23; and more) Renewing of your mind in the Spirit of Christ. Your feet walk according to your mind.

Shod – covering. 5265 in Strong's meaning to "bind under one's feet". Sounds like a foundation.

To wrap your feet securely in the Foundation of the Gospel of Peace. Okay. So.... having your feet or rather having every step you take be Ready to go, having been anchored and secured in the Foundation of Gospel which is Jesus Christ. (Hebrews 5:12-14, Hebrews 6:1-3)
But it says to have your feet shod WITH THE PREPARATION OF.... So how can your feet be secured in the Preparation. What is the Preparation? Awwww.... now we come to the fun part...

The Preparation is all in the BIRTHING or BEING BORN AGAIN process. PREPARATION OF is the WASHING OF THE WATER BY THE WORD.

Once you have been "prepared"... made ready by the washing of the water by the word... you then being born again can go forth.... covered and secured and grounded steps in God's love....

Your feet are clothed in the "preparation"... The Prophet Elijah was to be the one to come and PREPARE the way for Jesus to be manifested to Israel as the Lamb and King and Priest....

Once that was done, Jesus took over that role of Prophet, who WASHES us... and PREPARES us to RECEIVE the SON, KINGDOM, and FATHER.... AND.... THAT...IS...HIM.... RECEIVING.... US. ENTERED IN TO THE KINGDOM OF GOD BY BEING WASHED AND CLEANSED IN HIS BLOOD AND WORD, SPIRIT, AND WATER.... OHHH HAPPY DAY! WHEN JESUS WASHED OUR SINS AWAY!!!

So, Now, allow the Lord to WASH You in His Word which is the Gospel of Peace. In this He is washing your feet as He did to the disciples and commanded them to wash one another's feet... forgiving one another. Look at this....

John 13:3-11
3 Jesus knowing that the Father had given all things into his hands, and that he was come from God, and went to God;
4 He riseth from supper, and laid aside his garments; and took a towel, and girded himself.
5 After that he poureth water into a bason, and began to wash the disciples' feet , and to wipe them with the towel wherewith he was girded.
6 Then cometh he to Simon Peter: and Peter saith unto him, Lord, dost thou wash my feet ?
7 Jesus answered and said unto him, What I do thou knowest not now; but thou shalt know hereafter.
8 Peter saith unto him, Thou shalt never wash my feet . Jesus answered him, **If I wash thee not, thou hast no part with me.**
9 Simon Peter saith unto him, Lord, not my feet only, but also my hands and my head.

10 Jesus saith to him, He that is washed needeth not save to wash his feet , but is clean every whit: and ye are clean, but not all.
11 For he knew who should betray him; therefore said he, Ye are not all clean.

Look at what Jesus did.... it is all symbolic of what He was about to do then and how it would affect them ... and now us.
* He took off his garments: laying down His life for all
* Stood up as the New Life being the Resurrection & Life for all that would receive Him
* Towel (linen)was symbolic of Righteousness – Truth and Life
  As a Priest, he poured the new water in a clean bason – Washing of the Water by the Word. John 15:3 Jesus declares that they are clean through the word He has spoken to them. Also in John 17... word of truth....sanctifed. And WASHED us in new life: HIS New Life and Identity as The New Priest and King sanctifying and justifying them.

The earth is the Lord's footstool, and blessed are the feet of those that carry the gospel... and Jesus is that Water of Life to WASH THE WORLD.... but only to those that HEAR THIS GOOD NEWS and RECEIVE HIM can they benefit of it....

Romans 10:13-15 And how shall they preach, except they be sent? as it is written, **How beautiful are the feet of them that preach the gospel of peace, and bring glad tidings of good things**!

SOOOO... He is SENDING YOU AS A PREPARED PEOPLE.... to STAND in the full Armor of God.
Let God Be Glorified In His Saints.... God's Habitation and Family.

Revelation 12:10-11 And I heard a loud voice saying in heaven, **Now is come** salvation, and strength, and the kingdom of our God, and the power of his Christ: for the accuser of our brethren is cast down, which accused them before our God day and night.

And they overcame him by the blood of the Lamb, and by the word of their testimony; and they loved not their lives unto the death.

Amen.
RPJ

REVELATION 85
Apocalypse: Revelation of Jesus Christ

The word Revelation in Revelation 1:1 means "disclosure; to remove the cover; to unveil something that is hidden". This word Revelation is the Greek word "apokalupsis."

It is amazing how so many people want to turn this into a "sensationalism theology" rather than what it really is.

Revelation 1:1-2 The **revelation** of Jesus Christ, which God gave unto him, **to show unto his servants** things which **must shortly come to pass**; and he sent and signified it by his angel unto his servant John: who bare record of the word of God, and of the testimony of Jesus Christ, and of all things that he saw.

The Revelation... the unveiling of the beginning and the end, Jesus Christ. To give Understanding to his servants of what "**must shortly come to pass**"..... in that generation.

Apokalupsis is what many false teachings have used to express their false end of the world or end time theories. Apokalupsis is where they get the word Apocalypse. It only means to "disclose or uncover". And in this instance it is speaking of Jesus Christ.

The unveiling of the hidden mystery... Look at Colossians 1:25-27 "Whereof I am made a minister, according to the dispensation of God which is given to me for you, to fulfil the word of God; Even **the mystery** which hath been hid from ages and from generations, but now is **made manifest to his saints**: **To whom God would make known what is the riches of the glory of this mystery among the Gentiles; which is Christ in you, the hope of glory**:..."

Now back to Revelation 1:1-2... It was the revealing of what was about to happen "shortly" in their generation which was about

Jesus Christ bringing an end to that "world" or "age" and birthing in the New Order: New Heaven and Earth where God would dwell. The Regeneration that Jesus spoke of in Matthew 19:28. A Change of the Blood Covenant, Priesthood, Law, everything happening in that generation.... Hebrews 10:9 reveals the removing the first to establish the second.

They were in transition and it was the worst tribulation that had ever been nor ever would be.... Matthew 24:21 (Jesus speaking) For then shall be great tribulation, such as was not since the beginning of the world to this time, **no, nor ever shall be**." WOW!

"This Time" was them in That Generation. We live in the "nor ever shall be" ages. See... Jesus told them it was going to happen in their generation, not ours. There had to come the "judgment" from that law before it was closed, fulfilled, completed, and before Jesus could fully birth in the New Order after Melchisedec Priesthood, rules, law, etc.

Jesus fulfilled all Righteousness, Judgment, and Payment of Sin/Death for all under that order of the law of sin and death. That law was a working of the flesh; so God in the flesh man - Jesus Christ - came and FULFILLED every fleshly ordinance for us all under that order!!!!

That old law could not cleanse the conscience, so a better covenant of blood, and promises were made and revealed in and of and by Jesus Christ: The Last Adam - The Lamb of God that lives for ever as our Intercessor and Redeemer.

He Stands at (as) the door of Death and Sin that is of the old and Declares it Fulfilled and Shut..... He Stands as the Door of Life and says it is open to all that receive me, the Son of God, the Lamb of God. Come Through Me to ENTER. Oh please hear this!

He is the veil which is the flesh that was given for the world, so that all that receive and eat His Flesh/Word/Bread (water) and Drink His Blood/Life/Wine (Spirit) may ENTER in to His Kingdom and live for ever.

Receive His Testament that the Father is speaking to you.

What He has shut, none can open. What He has opened, none can shut. He is the KEY to all. Hallelujah, so much to say here... Perhaps another time... Let's continue.

The Father draws whom He will to the Son, and the Son reveals the Father to whom He pleases. (John 6:44; John 6:65; John 6:53-58; Matt 11:17; Luke 10:22)

Hebrews 10:20 By a new and living way, which he hath consecrated for us, through the veil, that is to say, his flesh;...

Now, the new is established and we press into His Kingdom of Righteousness, Peace, and Joy that is in His Holy Presence/Spirit. Now, under the New Order and Covenant we are secured in His Blood and Grace is Abounding through His Righteousness so we may have His Divine Eternal Life working in and thru us. Our Deliver. Our New Life. It IS a process and working of Grace, but He has secured our success. Each Will Be Changed.

Now let's look at Revelation again... Revelation is the Apocalypse "The Disclosure" to the saints back then. To Give them an understanding of what was about to happen. To give warning and an opportunity to those certain churches and their "angels" Pastors to Repent....

It was for THAT GENERATION and those churches. It happened. It is completed. It is Finished. It is Done.

Now, Today, Receive Jesus Christ in all that He Has Accomplished, and YOU TOO ENTER into His Kingdom that is already established: Righteousness, Peace, and Joy IN His Holy Spirit IN YOU.

Thank You Father and Lord!

Amen.
RPJ

(Write your notes here)

REVELATION 86
Did You Pass The Test? : Tried and Proven

God’s Training and Strengthening is not always easy. Probably lots of hands and voices of amen here. But God never tempts us. Yet God does train us by taking us through tests of faith that will prove us in our Faith and Trust of God. “Grounding us in Truth” is another way to say it. That’s why we need God’s Teachers.

This causes our Roots to be anchored and our steps established in His Righteousness and Provision. This causes us to be born again, and enter into His Kingdom, and be Set in His Kingdom as Trees of Righteousness. His kingdom is Righteousness, Peace, and Joy in the Holy Spirit (Romans 14:17), and only by being born again of His water and Spirit can we see and enter His Kingdom. (John 3:3-5)

Jesus went outside the camp to be crucified, so we seem to be outside the kingdom as God causes us to experience His cleaning, sanctification, and perfection into the maturity of Christ’s character. Yet, the Kingdom is WITHIN us if the Holy Spirit is In you (Luke 17:20-21).

Now God is washing us, cleansing us, and sanctifying us in the blood and word that is the Lamb of God, Jesus Christ. Now the Kingdom Of God begins to swallow up our mortality, and the new creature starts to be revealed from the earth. Oh Hear the wisdom of God!

It is amazing to see the Wisdom of God at work. Ask for His understanding and He will give that to you too. God perfects us or completes us by the His own Seed having accomplished all things of Salvation and Victory and Redemption for us. But we have to Grow Up into the Head (Ephesians 4:11-32) which is Jesus Christ.

Growing up in Christ is allowing God to take you through the obstacles, situations, etc that He causes to be there..... It's All In His Plan for You.

It may seem like the devil, but it isn't. It is God's wisdom perfecting you. Yet there are some people that are in what may appear to be a working of God but it is not!!! They have stepped out of God's will and/or have made the wrong choice along the path and have opened themselves up to some "yucky" situations that are allowing all kinds of evil to work in their lives. But I declare the blood of Jesus Christ on your life, if this is you, and ask God to close the door to the evil and set your feet back in His path of Righteousness. If that is you, remember where you made the bad choice, and apologize to God for it, and receive His Forgiveness.

Nurture that precious relationship with God again Daily.... Daily is important. Let Him be the apple of your eye, and the front of your thoughts and deeds... Be First in your life of importance. Submit to God, then you will be resisting the bad spirit, and that bad spirit will flee.

The devil is already defeated, but if you don't know that, then you'll keep fighting it, rather than abiding in Christ's Victory. (Hebrews 2:14; 1 John 3:8-9)

This is why we need to be in fellowship with those that are Holy Spirit filled and led!!! So each and every one of us can have the body watching out for each other... Not controlling

.... Just loving and making sure everyone is taking the right step and not being led astray. This truly is the office of the Shepherd. The Gift of the Hand ministries here too: Apostles, Prophet, Evangelist, Pastor, and Teacher.

Hebrews 5:12-14 says,
12 For when for the time ye ought to be teachers , ye have need that one teach you again which be the first principles of the oracles of God; and are become such as have need of milk, and not of strong meat.
13 For every one that useth milk is unskilful in the word of righteousness: for he is a babe.
14 But strong meat belongeth to them that are of full age, even those who by reason of use have their senses exercised to discern both good and evil.

And Psalms 23:3 tells us,
3 He restoreth my soul: he leadeth me in the paths of righteousness for his name's sake.

You say you want to have "more of God".... rather you want more of God's character and glory to be able to flow through your soul. To be skillful in the word of righteousness, you must have the Holy Spirit Teach you of Jesus Christ which only comes by revelation. Man's doctrine and understanding will mislead you and produce nothing of value. Receive of God's Shepherd and Gifts, AND GIVE as God's Shepherd and Gifts are once matured in you, GIVE.

God taught me a long time ago that once He brings me into my land (the place in Christ Jesus that He prepared for me: the place of maturity and understanding in wisdom of Christ Jesus) to then Go back at His leading to help others come in to their land (of Christ). This has not always been enjoyable, but the after affect is of much reward and joy in the Lord. Almost like a multi level business, except the top feeds the bottom, not the bottom the top.

Joshua 1:10-15 15 Until the Lord have given your brethren rest, as he hath given you, and they also have possessed the land which the Lord your God giveth them: then ye shall return unto the land of your possession, and enjoy it, which Moses the Lord's servant gave you on this side Jordan toward the sunrising.

So the journey continues for them He has called and chosen.... bring in the harvest for each age. Then again planting for the next season and age in the Lord.

Being established in the present truth (2 Peter 1:1-12), learning the first principles of God (Hebrews 5:12-14, 6:1-3*), getting the foundation of Jesus Christ laid properly, then going on to eat of the meat that is doing the work you are trained for.

Hebrews 5:14 says that strong meat belongs to them that are of full age... maturity. Like in Ephesians 4:11-16 shows us.

Hebrews 5:14 continues to explain that full age is those who by reason of use... KEY HERE... Exercised discernment through the experiences that our Father God prepares for us to go through... that by reason of use have their senses exercised to discern both good and evil.

Maturing in Christ is a process, and God will not force us to do anything. But as a perfect Father, He will make us willing, by our own uncomfortableness in disobedience... if that is what it takes. I'd rather agree with my Father and work in Harmony with Him. That is my choice.

So daily we should keep ourselves open to only Him, having your senses exercised and knowing the difference between good and evil, and Eternal Life.

Thank You Father for your tests to prove us and establish us in your present truth. What you have begun in us, you will complete... till you see Your Son come forth in and through our souls...His many-member body in this earth.

Psalm 66:10 For thou, O God, hast proved us; thou hast tried us, as silver is tried.

Amen.
RPJ

(Write your notes here)

REVELATION 87
God's Will Be Done

Having Faith in God's Will for the day is the better way to walk.

Many think to do this and to do that, and that God will do according to their faith. But it is the better choice to find out what God's plan is for your day, and then to step out having Faith in God for the outcome of your day.

God does tell us to ask and you will receive. But the scriptures show us that many ask and don't receive because they are asking out of their own lusts and gain, rather than according to God's good pleasure for themselves and the body of Christ.

When God prospers you, it will be for His pleasure so that you have what you need.... and so you can then be able to go and bless His Body. It's not so you can "look" better blessed than anyone else. It is for the welfare of all those He has put with you or you with them and for yourself. Helping one another in brotherly love .... according as the Holy Spirit is instructing."

Have Faith in God. Moses did not just move out in the waters... He sought out God's plan first, then acted in Faith according to God's plan. Waiting when needed to wait. Moving when needed to move.

God is and has placed "certain ones" in today's time to do just that for the body of Christ. But you can still seek God for yourself, and listen for His word for you today.

He Will instruct you and guide for His good pleasure, so that you may receive and enter His holy kingdom of righteousness, peace, and joy in His holy Spirit.

" 'My Life In You' by Jesus Christ"

Have Faith in God. Mark 11:22-26. Jesus only did what the Father did ... showed Him. Seek the Father and Nourish that relationship.

Welcome those Gifts of the Apostle, Prophet, Evangelist, Pastor, and Teacher, and many other Gifts of the holy Spirit that God will send to you for your benefit and edification and instruction... and if necessary, correction in Love. God wants you to be successful: to Enter His Kingdom and be established in Him, the present truth. Those Gifts will help build you up in God's perfect Plan for you.

Ephesians 4:11-16 v12 For the perfecting of the saints, for the work of the ministry, for the edifying of the body of Christ:....

Find out what God's direction, instructions are for your situation. Seek God. Then when the answer comes... GO in Faith of God's word, will, and love for your good pleasure. Then your asking will be done according to God's will and plan for you.

Sure, God can do whatever your heart desires, because He loves you and cares about even the smaller things that are a pleasure to you. So it is okay to ask for even those things. I asked God to be my valentine one year, and He ended up giving me a "real" miracle that day! He wants you to be happy and in His joy. God loves and cares for you.

So, Go in Faith of God's Will, Seek Him and His Kingdom, and you Will prosper.

Amen.
RPJ

REVELATION 88
Who You Know Matters

All things are delivered unto me of my Father: and no man knoweth the Son, but the Father; neither knoweth any man the Father, save the Son, and he to whomsoever the Son will reveal him. Matthew 11:27

To Know Him, is to birth forth after His Seed, which is Christ Jesus. That only comes from an intimate planting (revealing) of His Son in your Soul and mind, by His holy Spirit revealing Him.

James 1:18-21
v18 Of his own will begat he us with the word of truth, that we should be a kind of first-fruits of his creatures...
v21 Wherefore lay apart all filthiness and superfluity of naughtiness,and receive with meekness the engrafted word, which is able to save your souls.

John 17:2-3
As thou hast given him power over all flesh, that he should give eternal life to as many as thou hast given him.
And this is life eternal, that they might know thee the only true God, and Jesus Christ, whom thou hast sent.

John 14: 20-24 ... and will manifest myself to him. (make known Jesus to you)

Adam "knew" Eve and conceived.... likewise, allow the Lord to produce His Word (seed) in you and bring forth His Son through your Soul and Body.

Many membered body of Jesus Christ, God's habitation... being revealed in the earth. (Hebrews 12:21-29; Revelation 21:1-3; 1 Corinthians 12:20,27)

John 1:12-14 But as many as received him, to them gave he power to become the sons of God, even to them that believe on his name: which were born, not of blood, nor of the will of man, but of God. And the Word was made flesh, and dwelt among us,....

Hallelujah! Be Encouraged and Continue... In the Lord.!

Amen
RPJ

REVELATION 89
Reverence to the One and Only

To God only be all Praise and Honor!

Both testaments of the bible clearly instruct that there is only One God, and only One God is to be worshipped.

In 1 John 5:20 we see witness that Jesus Christ is God having come in the form of the flesh man. In many other scriptures the same witness is true. For purpose of today's message, I'll use a couple of scriptures that come to mind.

1 John 5:20 And we know that the Son of God is come, and hath given us an understanding, that we may know him that is true, and we are in him that is true, even in his Son Jesus Christ. This is the true God, and eternal life.

1 Timothy 3:16 And without controversy great is the mystery of godliness: God was manifest in the flesh, justified in the Spirit, seen of angels, preached unto the Gentiles, believed on in the world, received up into glory.

By God's own arm He brought to us our full salvation. Done. Now as age passes on to age, this good news (gospel) is preached and by faith in Jesus Christ, God in the flesh having brought to us salvation, we Enter in to His Presence and Kingdom... to live forever more with Him and the spirits of just men made perfect also.

Jesus Christ, the Son of God, the Lamb of God... God's Soul which is and was selected to accomplish the task needed for all of us. That soul tasted death for us. Yet because it was without sin, it was revived or could say raised again unto life victorious. Now never to have to experience death anymore, for it overcame death for Himself and for all mankind. Now having obtained All

Promises, He has been given by inheritance a greater name than any other. Yeshua, Immanuel, Jesus Christ has obtained our salvation and is readily able to give to all that the Father draws to Him... fullness of Victory.

Soooo... Reverence... He owns all. He has obtained all victory and blessings. He owns all that is God's.... being one with God... that is God's choice for Him.

Only through the Son of God can any of us obtain this wonderful salvation and victory and blessings. But even Jesus said to worship God, not Him. But God demands us to Reverence the Son, because we have no hope to come to God or to be one with Him in His family, except coming through the Son, which is God's word and promise of our salvation. He is the Way, the veil which is His flesh and blood... the Way to the Father. Restoration, Redemption, Reconciliation. That's a heavy Truth. Jesus Christ is God's Word and Promise of our Salvation which is LIFE. To bring us "home." All of our earthen realm and heavenly realm functions by the Son, of the Son, and from the Son... mortality is swallowed up of Life. (2 Corinthians 4:14-15; 5:1-5; 1 Cor 15:28)

So unless you by faith, accept, receive, reverence the Son of God, which is God's Promise of Eternal Life, then you have no possible chance of eternal life. It is God's word to You... your security and assurance of victory, and eternal life.

Blessings and Honor come by God' Word abiding In You and You in Him. Only through the Son, By the Son, and Of the Son can any of us be able to have any blessings, honor, glory and or victory of any kind.

Give all that you have to the Lord: Honor, Respect, Reverence to the King of kings, and Lord of lords.

From, By, and Of Him alone, can we be blessed.

" 'My Life In You' by Jesus Christ"

If all will Subject and Submit themselves to Jesus Christ, and Give Him the Honor, Respect, and Praise that He is Lord and King over ALL....

Then you will see and experience a change for the better in your own life, and as we are united in the Head, Jesus Christ, even the neighborhoods and nations and universe will produce this blessing of Life. Hallelujah!

To Him Only, God, All Bow and Give Reverence Today! Amen.

From, Of, and By Him Does All Blessings Come.

1 Corinthians 8:6 But to us there is but one God, the Father, of whom are all things, and we in him; and one Lord Jesus Christ, by whom are all things, and we by him.

Receive the Son of God and Give Reverence to God the Father and You will Receive Your Blessings...
A Change For The Better.

Amen.
RPJ

REVELATION 90
Who to Obey

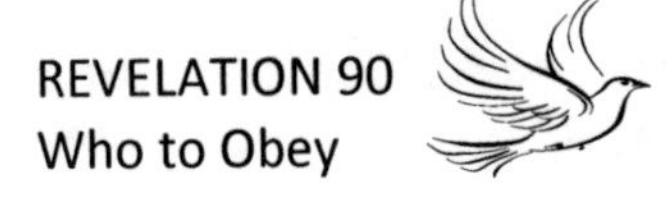

In reading Jeremiah 35 there is a lesson for all to partake of...

When God says to "drink the wine" and your parent or parents say to do something else, or the "traditional church" says to do something else... who will you obey?

Obey God, Please! Let go of your reputation, let go of your upbringing in the religious environment, and run to Obey what the Lord is saying to you, then Go.

In Jeremiah 35 the father had told them NOT to drink wine, etc. So they were obedient to their natural father to do just that. But they were so obedient to their natural father, that when God sent His prophet to instruct them to "Drink the Wine" that they ended up in rebellion to God.

Summary.... Obey God, Please! Do not let the traditions of man Hinder You from receiving and drinking of God's Wine, the True Word, the refreshing from the Lord today in the Spirit of Life in Christ Jesus.

Break out of the traditions of man, and walk in the blessings of the Lord.

Amen.
RPJ

“ ‘My Life In You’ by Jesus Christ”

REVELATION 91
Restoration Back to the Father

John 6:53 Then Jesus said unto them, Verily, Verily, I say unto you, Except ye eat the flesh of the Son of man, and drink his blood, ye have no life in you.

When Adam sinned, life left Him. Adam was dead. He died.

That's what God told him would happen if He ate the fruit of that tree of the knowledge of good and evil.

Yet Adam still walked..... but in a different mindset... a different realm.... dominion... outside the garden (God's mind).

Let's look at this for a moment....
Adam was in the Garden... placed in God's special place of communion (God's mind).
Here he was accountable to God only, and God provided all for him, yet he was to be obedient to God.

A place of Life: When Adam disobeyed God (sinned), he died and they were cast out of the garden... kingdom... the place of righteousness, peace, and joy IN the Holy Ghost.

The Place where we can communion with God; where we receive from God...outside the garden/kingdom it was a “struggle.” Life had left Adam. Death ruled in him now.

Only by having the Holy Spirit within us, can we have any HOPE of knowing or understanding the things of God. This Spirit IS God. This Spirit Is Eternal Life. It is the Spirit of the Son.

His arm reached into our soul and ANCHORS us, as He reconciles us to Himself.... causes Us to ENTER through the veil of the temple, which is the body and blood of Jesus Christ, who is the last Adam that in His righteousness and obedience, perfected the WAY back to the Father and kingdom for all that would believe in Him.

In the old testament only the High Priest was able to enter this place, through the door/veil and with many instructions in doing so.

Today, we have Jesus Christ, our High Priest and King, after the order of Melchisedec, consecrated by God's word/oath to be our Priest forever.

That Priest enters into communion with the Father always on our behalf: Intercessor, Mediator between God and Man. But then even Jesus told the apostles, you can pray to the Father yourself now, once I'm gone. In my name, my authority, my blessing, etc.... In respect of me, and by my power you are granted the riches of my glory.

We can come boldly unto the throne of grace, by the blood of the Lamb, in the name of the Son, your High Priest... we come through the door, the veil which is the FLESH OF THE SON, AND EAT AND DRINK OF HIM AS WE ENTER INTO THAT PLACE OF COMMUNION WITH GOD THE ALL MIGHTY ONE AND ONLY.

ENTER INTO ETERNAL LIFE.... That Place of Communion and Rest and Provision again.

The Place where LIFE Swallows up our mortality – death. And we are restored, reconciled, redeemed back to the Father of spirits, the Father of light, and can Walk in Life and Life In Us abounds again.

We are Restored back to the Father..... with our mind full and occupied by the presence of the Lamb: the blood and body of Jesus Christ.

When Adam sinned "LIFE left him".... The Father Left Him... Jesus was on the cross, The Father left Him at that moment that Sin had entered in... He became sin for us, who knew no sin.... only then would the Father Ever Leave or Forsake Him. It was Evident now, It was Done. Finished. The Lamb had taken on the sin of the world... death was accomplished. The full payment of Sin was PAID IN FULL for the benefit of all that would Receive HIM. (John 1:12, 2 Cor 5:21, and many, many other scriptures)

Now as you receive Jesus Christ, the Lamb of God, YOUR debt of Sin is PAID IN FULL too. And as the appearing of the RESURRECTION, Jesus Christ, in Your Soul is encountered and experienced, then you can step OUT of your prison of defeat (whatever mindset: spiritual or physical or natural)you may have and STEP INTO THE GARDEN OF GOD, God's kingdom. Eternal Life will swallow up all death, and the struggles are overcome in Victory.

Now the Restoration could commence.... In Your Soul, which is God's property, with or without sin... it belongs to God. This is God's Garden.... every soul. That is why there needs to be a renewing of your mind, so your soul may Produce LIFE ETERNAL... BRING FORTH THE SON, Jesus Christ. His identify and thinking and character..... But this can only be done by THAT HOLY SPIRIT.. the same one that RAISED Jesus from the grave... if that one be in you, then you too ARE BEING BROUGHT FORTH of that same seed, which is Christ. His Life will be revealed through you. Romans 8:9-11

But even Today in Grace of Jesus Christ, any Soul that has not RECEIVED LIFE, is still Dead... for sin still works in the un-regenerated soul. Let Jesus Christ forgive you.... free you from death, decay and those carnal spirits that cause the problems in the world. Let's clean up God's land! RECEIVE JESUS CHRIST and ENTER INTO the Kingdom by the Lamb of God that takes the sin of the world away.

Then we all can ENJOY our neighborhoods and each other even more.
Be Reconciled to the Father, and enjoy His Kingdom Life Today.

Amen.
RPJ

REVELATION 92
God's Garden of Gardens

Every Soul is God's property. Whether with sin or without, every soul belongs to God.

Every Soul has a mind. Let your mind be renewed in LIFE ETERNAL, Jesus Christ. Allow His holy Spirit to Reign and Rule within you. Submit to Him only.... as a wife or bride or woman.

There is neither male nor female in God, but for understanding, your soul produces, in example the woman a child, or the garden a produce and harvest. So let your soul be impregnated by the holy Spirit with the seed (word) of God: Jesus Christ His Son the Lamb of God our Salvation and Saviour.... Then Produce After THAT SEED.

Let the Son of God be manifest through your soul .... let that mind be in you, producing from the garden the best fruit – the Fruit of the Son – holy Spirit. (Galatians 5:22-23)

Galatians 5:22-23
But the fruit of the Spirit is love, joy, peace, longsuffering, gentleness, goodness, faith, Meekness, temperance: against such there is no law.

The assembling together of the tabernacles...The joining together of God's Souls that have been redeemed by the blood of the Lamb...the spirits of just men made perfect... the revealing and appearing of the Son of God.

The many-membered Son of God appearing in the land. God's habitation and temple.

His Kingdom is established and from generation to generation all that He calls are entering into the promised land (Luke 16:16) and being assembled by one Spirit, the Holy Spirit that raised Jesus from the dead.

Your Soul is God's and He desires to PLANT His Son in it. To eat and drink of you daily. And to distribute to the world their daily bread.... if they will receive His Son, which now your Soul produces (allows to manifest through you). Yet all this is done by the Father's holy Spirit.... nothing of self is able to do anything without the Spirit of the Son. (John 15:1-8)

It almost sounds like a multi level business, but one difference is the last receives as the first, so there is equality in the receiving of salvation and the benefits of the Son. The first ones in don't get more than the last ones. Eternal Life is for all.

But as far as levels of authority, gifts, and the working of His kingdom's reign, yes, there are differences of services, operations, and workings. (1 Cor 12)

Your Soul is God's garden to plant and produce after HIS SEED.

Let the gardening begin... or continue. Be a good steward of the produce and distribute to those that need the Lord. Work on gently removing the weeds, or just wait for the time of the harvest.

Your soul that is occupied of the Holy Spirit and is now become part of God's garden: His purpose, His vision, His planting... all according to His Will being done towards all. Many-membered sons of the One and Only Son, all going forth as His Mind (Holy Spirit) desires to do, and say.

You are being redeemed and reconciled to the Father. That means your heaven and earth are also being brought together, harvested, in One – the Lord Jesus Christ, thus being set in heavenly places as you are walking in the earth. In Jesus Christ, all heaven and earth are brought together in Him.

So we all are of one Spirit, and assembled together by one Holy Spirit, forever together in the Lord, Today. Is so be that you have that same Holy Spirit in you that was in Jesus Christ.
(1 Cor 12; Heb 9:14-15, 24-28; 1 Cor 15:24-28; 1 Thess 4:17)

Amen.
RPJ

REVELATION 93
Where Two Ways Met

This is going to be a short one, but from the Lord...there's a few revealing here but here is only one or two:

Mark 11:1-4
And when they came nigh to Jerusalem, unto Bethphage and Bethany, at the mount of Olives, he sendeth forth two of his disciples,

And saith unto them, "Go your way into the village over against you: and as soon as ye be entered into it, ye shall find a colt tied, whereon never man sat: loose him, and bring him.

And if any man say unto you, Why do ye this? say ye that the Lord hath need of him; and straightway he will send him hither.
and they went their way, and found the colt tied by the door without in a place where two ways met; and they loose him."

There was the need of a colt that had never been rode, and just as there was need for food or tax money, provision was made very easily for the ministry's need as well.

"Where two ways met" is the PLACE where Jesus Is = Heaven and Earth having come together in One. (Ephesians 1:10; Colossians 1:20) He is the Mediator, the Intercessor.

This is Power. This is Provision. And to those that have ears to hear more.... Hear the Heart of the Lord for you IN Him.

Stand fast in Jesus, your Place of Provision. HEAR His instructions for your situation. GO in obedience and His Grace will manifest the provision in the Earth for you.

The Father knows what you have need of, so continue to follow Matthew 6:33.

Matthew 6:32-33
...for your heavenly Father knoweth that ye have need of all these things. But seek ye first the kingdom of God, and his righteousness; and all these things shall be added unto you.

Know Where You Stand.... and Know Who Is Standing for (in) You.

Amen.
RPJ

REVELATION 94
It's a Wonderful "Life" when God is your "home"

"It's a wonderful "life" when God is your "home." Home... true Home... is a place of safety, rest, peace, comfort, and many other wonderful things that I have only found IN HIM. IN HIM I live and move and exist by. I am blessed coming and going. I am never without Him. He's bigger and stronger than any other power, principality, dominion, and might... including opinions too. He is all wisdom, understanding and knowledge over all that is in heaven and earth. He is my head, authority and is my protector and defender and provider. He is my Comforter. Whether you see me anymore, or not, just know that my soul rests at home in the Lord. Feel free to join us... but you'll have to come through the door of fire, the veil of His flesh, the blood that was shed, for it will wash and separate you from the filth of the unregenerate creature .... Today, be washed in His Word, the Water of Life, and Enter Into your rest, the Home of the Redeemed Ones... Welcome Home and truly Rest.

You'll not feel comfortable with the mind of the world anymore, yet you'll understand that it was God's love for the world that caused Him to have His own flesh sent to redeem the world. So it is done. What a great victory we have in Him. Make someone free Today, for the Lord is come... and in the fullness of Him who is Power, Truth, and Love. Jesus Christ the same yesterday, today, and forever.

Make someone Free, today! Jesus Christ, the Lamb of God is Come In You, and has swallowed up your mortality, and has brought you into His dwelling place... the place prepared for you within Himself (God's Temple). This is so that you can enter your rest... yet, only to go out and help others that He is calling to do the same, and enter their resting place.
Joshua 1:14-15 ... but ye shall pass before your brethren armed, all the mighty men of valour, and help them; Until the Lord have

given your brethren rest, as he hath given you, and they also have possessed the land which the Lord your God giveth them: then ye shall return unto the land of your possession, and enjoy it, ...

Be at Home in the Lord. Get your rest and strength, but go back out there and help others enter into God's kingdom.

John 15:4-5 Abide in me, and I in you. As the branch cannot bear fruit of itself, except it abide in the vine; no more can ye, except ye abide in me. I am the vine, ye are the branches; He that abideth in me, and I in him, the same bringeth forth much fruit: for without me ye can do nothing.

Amen.
RPJ

REVELATION 95
God's Debit Card: Direct Line to His Account

To pray for someone and nothing happening is like a person making a purchase and not having the money to take it home.

Miracles: the impossible happening for ones provision or "good."

Credit is "You will pay back later, because you don't have it Now"

God's Spiritual Wealth & Health Plan is "Cash in Hand for every Need."
"Use the Debit "Faith" Card (not credit) because it (God's provision through Jesus Christ) has already provided a balance in the Account for you to use as you need it. And as you use that, More is put in. It never goes empty." Faith draws upon it....

The Name on the Account is that of the Son and Father. All that come to the Son, and in honor of the Son, can receive of the Son. That is the Father's Will. Only in the Son's name: authority and responsibility, can any reap of Him or distribute of Him. The Son has acquired the benefits and provision, and only through Him can you receive such.

In Him, Yes and Amen, you can withdraw at any time. It is a "Joint Account."
Abundance... Abundance... Abundance.... A well that never, never runs dry.... God's Provision.

Today the Lord is causing some to be His Distributors, Administrators, which will be Responsible with Him, for the distribution and administration of His wealth, health, and provision to all. Only by the will of God can ones name be added to this account, which give them authority, permission, and responsibility to administer God's wealth, health, and provision to others. Not by will of man or any other will can their names be added. Only by His own will and purpose will certain ones share in the responsibility of distributing God's good will to others. These ones know all that they had to go through at the hand of God, to and for the preparation of this ministry.

Joint heirs... Co Heirs... the Son of God. (Hebrews 1:1-9 *2)

Miracles and healings and gifts will be working as always, but there is a movement of the Lord that will operate a bit uniquely than what has been seen before.

To God is all Glory.

Amen.
RPJ

REVELATION 96
God's Garden

All Souls belong to the Lord. Ezekiel 18:4 **Behold, all souls are mine**; as the soul of the father, so also the soul of the son is mine: the soul that sinneth, it shall die.

Our minds are a creative element of our being, just as God thinks then speaks to create it. The scripture reveals that out of the heart (mind) man speaks, revealing what is in the heart (mind).

So the mind, the soul together create.... as God made man in His image and likeness.

The Mind is the male, the Soul is the female. Whatever Spirit is in the soul is what produces thoughts. So as a man/woman thinks in his/her heart, that is what they do or say, according to the spirit of their mind in their soul. This is why we need to allow the Lord to wash us in His Word, and Blood so that the body of sin is cut off and the carnal mind removed. Then the mind of Christ is the only mind operating within: single vision.

(Now, if you have not the Spirit of Christ, then you are not of the mind of God (Christ Jesus) nor of His family. Yet God is still King over you and your soul is still God's possession, but you are in rebellion because of sin. Only having received the Spirit of Christ can you be free from sin and dwell in His kingdom of heaven. (Romans 8:9-11))

So if you have received the Spirit of God which is Christ Jesus, then His righteousness in you sanctifies you and begins and finishes your purification (washing, birthing) and causes you to enter His Kingdom and enjoy His Inheritance... co-heirs with Christ.

It is a process that is anchored and assured in Him. But the process of washing and cleansing you in His Word, causes your vision and hearing to change so that you see and hear of the Father's doings.... for you are passing through the veil which is the flesh of Christ, the Lamb, and entering in to the holy place which is the dwelling of the Father. (Galatians 4:1-7; 1 Corinthians 14:20-24)

Every Soul will produce His Fruit now... Producing according to the Spirit within their mind. Having now been redeemed, cleansed, and renewed in the spirit of their mind.... by that Holy Spirit which is Christ Jesus and the Father (1 Corinthians 14:20-24). They make their abode in your Soul, and mind.

Now, the Mind of Christ is the Mind and Spirit that works in you to produce His Fruit: Galatians 5 (all): 16-26).

Galatians 5:22-23 But the fruit of the Spirit is love, joy, peace, longsuffering, gentleness, goodness, faith, Meekness, temperance: against such there is no law.
v24 And they that are Christ's have crucified the flesh with the affections and lusts.
v25 If we live in the Spirit, let us also walk in the Spirit.

"If we live in the Spirit" – since you have received Jesus Christ as your Saviour, you now are living in the Spirit. And because you have the Spirit of the Son in you, you now dwell in Him. And if you are dwelling in Him and are yielded to obey Him daily, then you will also begin to WALK IN The SPIRIT...... That means you will PRODUCE HIS FRUIT Out of YOUR MIND which has NOW BECOME ONE WITH AND AS THE MIND OF CHRIST JESUS... GOD'S SON WORKING IN YOU AND THROUGH YOU to this age and all ages to be.

Let this mind be in you which is also in Christ Jesus (Romans 8:6; 1 Corinthians 2:9-16; Philippians 2:5-11; Titus 3:3-5...)
Phil 2:5-11
5 Let this mind be in you, which was also in Christ Jesus:

6 Who, being in the form of God, thought it not robbery to be equal with God: 7 But made himself of no reputation, and took upon him the form of a servant, and was made in the likeness of men: 8 And being found in fashion as a man, he humbled himself, and became obedient unto death, even the death of the cross. 9 Wherefore God also hath highly exalted him, and given him a name which is above every name: 10 That at the name of Jesus every knee should bow, of things in heaven, and things in earth, and things under the earth; 11 And that every tongue should confess that Jesus Christ is Lord, to the glory of God the Father.

Titus 3:5-7
5 Not by works of righteousness which we have done, but according to his mercy he saved us, by the washing of regeneration, and renewing of the Holy Ghost; 6 Which he shed on us abundantly through Jesus Christ our Saviour; 7 That being justified by his grace, we should be made heirs according to the hope of eternal life.

Whatever you do, do it unto the Lord...
Colossians 3:23 23 And whatsoever ye do, do it heartily, as to the Lord, and not unto men;...

Amen.
RPJ

REVELATION 97
GRACE Vision – Not Sin Vision

"I want you to have GRACE vision, not Sin vision." GRACE stops the working of sin in your life: the decaying factors of death ceases, and is completely removed.

GRACE comes in and Heals, Delivers, and Provides an Eternal Comfort and Protection and New Standard to live by, of and as you travel in and through your life INTO His.

You were already dead.... sin was revealed and death began to work in you... walking dead – separated from LIFE (God).

Now He is raising you up into a Higher Vision AND Understanding AND Experience of His Dwelling place and Kingdom.

TODAY is your Day of GRACE, IF you are Hearing this word of God. This IS for You.

His Blessings and Benefits are Yours THROUGH the HEARING and RECEIVING of His Son, Yeshua – Immanuel - Jesus Christ. BEHOLD Him and be changed out of death garments, and into Eternal Life (1 Corinthians 15:51-57; Philippians 3:21; 2 Corinthians 3:16-18; and others).

Amen.
RPJ

REVELATION 98
Not a Statement, But a Discovery in Present Truth

Subduing all things unto Himself....

1 Corinthians 15:19-28
19 If in this life only we have hope in Christ, we are of all men most miserable.
20 But now is Christ risen from the dead, and become the firstfruits of them that slept.
21 For since by man came death, by man came also the resurrection of the dead.
22 For as in Adam all die, even so in Christ shall all be made alive.
23 But every man in his own order: Christ the firstfruits; afterward they that are Christ's at his coming.
24 Then cometh the end, when he shall have delivered up the kingdom to God, even the Father; when he shall have put down all rule and all authority and power.
25 For he must reign, till he hath put all enemies under his feet.
26 The last enemy that shall be destroyed is death.
27 For he hath put all things under his feet. But when he saith, all things are put under him, it is manifest that he is excepted, which did put all things under him.
28 And when all things shall be subdued unto him, then shall the Son also himself be subject unto him that put all things under him, that God may be all in all.

Romans 8:9-11
9 But ye are not in the flesh, but in the Spirit, if so be that the Spirit of God dwell in you. Now if any man have not the Spirit of Christ, he is none of his.
10 And if Christ be in you, the body is dead because of sin; but the Spirit is life because of righteousness.
11 But if the Spirit of him that raised up Jesus from the dead dwell in you, he that raised up Christ from the dead shall also quicken your mortal bodies by his Spirit that dwelleth in you.

This is not a statement of facts, but of the reality of Truth in Action.

An Experience of the Lord In You.

Today, if you hear His Voice.... come forth.

Amen.
RPJ

REVELATION 99
Blessed In His Kingdom

Luke 14:15 And when one of them that sat at meat with him heard these things, he said unto him, Blessed is he that shall eat bread in the kingdom of God.

Jesus said I will not drink of the fruit of this vine until I do it new with you in my Father's kingdom.

Luke 17:20-21 And when he was demanded of the Pharisees, when the kingdom of God should come, he answered them and said, The kingdom of God cometh not with observation: Neither shall they say, Lo here! or, lo there! for, behold, the kingdom of God is within you.

The Pharisees had within their minds the kingdom of God, but God was about to end one order and begin another one.

Matthew 13:11-12 He answered and said unto them, Because it is given unto you to know the mysteries of the kingdom of heaven, but to them it is not given. For whosoever hath, to him shall be given, and he shall have more abundance: but whosoever hath not, from him shall be taken away even that he hath.

They did not understand what God's kingdom was about. They had the keys but did not enter, nor did they allow others to enter. So God removed the first to establish the second.

Luke 9:27 But I tell you of a truth, there be some standing here, which shall not taste of death, till they see the kingdom of God.

Matthew 16:28 Verily I say unto you, There be some standing here, which shall not taste of death, till they see the Son of man coming in his kingdom.

Mark 9:1 And he said unto them, Verily I say unto you, That there be some of them that stand here, which shall not taste of death, till they have seen the kingdom of God come with power.

So all these scriptures clearly say that there were people back then that were going to see the kingdom of God come with power.... and those people are not here today, so they must have seen the Kingdom of God come with power back then. So, the Kingdom of God came.

Luke 22:12-30 (Passover was at hand) v15-17 And he said unto them, With desire I have desired to eat this Passover with you before I suffer: for I say unto you, I will not any more eat thereof, until it be fulfilled in the kingdom of God. v17 And he took the cup, and gave thanks, and said, Take this, and divide it among yourselves: v18 For I say unto you, **I will not drink of the fruit of the vine, until the kingdom of God shall come**.

Mt 26:29 and Mark 14:25 also say: But I say unto you, I will not drink henceforth of this fruit of the vine, until that day when I drink it new with you in my Father's kingdom.

Then after the Lamb went to the cross and became our Passover for us, He arose and walked on the earth as the Second Man walking, the Lord from heaven, the quickening Spirit. Then He appeared to many, did more miracles, and ate and drank with them again, for the Kingdom had come.

Luke 24:30-31, 35 **And it came to pass, as he sat at meat with them, he took bread, and blessed it, and brake, and gave to them**. And their eyes were opened, and they knew him; and he vanished out of their sight. and they told what things were done in the way, and **how he was know of them in breaking of bread.** Also Luke 24:42-45.

Acts 10:40-41 Him God raised up the third day, and showed him openly; Not to all the people, but unto witnesses chosen before of God, even to us, **who did eat and drink with him after he rose from the dead.**

This was in His Kingdom, for it was accomplished. (Lk 18:31)
Luke 22:29-30 That ye may eat and drink at my table in my kingdom, and sit on thrones judging the twelve tribes of Israel.

Luke 14:15 And when one of them that sat at meat with him heard these things, he said unto him, Blessed is he that shall eat bread in the kingdom of God.

John 6:21-71 v 56-57 He that eateth my flesh, and drinketh my blood, dwelleth in me, and I in him. As the living Father hath sent me, and I live by the Father: so he that eateth me, even he shall live by me.

1 Corinthians 10:16-17 The cup of blessing which we bless, is it not the communion of the blood of Christ? The bread which we break, is it not the communion of the body of Christ? For we being many are one bread, and one body: for we are all partakers of that one bread.

We are blessed to Eat of the Lord's body and drink of His blood as our Passover In to the Kingdom of God.

Amen.
RPJ

REVELATION 100
God's Kingdom

* In Romans 14:17 we find that the kingdom of God is righteousness, peace, and joy in the Holy Ghost.

* In Luke 16:16 we find that since John, the kingdom of God is preached and every man presses into it... into the kingdom of God that is in the Holy Spirit (and in you if you have received Him, and now you are pressing into it).

* In Luke 17:20-21 we find that the kingdom of God "is in you"... in those that had the truth at that time, and today in those that have received the Holy Spirit.

* In John 3:3-5 Jesus tells all that unless you are born from above you cannot "see" the kingdom, and unless you are born of the water and Spirit you cannot enter the kingdom of God (which is righteousness, peace, and joy in the Holy Spirit).

* In Hebrews 12:28 we are told that they were receiving a kingdom which cannot be moved...

* In Luke 12:32 Jesus tells us that it is the Father's good pleasure to give us the kingdom.

So the Kingdom of Heaven, the Kingdom of God is not natural Jerusalem, or mount Zion anymore... but it is in the Holy Spirit and has been birthed forth in the regeneration during Jesus' day, and is from age to age, generation to generation being established in the hearts and souls of mankind by that same Holy Spirit that raised Jesus from the dead and grave.
The kingdom of God has more to it than any of us have experienced, but we know that God plants His kingdom in the hearts and souls of mankind by the imparting of His Holy Spirit

within them. Those that have received the testimony of His Son Jesus Christ, are sealed with that Holy Spirit of the Son and Father. Now God makes His abode within us. (Many scriptures on this but here's a few more to add to the ones above: Ephesians 1:12-14, John 14:20-24, Luke 17:20-21, John 18:36-37, John 4:20-23,...)

No more is the natural Jerusalem or Mount Zion or Israel the place of God's kingdom.... so please stop wasting God's time trying to rebuild God's temple in the natural place that He put an end to. Read John 4:20-23, John 18:36, Hebrews 11:16, Hebrews 12:22-29, Hebrews 7:12-16, Hebrews 10:1-10, and many others... You'll find some of them in this article.

Hebrews 12:22 says "But ye are come unto mount Zion, and unto the city of the living God, the heavenly Jerusalem...." Not the natural Jerusalem or Mt Zion, but the heavenly, spiritual city and country of God.

Hebrews 10:9-10 Then said he, Lo, I come to do thy will, O God. He taketh away the first, that he may establish the second. By the which will we are sanctified through the offer of the body of Jesus Christ once for all.

John 18:36 is Jesus talking to Pilate and declares to Pilate that His kingdom is not of this world.... so why would the Jews then, and those people today insist again that the kingdom of God is to be in natural Jerusalem, when Jesus clearly says it is no longer going to be there anymore. That was a shadow of what truly is. The real kingdom of God is come. Jesus birthed it forth back then. And today His kingdom which is righteousness, peace, and joy in the Holy Spirit is being established in souls throughout all ages and generations. His Kingdom will never end. It is come, and is established, and is receiving many that have received Him and His Righteousness, Peace, and Joy. Be established in His Kingdom. Look at these scriptures and hear the voice of the Lord:

John 18:36 Jesus answered, My kingdom is not of this world: .....

John 4:20-23 Our fathers worshipped in this mountain; and ye say, that in Jerusalem is the place where men ought to worship. Jesus saith unto her, Woman, believe me, the hour cometh, <u>when ye shall neither in this mountain, nor yet at Jerusalem, worship the Father</u>.... WOW...is this clear enough?. Then Jesus says in verse 23 But the hour cometh, and now is, when the <u>true worshippers shall worship the Father in spirit and in truth</u>: for the Father seeketh such to worship him....

God's Kingdom is Righteousness, Peace, and Joy IN THE HOLY SPIRIT.

If you have received the Father's holy Spirit, then you are sealed with the mark of the Lord Jesus Christ and the kingdom of God is within you.

Now as Luke 16:16 states: ...since John the kingdom of God is preached and every man presses into it. Now you are being washed and cleaned up, your mind being renewed by the Spirit of the Lord In You. You are being presented and set in the body of Jesus Christ, who has prepared a place for you in Himself in His kingdom. You are set in Him who is IN THE KINGDOM AND SITTING ON THE THRONE OF HIS KINGDOM.... He is ruling and reigning in His Kingdom... now in the earth, through those that have received HIM.

It is a mystery, and only by His Holy Spirit can any of us attempt to understand the all of His Kingdom.

Galatians 2:20 I am crucified with Christ: nevertheless I live; yet not I, but Christ liveth in me and the life which I now live in the flesh I live by the faith of the Son of God, who love me and gave himself for me.

Revelation 5:9-10 And they sang a new song... hast redeemed us to God by thy blood out of every kindred... And hast made us unto our God kings and priests; and we shall reign on the earth.

Ephesians 5:25-27 ...loved the church, and gave himself for it; That he might sanctify and cleanse it with the washing of the water by the word..... (this is how Jesus is cleaning you – preaching of His testimony by that Holy Spirit and witness of the Father speaking in your spirit and soul.)
v27 That he(Jesus) might present it to himself a glorious church, not having spot, or wrinkle, or any such thing; but that it should be holy and without blemish.

You are entering His kingdom, through the FLESH OF THE SON (the veil to the Holy Place where the Father dwells), as you are partaking of His Testimony and receiving Him, you are being presented to the Father and all things are put under your feet, for you "are" now become One with the Son and now through the Son joined unto the Father. (Hebrews 6:19-20, chapters 7,8,9,10; 1 Corinthians 15:22-28, 52-28; Eph 1:22-23; Eph 2:4-7; Hebrews 12:22-29....)

There is so much to learn about our new place of dwelling in the Lord Jesus Christ.

The Father has purposed this from the beginning. So, that TODAY if you hear His Voice calling you, don't be stubborn, but take that step and allow the Father to bring you to His Son Jesus Christ and establish your soul in the liberty she belongs in with Him: co-heirs with Him as He is King and Priest over all.

Present Truth.

2 Peter 1:11-12 For so an entrance shall be ministered unto you abundantly in to the everlasting kingdom of our Lord and Saviour Jesus Christ. Wherefore I will not be negligent to put you always

in remembrance of these things, though ye know them, and be established in the present truth.

Amen.
RPJ

(Write your notes here)

REVELATION 101
Where is Heaven...? What is Heaven? 

(This is not a complete understanding of heaven, but rather an understanding thus far revealed. There is so much more to see and enjoy! Thank You Father and Lord!)

In John 3: 13 Jesus was standing in heaven while standing in the earth. In Him and by Him heaven and earth was brought together. He filled in the gap. Yet in John 3 Jesus was talking and saying that "the Son of man which is in heaven"... speaking of himself as He dwelled in the earth also. So there was an understanding of what and where heaven truly was and is.

John 3:12-13
12 If I have told you earthly things, and ye believe not, how shall ye believe, if I tell you of heavenly things? 13 And no man hath ascended up to heaven, but he that came down from heaven, even **the Son of man which is in heaven**.

Where is Heaven...? God is Spirit. So is heaven. So if Jesus Christ is in heaven, and He is IN you, then heaven is there in you too... yet you are also in heaven.... but not all of heaven is revealed to you yet, because it is too awesome to take in at one moment. Read on to understand more.

Have you ever been in a meeting or just in your private time with the Lord, and the anointing begins to flow?

It is a dominion of Righteousness, Peace, Joy and contentment as the Holy Spirit carries us into God's presence. You are "raptured" "caught-up" "swallowed up" into the presence of the Lord and His kingdom, yet, you are still in the earth and natural body.

The Lord is swallowing up your mortality in eternal life. In that moment, twinkling of an eye, a change takes place... Yet you are experiencing His presence that takes away all bondages, and sets your feet in His dominion where all sorrow flees, all lack disappears, and all is content. Our hearts are filled with love, real love for each other. Bodies are healed, miracles appear, situations and problems get corrected and fixed... eternal life abounds through the righteousness of Jesus Christ that affects all things. And no one wants to leave that meeting and go back to their natural "home."

Home is where the Lord is, and the Lord is in heaven, now having made His home in our souls, causes us to be joined unto the Father which is in heaven too: Heaven and Earth brought together now in each of you, as His testimony and presence is manifested in and to you.

John 14:20-23 (Jesus is speaking) "At that day ye shall know that I am in my Father, and ye in me, and I in you. He that hath my commandments, and keepeth them, he it is that loveth me; and he that loveth me shall be love of my Father, and I will love him, and will manifest myself to him.... and we will come unto him, and make our abode with him."

This is the place and dominion where the saints that have gone on before us, now assemble with us, even though we are still alive and remain in the earth. But Jesus Christ has made provision to bring us and them together, heaven and earth and all that is within them (Colossians 1:16-29). It is done.

Yet we can only enter if we have been redeemed by the blood of the Lamb, born again of His water and Spirit (John 3:3-5). In the twinkling of an eye is the time it takes to change us all, yet each of us in the Father's own order (1 Corinthians 15:23,52).

The maturing part is a process of growing through experiences that the Father allows for our growth. We are growing up into the head, Ephesians 4 tells us. We are changing in every step and experience which the Lord puts before us to go through. Each step is an experience of the revealing of His Son to us. We go from Faith to Faith... Glory to Glory... and Victory to Victory. A little at a time we press into His kingdom.

Receiving the Lord's kingdom is an awesome and powerful experience, so a little at a time the Father causes us to behold Him so we too may be changed out of our death clothes and into the garments of Jesus Christ – Righteousness.

As we behold Him, we are changed into the same image, yet it is by the Holy Spirit (Phil 3:21; 2 Cor 3:16-18*) We are raised out of our graves of death and sin, and resurrected by Eternal Life, that Holy Spirit working in us, just as He did in Jesus.

We are entering into the Kingdom of heaven where the Lamb of God sits upon His throne of Authority over all. God our Father is setting each of us within the body of His Son as it pleases Him... all for His purpose and working.

The Second Man has been raised from the grave... now we who Hear His Voice are being joined to the Head who is already risen, assembling together in this age, to allow the Saviour to appear in and through His multi-membered body on earth and in heaven. We are His church, bride, wife, and body. He is the Head of us all. Our souls are the Lamb's purchased possession.

The Anointing breaks the yoke of traditions, and barriers between the world of the earth and heaven.

The Holy Spirit is God our Father in the full salvation and victory of the Son for us. He is able to deliver us, and bring us fully cleansed and ready to experience the dominion of the Father and Son, even as we that are alive and remain interact with those that have gone on before us... yet only as the Father desires.

He has made spirits angels and ministers flames of fire, to work on our behalf, so that we may receive the fullness of our Salvation through Jesus Christ, Immanuel, God's Son, Our Saviour and Lord. Yet, Jesus tells us to worship the Father, ask of the Father in the name of the Son...or could say in the acknowledgement of all that the Son has done and Is. Now that is Respect and Honor to the King!

So if, in and through the Son of God, we are redeemed and have been joined unto the head, which is Christ Jesus, and have the Spirit of Christ in us... we walk in the earth with the Lord in us, then we also abide in the Lord who is in heaven. This is how Jesus walked on the earth, yet was in heaven, as it speaks in John 3:13. The Spirit of the Son was the Father in Him, doing the work and never leaving Him. Jesus was reconciling... bringing the two worlds together, within and through Himself.

Colossians 1: 16-29 (pls read) For by him were all things created, that are in heaven, and that are in earth, visible and invisible, whether they be thrones, or dominions, or principalities, or powers: all things were created by him, and for him: And he is before all things, and by him all things consist. And he is the head of the body, the church: who is the beginning, the firstborn from the dead; that in all things he might have the preeminence. for it pleased the Father that in him should all fullness dwell; And, having made peace through the blood of his cross, by him to reconcile all things unto himself; by him, I say, whether they be things in earth, or things in heaven..... Christ in you, the hope of glory....

What a Mystery!!!

So it is possible for those ones that have received the Spirit of the Son in their own hearts, and worship the Father in spirit and in truth, to also walk on this earth, yet be in heaven also.

As Hebrews 12:22 begins to tell us "We are come unto Mount Zion..."…. It is a Mystery to many, but to the ones that have the Spirit of Christ in them, He will give you the understanding AND Experience of this present Truth.

1 John 5:20 And we know that the Son of God is come, and hath given us an understanding, that we may know him that is true, and we are in him that is true, even in his Son Jesus Christ. This is the true God, and eternal life.

Don't let this shatter you... but instead REJOICE as the anointing is flowing and all hearts are praising the Lord for the Victory of the Lamb has made provision for us all... not just in heaven, but in this earth too: spiritually, materially, and monetarily.

He has redeemed us by the Blood of the Lamb, and the word of His Testimony is flowing from the Father in heaven into the earthen realms to declare the Righteousness of the Son.

God will not allow us to experience anymore than we can handle, yet He desires for you to receive all His kingdom and the kingdom you. This is powerful. This is home... our place to rest with Him ... in the Son.

So the next time you are praising the Lord, remember you are opening the gates of praise so the King of Glory can reveal Himself to you…. Expect It.

For the Lord is dwelling in you... in His many-membered body, in the mountain that He so loves…….. the place called heaven.

It's not the all-ness of heaven, but it is *an experience* of what is going on in heaven. "...thy kingdom come, thy will be done on earth as it is in heaven..."

He birthed forth His kingdom, now certain ones are entering in to His kingdom... Luke 16:16, Luke 17:20-21, Hebrews 14:17....

Kingdom of Heaven can only be seen with the Eyes of the Born from Above ones. (John 3:3-5)

Psalm 24:7-10
v7 Lift up your heads, O ye gates ; and be ye lift up, ye everlasting doors; and the King of glory shall come in.
8 Who is this King of glory? The LORD strong and mighty, the LORD mighty in battle.
9 Lift up your heads, O ye gates ; even lift them up, ye everlasting doors; and the King of glory shall come in.
10 Who is this King of glory? The LORD of hosts, he is the King of glory. Selah.

Psalm 118:19-24
19 Open to me the gates of righteousness: I will go into them, and I will praise the LORD:
20 This gate of the LORD, into which the righteous shall enter.
21 I will praise thee: for thou hast heard me, and art become my salvation.
22 The stone which the builders refused is become the head stone of the corner.
23 This is the LORD's doing; it is marvelous in our eyes.
24 This is the day which the LORD hath made; we will rejoice and be glad in it.

Psalm 87:2
2 The LORD loveth the gates of Zion more than all the dwellings of Jacob.

Psalm 100:4
4 Enter into his gates with thanksgiving, and into his courts with praise: be thankful unto him, and bless his name.

Ephesians 2:5-6 Even when we were dead in sins, hath quickened us together with Christ, (by grace ye are saved;) **And hath raised us up together, and made us sit together in heavenly places in Christ Jesus**:

Amen.
RPJ

REVELATION 102
Certain Ones have become God's Place of Rest

We, that have received His Holy Spirit, are His holy habitation and His eyes that look over all the land and inhabitants.

Through us the Lord is the Keeper of the land. As He had put the first Adam in charge, now the 2nd man the Lord from Heaven, the quickening Spirit IN US is in charge of all the land and creature everywhere.

God has made us His habitation through the giving of His promise, His holy Spirit. By the blood of Jesus Christ that testimony has enjoined us to the Father for His place of rest, dwelling and enjoyment. From this place the Lord looks out over all things, and intercedes for all according to the Fathers will and pleasure and purpose.

Oh give Honor and Praise to the King and Lord of all! Let every soul give thanksgiving and honor to Him only!! For God Is IN His Holy Habitation and Is Ruling and Reigning over all!
The Eyes of the Lord are watching all! and the intercession of the Son is going forth.

Psalm 132:13-18 v13-14 For the Lord hath chosen Zion; he hath desired it for his habitation. This is my rest for ever: here will I dwell; for I have desired it.

Psalm 33:14 From the place of his habitation he looketh upon all the inhabitants of the earth.

Jesus reveals a change in the place of God's rest and dwelling.... out of the natural Zion and now the Spiritual Zion in us! Our Souls are His Inheritance to dwell in for all eternity! He has acquired This land, bought and paid in full by His own Son's blood. !!! Oh, so much can be said on this! Hallelujah!

John 4: 20-24 Jesus saith unto her, Woman, believe me, the hour cometh, when ye shall neither in this mountain, nor yet at Jerusalem, worship the Father. Ye worship ye know not what: we know what we worship: for salvation is of the Jews. But the hour cometh, and now is, when the true worshippers shall worship the Father in spirit and in truth: for the Father seeketh such to worship him. God is a Spirit: and they that worship him must worship Him in spirit and in truth.

Zion was that mountain of worship... now it is those (us) that have received His Holy Spirit by receiving the testimony of the Son.

If you have not received His Son Jesus Christ, then you are not part of God's family.... the certain ones. Only those that have received That Seed of God in their souls (engrafted word) can become sons of God.

John 1:12-14 But as many as received him, to them gave he power to become the sons of God, even to them that believe on his name: which were born,..... of God, ...

1 Peter 1:22-23 v23 Being born again, not of corruptible see, but of incorruptible, by the word of God, which liveth and abideth for ever.

Ephesians 5:26-27 That he (Jesus) might sanctify and cleanse it(the church, bride) with the washing of the water by the word, That he might present it to himself a glorious church, not having spot, or wrinkle, or any such thing; but that it should be holy and without blemish.
NOW THAT IS A Baptism in heavenly water!!!

As John 3:3-5 reveals to us how to be born again... Jesus says... Except a man be born of water and of the Spirit, he cannot enter into the kingdom of God.

Allow Him to Wash and Cleanse you and Birth you forth by the revealing of Son in your Soul. Not in letter, but in and by His Spirit. Thus becoming set in His body. Married to the Head of the Family.!.

A new name you receive, and new identity comes forth.... That which is in the full maturity and character of the Son of God. Amen.

Now in Romans and other scriptures reveal that those that have the promise of the Father, the Spirit and Word of the Son IN them are the habitation and house of God.

Romans 2: 28-29 For he is not a Jew, which is one outwardly; neither is that circumcision, which is outward in the flesh: But he is a Jew, which is one inwardly; and circumcision is that of the heart, in the spirit, and not in the letter; whose praise is not of men, but of God.

Matthew 3:9 And think not to say within yourselves, We have Abraham to our father: for I say unto you, that God is able of these stones to raise up children unto Abraham.

Ephesians 4:4-7 There is one body, and one Spirit, even as ye are called in one hope of your calling; One Lord, one faith, one baptism, One God and Father of all who is above all, and through all, and in you all.

1 Corinthians 6:13-20 v19 What? know ye not that your body is the temple of the Holy Ghost which is in you which ye have of God, and ye are not your own? For ye are bought with a price: therefore glorify God in your body, and in your spirit, which are God's.

1 Corinthians 12:12-27 For by one Spirit are we all baptized into one body... have been all made to drink into one Spirit. For the

body is not one member, but many...But now hath God set the members every one of them in the body, as it hath please him....But now are they many members, yet but one body....Now ye are the body of Christ, and members in particular....

<u>Gal 4: 1-7</u> ...But when the fulness of the time was come, God sent forth his Son, made of a woman, made under the law, to redeem them that were under the law, that we might receive the adoption of sons. And because ye are sons, God hath sent forth the Spirit of his Son into your hearts, crying , Abba, Father. Wherefore thou art no more a servant, but a son; and if a son, then an heir of God through Christ.

Christ Jesus is the intercessor and mediator for all, yet this is God, this is the Holy Spirit in the Earth. God's blessing to all is through THAT SEED WHICH IS CHRIST, and only through the Son of God which is Immanuel, God with us, Jesus Christ ... only through this Certain One can the world be changed.

Now ye are the body of Christ, and members in particular.... That Seed which is Christ is abiding IN YOU, and is working His will Through you, for you and Him have become ONE.

<u>Galatians 2:20</u> I am crucified with Christ: nevertheless I live; yet not I, but Christ liveth in me: and the life which I now live in the flesh I live by the faith of the Son of God, who loved me, and gave himself for me.

<u>Romans 8:18-21</u> ...with the glory which shall be revealed in us. For the earnest expectation of the creature waiteth for the manifestation of the sons of God. For the creature was made subject to vanity, not willingly, but by reason of him who hath subjected the same in hope, Because the creature itself also shall be delivered from the bondage of corruption into the glorious liberty of the children of God.

Psalm 33:12 Blessed is the nation whose God is the Lord; and the people whom he hath chosen for his own inheritance.

Amen.
RPJ

(Write your notes here)

REVELATION 103
The 2nd and 3rd Day: Revival & Resurrection Day 

What day of the Lord have you been awakened unto, and have entered into? Awaken Unto His Righteousness, and Enter Into His Kingdom... The New Life...

Hosea 6:1-3 After two days will he **revive** us:
in the third day he will **raise** us up,
and we shall **live** in his sight.
Then shall we **know**,
if we follow on **to know the Lord:**
his going forth is **prepared** as the morning; and **he** shall come unto us as the rain,
as the **later and former rain** unto the earth.

After Two Days: Jesus has AWAKENED you unto His presence which is Your Righteousness: Your ability to overcome death and sin and be cleansed and released from the effects of that. Like Lazarus was brought back to life, but still had his grave clothes on, so you are awakened unto life, and are being cleansed from all sin and death (released from your grave clothes).... as the third day approaches.

Now the third day approaches....

In The Third Day: Resurrection... Jesus raises us up in to the New Life in Him. We leave death and sin behind.

We LIVE with Him where He is, even though we may still be in the natural realm. Whether alive and remain, or in spirit only... we are together with Christ where He is.

It is our spiritual body, and natural body that belong to the Lord. Jesus Christ has brought these two worlds back together ... now it is as one King-dom reigning, and one God that is Christ, ruling over all kingdoms. (Psalms 103:19)

Not all are awakened unto this yet, because they are still in the understanding of the first day.... Jesus died for their sins.

Now see and **KNOW** Him in the second AND third day of His cross for our sins. **SEE HIM** ... meaning to **UNDERSTAND** what He has Done and Who He is. Then **RECEIVE HIM**, the Resurrection that is without sin, and receive your fullness of Salvation... the **full affect** of the Death, Burial, and Resurrection of Christ Jesus.

Paul writes in Galatians 4:19 My little children, of whom I travail in birth again until Christ be formed in you,...

The forming of Christ IN YOU, is the awakening. As the Father reveals to you the Son, by the writing in your heart, and putting in your mind the Lord Jesus.... THAT IS THE LIVING WORD OF GOD abiding IN YOUR SOUL that makes you free. (Hebrews 8:10)

POWER HE IS. WISDOM HE IS. ETERNAL LIFE IN YOU! Hallelujah and AMEN. (John 17:2-3; 1 John 5:20, and many more).

Nothing is impossible for Him. Nothing is impossible for those that are abiding IN Him. In Him is the promises of God Yes and Amen.

He ENTERED YOU to clean and release you from all that separated you from the FATHER/LIFE.
YOU ENTER HIM, the RESURRECTION.... and HE JOINS YOU to the FATHER....

RESTORATION – REDEMPTION – RECONCILIATION is complete.

Go and Sin no more for He that is without Sin has made you ONE with Him and As He is... in this world. (1 John 3:2, and many more)

AMEN.
RPJ

REVELATION 104
With God all things are Possible

With God all things are possible.....
Even the saving of all souls.....
but all souls must be drawn by the Father to the Son and they must believe.....
So from Age to Age, Generation to Generation.....
The Gospel of Jesus Christ is Preached to all Souls .....
and what was lost will be found and raised up in Jesus Christ .....
Yet as the designated time of God is appointed for that Soul.....
For All Souls Belong to God.....

The Soul that sins, dies, and lives in death, separation from Life/God.

But God has provided HOPE...

If you are God's minister of HOPE, then the world is in need you!

Go forth at the leading of the Holy Spirit and allow our Father to REDEEM all souls in This Generation:.....
Through the simplicity of Preaching the Gospel of Jesus Christ by the Holy Spirit into the ears and Souls and Minds in the world.

By the Holy Spirit, those that are "ready" will hear, and those that it is not their time, will not. Don't be discouraged Ministers of God, but know the Lord is building the house, not you.

He has Succeeded and He will Succeed! Continue to follow His lead in all your affairs. God never fails. Love never fails.

All Souls belong to God. It is God's field, God's harvest, and in God's timing. Be patient and move with the Lord.

Mark 10:23-27
23 And Jesus looked round about, and saith unto his disciples, How hardly shall they that have riches enter into the kingdom of God!
24 And the disciples were astonished at his words. But Jesus answereth again, and saith unto them, Children, how hard is it for them that trust in riches to enter into the kingdom of God!
25 It is easier for a camel to go through the eye of a needle, than for a rich man to enter into the kingdom of God.
26 And they were astonished out of measure, saying among themselves, **Who then can be saved**?
27 And Jesus looking upon them saith, **With men it is impossible, but not with God: for with God all things are possible.**

Amen
RPJ

REVELATION 105
Your Cross to Bear 

Mark 8:34-38
34 And when he had called the people unto him with his disciples also, he said unto them, Whosoever will come after me, let him deny himself, and take up his cross, and follow me.
35 For whosoever will save his life shall lose it; but whosoever shall lose his life for my sake and the gospel's, the same shall save it.
36 For what shall it profit a man, if he shall gain the whole world, and lose his own soul?
37 Or what shall a man give in exchange for his soul?
38 Whosoever therefore shall be ashamed of me and of my words in this adulterous and sinful generation; of him also shall the Son of man be ashamed, when he cometh in the glory of his Father with the holy angels.

Mark 10:21
21 Then Jesus beholding him loved him, and said unto him, One thing thou lackest: go thy way, sell whatsoever thou hast, and give to the poor, and thou shalt have treasure in heaven: and come, take up the cross, and follow me.

Luke 14:27
27 And whosoever doth not bear his cross, and come after me, cannot be my disciple.

Bearing YOUR Cross can be a heavy experience. Jesus is our example, and bore the cross of crosses. No other cross can compare. No other cross is necessary for our salvation. So what cross are we to bear, if no other cross is necessary for our salvation?

The carrying of His Gospel, and the daily ministering of His Grace to all, through His Spirit of Power and Love.

If you are carrying your cross that the Lord has destined you for, then your cross is the life that you are living in Him: The Testimony of Jesus Christ made manifest as your life for all to "see" and "read." You are become one with God's Book of Life (Jesus Christ). Your name written in Him and His name written in you. You have lost your identity, and are married to the Son, and have taken on His name and identity... yet He is always the Head.

At the cross of Jesus, He dealt with ridicule, suffering of every kind, and the chatting voices of those that had no faith.... crying out "where is your God" "If you are the Messiah, then save yourself".

So perhaps today you are beyond carrying your cross and now you feel you too are hanging there before your enemies, and they are not helping you, they are not giving you something to drink, they are not wanting you to be relieved of your pain, but rather they are just waiting to see what will happen next.

"Is this God you confess 'real'?" "Will He deliver you or let you die?" Oh, and so many other exclamations they would make. Trying to add to your misery rather than lighten your load. BUT JESUS KNEW THE JOY THAT WAS BEFORE HIM, SO HE LOOKED FORWARD AND FORGAVE THEM... HIS TRUST WAS IN THE FATHER'S WILL AND LOVE FOR HIM. So likewise for you to continue forward...

I'm here to tell you to declare your love for your Father, and know that He sees and knows all that is going on. And if you have given all of your life for Him to live through, then hold on for You Will Rise Again. Look to the Joy He has for you. For the suffering of the present time will reap a greater harvest. Jesus knew that the suffering He was going through would be for our Joy and Liberty. ! ! ! Oh Thank you Lord!!! And no one will have to go through that again. It is done.

Yet, as we are His body in this generation and age, He causes us to go through certain “cross bearing and sufferings” that is producing a greater birthing and glory of His presence for us all to reap of Today.
You’re almost there. Joy comes in the morning!

Amen.
RPJ

REVELATION 106
Awake to Christ

"Awaken – Wake up to the Presence of Jesus Christ – And if you have received Him as Your Saviour – then Awake unto Him - That Divine Nature In You"

2 Peter 1:12
v2-3... According as **his divine power hath given unto us all things**...., **through the knowledge of him...**
v4 **Whereby** are given unto us exceeding great and precious **promises**: **that by these ye might be partakers** of the **divine nature**, having escaped the corruption that is in the world through lust.

Through the knowledge... the experience and encounter of Jesus Christ as your Saviour....

This is true "knowing" of someone. Not by the letter, but by the Spirit breathing LIFE within your soul, and a change within you is evidence of His Love.

Awake to His Presence In Your Soul. Awake to the Spirit of Life and Righteousness in you, that is Power to save and deliver and set you forever in His kingdom. He is the same Spirit that raised Jesus the last Adam from the grave and from death, and He is the Spirit that is God and Christ abiding in your soul, telling you or rather writing in your mind and putting in your heart the "blood covenant" of Jesus Christ (Hebrews 8:10).

By Grace, through Faith we Receive His Divine Power which transforms us into His Divine Nature and Likeness.... even as we still abide in this world. We Rise Up... with Christ and all the saints that have gone on before us. We assemble together (Hebrews 12:22-29) and abide in His present Kingdom, where Jesus Christ is ruling and reigning in all worlds, even through His many membered body that is the visible image of Him in this earth.

Awaken unto Righteousness…. HIS Righteousness that is abiding IN you, as the new creature you have and are becoming…. Christ Jesus as the head of all members as we all work in harmony with one another…. because each of us are following and being lead by that one Spirit which is Christ – Holy Spirit.

Walk in Faith of the Son… Hebrews 4:2 Enter in to His Rest. His Works have accomplished our liberty and Salvation and Sanctification and Justification unto all Righteousness. His Works are Completed. We rest with Him in His Victory. In Him, By Him, and of Him we live, move and have our being.

Awake to His Righteousness as our ability and sufficiency to become one with the Son and Father… in their divine nature that is without sin, sickness, decay, and death. Liberty and Victory is ours Because of His Righteousness.

1 Corinthians 15:34 Awake to righteousness, and sin not; for some have not the knowledge of God: I speak this to your shame.

"REACH OUT and GRAB AHOLD of His Righteousness". Embrace Him and Encounter and Experience The Word of God that was made into flesh man… Jesus Christ: God's full salvation for us. He has overcome sin and death, so that we can be free from sin and death and the affects of sin and death.

The lady with the issue of blood knew and believed He IS The One That Is Able to make her free and heal her. She knew if she reached out and touched… become one with…. she could be healed. The hem of the Rabbi's robe is a blue ribbon that represented "Righteousness." She reached to grab ahold of His Righteousness for her healing.

In His Righteousness is FORGIVENESS. In His Righteousness Is Healing, Health and the Cure for whatever "issue" you have.

THIS ONE is abiding IN your Soul... to make you free... and set you in His place that He has prepared for you that is without corruption. Allow your Faith to receive Him for your situation.

Philemon 1:6 That the **communication of thy faith** my become effectual **by the acknowledging of every good thing which is in you in Christ Jesus**.

Awake to His Righteousness and let your Faith Work.... Give Thanks to Him and Receive.

Faith without works is dead... As the body without the Spirit (Life) is dead. You were dead once in sin, now the Spirit of Christ in you has revived your soul unto life.... but the body is still dead because of sin...

Romans 8:9-11
v9 But ye are not in the flesh, but in the Spirit, if so be that the Spirit of God dwell in you. Now if any man have not the Spirit of Christ, he is none of his.
v10 And if Christ be in you the body is dead because of sin; but the Spirit is life because of righteousness.
v11 But if the Spirit of him that raised up Jesus from the dead dwell in you, he that raised up Christ form the dead shall also quicken your mortal bodies by his Spirit that dwelleth in you.

Now allow the Lord to raise up your body too, as it says in the verse noted above.... just as Jesus Christ was raised up, and even Lazarus. Now let the grave clothes, or clothes of death fall off, by PUTTING ON THE GARMENTS OF RIGHTEOUSNESS AND LIFE that is JESUS CHRIST. As you allow the Holy Spirit to teach you of Jesus Christ, this process is the washing and cleansing and birthing of the Son in your soul. The renewing of the mind. The regeneration (rebirth) by the Holy Spirit.

Through Faith in the Grace of God, the Holy Spirit is changing your clothes, garments: exchanging your 1st Adam's garment to the Last Adam's garments – the first man's clothes of identity to the second man's clothes of identity: Quickening Spirit, the Lord from Heaven. (1 Corinthians 15)

We are married to another: Jesus Christ. He is our head, authority, identity, and beloved of our soul. CHANGE for the better is a for sure happening when your eye or vision is Single on Him.

Awake to His Righteousness and let your Faith Work.... Give Thanks to Him and Receive....
He is that Divine Nature that has no sin or death, and has overcome the corruption that is in the world through lust.

Freedom... we are Free at last.

Amen.
RPJ

REVELATION 107
Giving Thanks

Giving Thanks to the Lord is showing respect and appreciation for all that He has done and IS for us. Yet, some people have asked me if they have to give thanks. Well.... no you don't have to give thanks to the Lord, but if you have ever encountered or had an experience of salvation, you can't help but Give Thanks! The Presence of the Lord will humble your soul, and the love will cause a heart in you that is expedient to give thanks to our Saviour and Father.

So if there is someone you know that doesn't or isn't willing to give thanks to the Lord, then pray to the Father for them to have an experience of His Grace. Then they will Thank Him over and over again.

Here are some scriptures of Jesus giving Thanks just before the miracle came forth... a lesson to learn from Him:

Matt 15:36
36 And he took the seven loaves and the fishes, and gave thanks, and brake them, and gave to his disciples, and the disciples to the multitude.

Luke 22:17-20
17 And he took the cup, and gave thanks, and said, Take this, and divide it among yourselves:
18 For I say unto you, I will not drink of the fruit of the vine, until the kingdom of God shall come.
19 And he took bread, and gave thanks, and brake it, and gave unto them, saying, This is my body which is given for you: this do in remembrance of me.
20 Likewise also the cup after supper, saying, This cup is the new testament in my blood, which is shed for you.

Anna the prophetess gave thanks as she came in the presence of the Lord:

Luke 2:36-38
36 And there was one Anna, a prophetess, the daughter of Phanuel, of the tribe of Aser: she was of a great age, and had lived with a husband seven years from her virginity;
37 And she was a widow of about fourscore and four years, which departed not from the temple, but served God with fastings and prayers night and day.
38 And she coming in that instant gave thanks likewise unto the Lord, and spake of him to all them that looked for redemption in Jerusalem.

The one leper that was healed returned to the Lord to show his appreciation and thankfulness for the healing (provision) given to him, and a greater miracle came forth to him because of his actions (another lesson to learn from):

Luke 17:11-19
11 And it came to pass, as he went to Jerusalem, that he passed through the midst of Samaria and Galilee.
12 And as he entered into a certain village, there met him ten men that were lepers, which stood afar off:
13 And they lifted up their voices, and said, Jesus, Master, have mercy on us.
14 And when he saw them, he said unto them, Go shew yourselves unto the priests. And it came to pass, that, as they went, they were cleansed.
15 And one of them, when he saw that he was healed, turned back, and with a loud voice glorified God,
16 And fell down on his face at his feet, giving him thanks: and he was a Samaritan.
17 And Jesus answering said, Were there not ten cleansed? but where are the nine?

18 There are not found that returned to give glory to God, save this stranger.
19 And he said unto him, Arise, go thy way: thy faith hath made thee whole.

Here are a couple more scriptures that reveals more reasons to always be of a thankful heart to the Lord our God and Father:
1 Cor 15:57-58
57 But thanks be to God, which giveth us the victory through our Lord Jesus Christ.
58 Therefore, my beloved brethren, be ye stedfast, unmoveable, always abounding in the work of the Lord, forasmuch as ye know that your labour is not in vain in the Lord.

2 Cor 2:14
14 Now thanks be unto God, which always causeth us to triumph in Christ, and maketh manifest the savour of his knowledge by us in every place.

Amen.
RPJ

REVELATION 108
Can God live in an Unclean Vessel?

The Wife joined to the unsaved Husband = a Sanctified Husband
The Husband joined to the unsaved Wife = a Sanctified Wife
Christ joined to an unclean vessel = Sanctified Vessel

So if the one that is sanctified is joined to one that is not then get ready ... cause all unrighteousness is about to get cleaned up.

That is the "Entering into your Promise Land" Experience. God cleans up His House.

The Holy Spirit (Father and Son together) buys your soul then comes to inhabit it, only to bring you through the being born again experience and process..... one step at a time.... until all of your Spirit man, Soul and Body are redeemed and freed from every spot and affect of sin and death.

Just like Jesus – Your Resurrection – So also, is HE (that same Spirit that raised Jesus from the grave is in you, to raise you up out of your grave of disobedience, sin, and death) raising you up ... in to Eternal Life.... Jesus Christ. ...your promise land. (John 14:2-3...prepare a place for you.)

So He washes you by His Word and Blood.... little at a time.... and with Fire..... a little at a time.... as you are being born again... or rather are entering into His Kingdom, which is Righteousness, Peace, and Joy in Him the Holy Ghost. (The example for us was the coming out of Egypt and entering the promised lands)

So if YOU have joined yourself to the Sanctified One (Jesus Christ/Lamb of God), then get ready to have allllll your unrighteous mindsets, behaviors, etc of the carnal nature dealt with..... because they are about to be Removed, and God's House Cleaned Up.

YET, even so, the Lord is GENTLE, to take us all through the fire a little at a time, pending His need to use us for His Glory.

John 17:17-24; Matt 3:11-12; Fire is God, and is good. God in Hebrews 12:29 is a consuming fire. We all go through "fire" as we are entering into God, and His Kingdom. The Son washes us, protects us, keeps us (preserves us) as we are going through that process of "being born again" so that we are not burned by that holy fire. That Holy Fire is God who consumes all unrighteousness as we enter in to dwell with Him. It's a process.... we couldn't handle this birthing all at once.... so He gently processes us, births us by His Spirit and Word through our Souls.

You see, nothing unrighteous can enter in to the Kingdom of God. Yet, being born again is God's way of bringing us Home. Being Born of His Word, Truth, Son, Blood... oh the revealing could go on and on ... and it does.

Look at this.... Luke 16:16 tells us that since John, or after John since Christ we "press into the Kingdom of God". Hebrews 12:22-29 tells us that receiving the Kingdom of God is a 'shaking' experience. A shaking of your physical and spiritual existence of everything that is unrighteous, leaving only that which is "Righteousness, Peace, and Joy" that is in the Holy Ghost... revealing the Kingdom of God, and You in God, and God in You. (Romans 14:17-18 tells us what the Kingdom of God is; John 14:20-24 tells of the Father and Son making their abode in you)

So, does God dwell in an unclean temple?......
The scriptures tell us that He quickens us together with Him, even when we were in our sins and uncircumcision of the flesh (Col 2:13 (9-15) and Ephesians 2:5 (4-6)). That means He joined with us in our filth to BE OUR SANCTIFICATION. Nothing else could sanctify us.

Only HIS Presence (seed) in us determines That value. BUT... HE then begins the clean up process, or rather the "born again" process in us... then His Nature (genetics, divine nature) begins to be revealed through us towards others..... a Transformation, Change takes place within, and then an outward expression of an inward glory. (Rom 8:17; John 17:21-24...)

We notice it in us, and little by little, others see it too and are affected by His Presence... cause once born again from above there is just no way to keep it hidden anymore.

A New Man (Creature) is birthed.... The 2nd Man, the Lord from Heaven has swallowed you up, and you and Him have become one. As He is, you are too. Same Mind, Behaviors, Identity,... etc... yet so He is the Head and we His Body. *(like the first Adam, yet now better/perfected, the 2nd Man with help mate – the body = the Lord from Heaven appearing in the earth, ruling & reigning, the Lord's Government abounding.... to those that have ears to hear what the Lord is saying)*

There are sooo many ways to explain this working and operation of the Lord. But I'm convinced you are hearing what the Lord is telling you in this.

So the Lord joins with us in our filth to be that catalyst that causes us to be changed, and that process from conception to inheritance is the "being born again" experience and process.... the "Entering into His Kingdom" experience. (John 3:3-5 tells us we cannot see nor enter Kingdom of God unless born again.)

So yes the Lord can attach himself to uncleanness, but the moment He does.... The Clean up begins. And during that process, that Grace abounds to sustain us always in God's Favor, thanks to Jesus Christ His Son.

Maybe He causes Himself in You to go into the midst of a "mess".... perhaps to be the catalyst Himself through you.... to begin the clean up process in another.

1 Cor 15 ...to every seed his own body. Allow the Lord to Create in You.... the stroke of the Artist's breath upon your soul.... (John 15:3; Eph 5:26-27; James 1:18,21 ....)

1 Corinthians 6:20 For ye are bought with a price: therefore glorify God in your body, and in your spirit, which are God's.

We've been bought, so our body and spirit/soul belong to God. Adam was a living soul but when he sinned, all was overcome by that same spirit of disobedience, and sin with death reigned over all... so our souls were no longer living.

We needed a new spirit to revive the soul and body (Romans 8:9-11.) So God by His own arm, sent us the Saviour, in our own likeness of nature, yet the Seed/Spirit within was different and Greater than the last...... His only begotten Son, Jesus Christ. Yet, He came as the last of that Adam nature, as the Quickening Spirit; and as the new Man – 2nd Man which is the Lord from Heaven. (1Corinthians 15:45-47)

A new generation was then about to be formed, brought forth from above... not as the first, but as the second Man, the Lord from Heaven.

God's Purpose and Plan in His Son, Immanuel, Jesus Christ... to redeem us.... The "Entering into Your Promise Land" experience.

The Holy Spirit (Father & Son together) have bought our souls through that precious Blood of the Lamb. Then inhabit you, only to bring you through the "being born again" experience and process.... one step at a time... until all of your spirit man (inner man), soul and body are redeemed and freed from every spot and affect of sin and death. And as said before, that Grace sustains us during the process.

Just like Jesus – Your Resurrection – So also is HE *(that same Spirit that raised Jesus from the grave is in you, to raise you up out of your grave of disobedience, sin, and death)* raising You up and bringing you in to Eternal Life.... Jesus Christ. ...your promise land. (John 14:2-3...prepare a place for you.)

He Washes you by His Word and Blood..... a little at a time, causing you, in and thru your Spirit, Soul, and Body, to completely experience all His Blessings and Glory of Salvation ....

So continue to press in, and receive the TRUTH, and LIFE for it is the only WAY in to God's glorious and wonderful Kingdom (Romans 14:17; Luke 17:21; Luke 16:16;).

And Yes, God can live in an unclean temple/body, but that is only to start the clean up process. Yet, His presence In You is your sanctification...not according to your works, but according to His and Who He is.

Ephesians 2: 5 (4-6)
Ephesians 5:26-27
John 14:20-24
John 15:3-5
1 John 2:5
Hebrews 12:27-29
Colossians 2:13 (9-15)
James 1:18,21
Rom 8:17
John 17:21-24
John 3:3-5
Romans 14:17
Luke 17:21
Luke 16:16

many more...........

Amen.
RPJ

(Write your notes here)

Glory to God!

Let us know how the Lord has blessed you, as you have received of Him in the reading of His revelations in this book.

You can also send your Prayer Requests to this address or to the email address below.

Ministry Services, LLC
Holy Spirit Family & Kingdom Ministries
PO Box 8222
Virginia Beach, VA 23450

Website: www.hsfkm.info
www.kingdomministry.info
Email: hsfkm@live.com

God's Blessings, Benefits and Best to You!

His Love for You,

Judith

" 'My Life In You' by Jesus Christ"

CONTENT by REVELATIONS (Alpha Order)

" 'My Life In You' by Jesus Christ"

* End Time Messages

" 'My Life In You' by Jesus Christ"

" 'My Life In You' by Jesus Christ"

CPSIA information can be obtained at www.ICGtesting.com
Printed in the USA
BVOW021803120212

282724BV00002B/2/P